SUMMIT BOOKS
New York   London   Toronto   Sydney   Tokyo

William and Jane
TAUBMAN

MOSCOW
SPRING

SUMMIT BOOKS
SIMON & SCHUSTER BUILDING
ROCKEFELLER CENTER
1230 AVENUE OF THE AMERICAS
NEW YORK, NEW YORK 10020

10   9   8   7   6   5   4   3   2   1

10   9   8   7   6   5   4   3   2   1   (PBK.)

LIBRARY OF CONGRESS CATALOGING IN PUBLICATION DATA

TAUBMAN, WILLIAM.
   MOSCOW SPRING/WILLIAM AND JANE TAUBMAN.—1ST TRADE
PBK.
     P.   CM.
   1. SOVIET UNION—POLITICS AND GOVERNMENT—1985–
   2. SOVIET UNION—INTELLECTUAL LIFE—20TH
CENTURY.   3. SOVIET UNION—DESCRIPTION AND TRAVEL—
1970–   4. TAUBMAN, WILLIAM—JOURNEYS—SOVIET
UNION.   5. TAUBMAN, JANE—JOURNEYS—SOVIET
UNION.   I. TAUBMAN, JANE.   II. TITLE.
[DK288.T38   1989]
914.704′854—DC20
                                        89-39100
                                         CIP

ISBN 0-671-67731-4
ISBN 0-671-70058-8 (PBK.)

*To our friends in Moscow
and beyond who made this
book possible*

ACKNOWLEDGMENTS

This is not the book either of us went to Moscow to write; it is what Soviet official jargon would call "overfulfillment of our plan." The scholarly research we went to Moscow to conduct, and hence our stay there as a whole, was supported in part by a grant from the International Research and Exchanges Board (IREX), with funds provided by the National Endowment for the Humanities and the United States Information Agency. Bill also held a Fulbright-Hays Faculty Fellowship administered by the U.S. Department of Education. None of these agencies is responsible for conclusions we reach in the research projects they supported. Even less are they responsible for views expressed in this book.

Our former Amherst College colleague George Kateb first suggested that we try our hand at writing this book. Betty Steele and her associates at the Amherst Computer Center helped us do it expeditiously. Aleksander Babyonyshev, Seymour Becker, Pavel Machala, Adele and John Simmons, Ronald Tiersky, and Alla Zeide read and criticized early drafts. The Simmons and Chernock-Abeles households "adopted" Phoebe when she returned to Amherst in early May. We would also like to thank Anne Freedgood, our editor at Summit Books, for wielding her blue pencil ruthlessly, and Lurline Dowell for swift and flawless word-processing.

Most of all, we thank Alex and Phoebe for being willing to share this adventure with us and for being patient while we wrote about it.

CONTENTS

INTRODUCTION

Moscow Spring—the changes that Gorbachev has been bringing to the USSR and that reached a crescendo in the first six months of 1988—may prove to be more revolutionary than the Russian Revolution itself. We didn't think so when we arrived in Moscow in January. We did when we left in June.

John Reed described the Bolshevik seizure of power in October 1917 as "ten days that shook the world." The Bolsheviks insisted their revolution *changed* the world as well. For a while, much of the world agreed. But increasingly, people have been wondering how much the Revolution changed even Russia itself. By the spring of 1988, many Soviets admitted to sharing those doubts.

Far from democratizing Russia, the Bolshevik Revolution strengthened the authoritarianism that had dominated its politics for centuries. A traditional autocracy was replaced by a modern dictatorship. The Russian people who were now supposed to practice self-government descended deeper into passivity and fatalism. Democracy rests on mutual trust and respect among politically equal citizens, on toleration of difference and a willingness to compromise. All these traits were underdeveloped in pre-1917 Russia's political culture. Soviet rule has made things worse. Stalin's terror not only exterminated millions of innocent people, it poisoned relations among those who survived by encouraging and at times compelling them to denounce and betray one another. The traditional Russian identification of freedom with license and democracy with anarchy was, if anything, strengthened by Stalinism.

Mikhail Gorbachev would agree with some of this indictment. Many of his supporters astonished us by accepting it all. When we arrived, they were debunking both Stalin and Brezhnev. Khrushchev, they said, had been a mixed blessing, a reformer who failed largely because of his own flaws. Leaving aside the short, sickly reigns of Andropov and Chernenko, that left only Lenin to legitimize Soviet socialism. Gorbachev justifies his reforms as a return to Leninism. But by the time we left Moscow, even Lenin was coming under attack.

We found ourselves in the middle of Moscow Spring because we are specialists in Soviet studies—Bill in political science, Jane in Russian literature—who went to Moscow in mid-January 1988 as participants in the thirty-year-old Soviet-American academic exchange, the oldest and most successful of the cultural exchanges. Bill was doing research for a political biography of Nikita Khrushchev; Jane was researching a biography of Kornei Chukovsky (1882–1969), well known to any Russian as literary critic, writer of beloved children's books, translator of Anglo-American literature, and author of classic works on children's language and creativity.

Both of us began our study of Russia and Russian at Harvard and Radcliffe in the early sixties; we are part of the post-sputnik generation of Soviet specialists who entered the field in the glory days of the thaw in the USSR and relatively good Soviet-American relations under Khrushchev and John Kennedy. The Cuban missile crisis, the test-ban treaty, the disenthronement of Khrushchev, the Sinyavsky-Daniel trial, the invasion of Czechoslovakia—all these landmarks we remember vividly from our years in college and graduate school.

In 1963 Jane was part of a group of Russian-speaking college students who traveled through the USSR and Eastern Europe in Volkswagen mini-vans for nine weeks. It was an era when Russians were first getting to know Americans again after the long cold war—friendliness and immense curiosity were everywhere. It was an exhilarating experience for a twenty-year-old college senior who had never been outside the United States before, and it hooked Jane forever on her chosen field.

Bill made his first trip to the USSR in the summer of 1964, when he was already a graduate student at Columbia University. Traveling with an Indiana University language-study tour, he visited nine cities in six weeks. Khrushchev was still in power in 1964, but by the time Bill returned to spend 1965–66 at Moscow State University, he had been toppled and the long Brezhnev era of "stagnation" was about to begin. There were enough sparks still flying that he briefly put aside the materials he'd collected for his dissertation on Soviet city government and turned his diary into a book, *The View from Lenin Hills: Soviet Youth in Ferment.*

We took our first joint research trip to the USSR in March 1973. It was then that we made some of the friendships that have continued to enrich our lives and our understanding of Soviet society. For many years, our contacts clearly fell into two distinct categories. "Bill's friends" were official contacts, largely Soviet scholars of America or of Soviet-American relations, whose attitude toward us was cordial but correct. They were generally

people on the up escalator at a time when holding
tightly onto the handrail was becoming more and more
important. "Jane's friends" were from the liberal and
literary intelligentsia, melting into the dissident community—people who were so alienated from the system
that they had nothing to fear by associating freely with
us; who hoped, in fact, that if anything dire happened to
them, we would be able to make enough noise about
their case in the Western press to protect them. These
friends introduced us to their friends. Twice we were
taken to see the late Nadezhda Mandelstam, widow of
Russia's great poet, whose memoirs, smuggled out of
Russia, offered a searing insider's account of Russia
under the purges.

We visited the USSR again in 1975, 1976, and 1982—
and Bill went alone in 1978—sometimes escorting
groups of students, sometimes taking part in conferences, always trying to squeeze in a little research. As
glasnost made such trips both easier and more interesting, the pace of our visits quickened; we went to Moscow in December/January 1985–86 and again in June
1987. In November 1987 Jane accompanied a group of
American liberal-arts college deans to Moscow, Leningrad, and Odessa.

Our children, too, were no strangers to Moscow. Alex
had twice come along when we took groups of students
in the mid-1970s. Phoebe made her first trip with the
rest of the family in December 1985, to spend Christmas
and New Year's with her uncle and aunt, who had just
been posted there as *New York Times* correspondents.
Both children came in June 1987, when Bill was co-
chairing a U.S.-Soviet conference on cold war history.
So when we went for five months in 1988 we wanted
the children to share the experience. Alex, a junior in
high school, would do his schoolwork on his own. He
found a job as a laborer at the American Embassy, where
help has been in short supply since the Soviet staff was

removed en masse in the fall of 1986. During the summit, he worked for one of the American TV networks as a "gofer." Phoebe, aged ten, attended a Soviet school for four days, until she came down with a bad case of Moscow flu, and for the rest of her stay went to the Anglo-American school.

As our lives became entwined with Moscow Spring, we had to struggle to keep pace. Americans who speak Russian have always been welcomed by Soviets thirsty for knowledge of the United States. This time they were more eager to hear our impressions of the Soviet Union. We were sometimes told that we knew more about Soviet history and politics than they did. By the spring of 1988, Moscow resembled a floating constitutional convention, debating such hallowed American institutions as the rule of law, the separation of powers, even a two-party system. "Bill's friends" talked almost as freely about these and other issues as "Jane's friends."

Together or separately, we took in the most talked-about films, plays, lectures, and art exhibits. Literary and cultural "evenings" centering around a taboo-smashing film, or in honor of a formerly banned writer, were for us the newest feature of Moscow intellectual life. Besides being witnesses to history, we became bit players in the drama. We were often invited to speak or be interviewed or televised, all in Russian that was fluent when we arrived but became even better when challenged. In the past, we would have feared our words would be twisted into propaganda. This time, progressive journalists used our criticisms of Soviet life to help themselves make the case for reform.

Moscow Spring represents a new beginning. *Perestroika* means "restructuring." Gorbachev originally aimed to revive the stagnant economy so as to safeguard Soviet status as a superpower. When economic reform failed to do the job, he embarked on restructuring polit-

ical institutions, and even ideas and consciousness.
Glasnost, the startling new openness in intellectual and
cultural life, is partly a means to the same economic end.
For some of the Soviet leaders, perhaps including Gorbachev, that's all it is. But for many reformers, it is an
end in itself. Either way, it is new, not just for Soviet
Russia but for Russia itself. Compared to Soviet censorship, the tsarist variety was relatively mild. Still, one of
the most distinguished American historians of old Russia, Edward Keenan, describes *neglasnost,* lack of openness, as a key feature of the Muscovite political culture.

Along with *perestroika* and *glasnost,* the third key
word of Moscow Spring is *demokratizatsiya.* Democratization occurred before our eyes—within strict limits,
for economic and foreign policy reasons as much as out
of a belief in democracy itself, but still enough to spark
a virtual civil war between champions and opponents of
change. The democracy that is emerging is not Western
liberal democracy. So say the Soviets. So we said before
arriving in Moscow. But we're not so sure anymore. The
Soviet leader and his more conservative colleagues want
to keep democracy within one-party limits. But many
reformers have reached a different conclusion: economic efficiency, not to mention human dignity, requires the freer political choice that only a multiparty
polity embedded in a rule of law allows.

These reformers understand the link between democratization and individual participation in the political
process. But not many Soviets do. It is difficult for a
society steeped in the primacy of the collective to understand that the essence of democracy is respect for the
individual. Soviets are brought up to believe that *we*
(the collective) will bring about *our* achievements. Too
often, this *we* has meant *they* (those in power), and that
has led to a feeling of individual powerlessness. Yet
even reformers who have no stake in the preservation of
one-party rule worry about the danger of "excessive in-

dividualism." For them, the paradox of Gorbachev democracy is how to empower the individual to release his creative and economic energies while not abandoning what is good in the collectivist ethic.

Yury Karyakin, a reform-minded philosopher, gave eloquent voice to the need for individual participation in one of the most outspoken and controversial articles of *perestroika*. It was published in September 1987, but friends insisted we read it as soon as we arrived.

> This really is a revolution. And it is *my revolution*. That means it depends on me, too. That means it is precisely *me* on whom it depends. It's not only whether and how much one should expect help from it, as much as helping it oneself, not asking for its coming, but going out to meet it. We have waited long for its beginning—that means you must do it yourself, in your own place, in your own work. What is vanishing at last is the intolerable, unnatural, debilitating bifurcation between what you firmly know yourself and see around you with your own eyes, what you think to yourself, and what you hear "from above," what you read in the newspapers, what ignoramuses in power keep dunning into you, or what your own internal censor frightens you with. And the most, most important thing now, the most decisive, is *my* responsibility, *my* courage and even more, it turns out, *my* "*liquidation*" of *my* "*illiteracy*"—in socialism, in democracy, and in history and in politics, and especially, in economics and law.

We watched around us the kind of education in democracy that Karyakin calls for here.

To list Moscow Spring's more moderate goals, let alone the hopes of its most radical supporters, is to see how important it is potentially. If it thrives and evolves, it could truly change Russia. Given the size and power of the Soviet Union, this would change the world as well. American foreign policy has long been predicated on a Soviet Union that is politically totalitarian, militarily threatening, and economically weak—and these are the qualities Gorbachev is trying to change. The word most often used in the West to describe what we saw in Moscow is "reform"; Gorbachev's most militant supporters are called "radical reformers." After our stay in Moscow, we do not think it an exaggeration to call Moscow Spring a revolution in the making.

Yet the obstacles to success are just as great—even greater we often found ourselves thinking—as Moscow Spring's potential. The effort to come to terms with the burden of the past brings deep pain and anger. While we were in Moscow, facts about Stalin's long reign of terror poured forth in the press—numbers of victims, details of their fates in NKVD torture chambers, profiles of the dead and their executioners. It is hard enough to explain how Stalinism could happen and why, especially to older people who identified all their lives with its ostensible triumphs and now find those lives devalued by its real crimes. It is almost harder to confront the questions raised by the Brezhnev era. Many of today's reformers were young idealists inspired by Khrushchev's de-Stalinization. Why did they acquiesce in the partial re-Stalinization-turned-corruption that occurred under Brezhnev? What will keep the same thing from happening again?

The forces that would turn back the clock are numerous and powerful. They are to be found almost everywhere—in the Politburo, in the bureaucracy, and among the people. The term we most often use for them is "conservatives," but that simplifies a complex situation. Some sincerely seek to conserve a more orthodox version of Communism, others to resurrect the pre-Communist Russian past. Others quite simply defend positions of power and privilege that democratization threatens. Reform-minded Soviet friends insisted that

selfish conservatives, whom they referred to as an entrenched "Mafia," far outnumber the more selfless variety. But we weren't so sure. If so, how to explain the fact
that so many ordinary citizens, with little power and
fewer privileges, resisted changes designed to give
them at least a modicum of each?

Reformers also come in several varieties, and their
contradictory feelings about their own cause constitute
yet another obstacle to its success. Some reformers, who
prefer merely cosmetic changes, are indistinguishable
from conservatives. Gorbachev himself is as radical as
any top Soviet leader is likely to get, but he too gives
signs of fearing to go too far. Even the most fervent of
his supporters ("liberals," we sometimes call them,
though relatively few fit the Western sense of that term)
are as nervous about democracy as they are desperately
committed to it. Either they don't think it can happen in
a country with Russia's history and political culture, or
they aren't sure it should, given the unpreparedness of
the people. These doubts risk becoming a self-fulfilling
prophecy. In the beginning we were impatient with the
reformers' seeming inconsistency. Gradually, we saw it
was the essence of Moscow Spring.

Gorbachev's revolution is a democratic revolution
from above, a contradictory hybrid that explains both the
force and the fragility of Moscow Spring. His power as
leader of a still centralized party allows him to ram
through reforms against the wishes of not only his party's entrenched apparatus, but many ordinary citizens as
well. Everyone is supposed to be learning democracy.
But meanwhile, as an American philosopher friend of
ours put it, "Freedom is being used to reject freedom,
and force is being used to impose it."

What are democracy's chances in the USSR? Too often
we in the West focus on the short run. In America especially, we personalize the struggle, we focus on the individual players, we ask whether Gorbachev can win,

and when. In fact, the outcome will not be known for a
generation. If Gorbachev stays on top another ten years,
his work will still not be done. Even if he disappears
tomorrow, his cause might yet prevail. All sorts of im-
personal forces are also at work, as we will try to show.

During the five months we were in Russia, we entered
more deeply into Soviet life than we ever had before,
but not deeply enough to cover every significant aspect
of Moscow Spring. A few of our friends were close
enough to the Kremlin to know what went on inside—
but not necessarily to tell us. Except for taxi drivers, we
had few conversations with blue-collar workers. Over
the years we've known quite a few dissidents and refuseniks, but many of them had emigrated. For obvious
reasons, extremist Russian nationalists and Stalinist conservatives have never cultivated our friendship. This
book, therefore, is *not* about life at the very top, or at the
very bottom, not about the dissident movement or the
far right. Most of our friends and sources were intellectuals—writers, academics, scientists. Most were reformers—more or less radical—and more knowledgeable
about the West than the average Russian.

It is hard to know how to refer to our friends and
sources in this book. In the past, we would have disguised them all for fear of compromising them. In Bill's
first book, he not only changed names but blurred char-
acteristics. But Russia today is a society that is at long
last speaking and hearing the truth about itself, its past
mistakes, the real cost of its vaunted accomplishments,
and the depth of the crisis from which it must now extri-
cate itself. It is still not speaking the truth fully, to be
sure, or even, always, speaking it from the love of truth.
In the Russian tradition, it is speaking truth with the
approval of, and even on orders from, those above.
Given all this truth-telling, shouldn't we at least refer to
people by their real names?

Alas, we think not. We will identify those who are

public figures. But for others, the choice is harder. Most others showed no fear of openly associating with us. But we, like they, are not yet convinced that the reforms are irreversible. For the sake of the uncertain future we have chosen to veil some of our sources by changing their names and, more rarely, their circumstances.

Obviously our story is biased by who we were, what our interests were, and what we *wanted* to see in the mass of evidence before us. But in the spirit of *glasnost*, we will not soften the truth as we saw it out of fear of offending. To those Soviets, and there were many, who paid us the compliment of telling us the truth about their country and themselves, we will return the compliment by trying to tell the truth ourselves. In doing so, we hope to make our own small contribution to the success of *perestroika*.

One last item of introduction. Bill almost didn't get to witness Moscow Spring. During our visits in the sixties and seventies, last-minute visa issuance was standard procedure; often visas had to be flown to Kennedy Airport to catch a group's departing plane. Visa rejections, too, could arrive at the last moment. We never had problems getting visas, but enough people we knew did to make it always a concern.

Our first post-Gorbachev trip was a holiday visit to Bill's brother, Philip, and sister-in-law, Felicity Barringer. We had never before requested visas as relatives of resident foreigners; we were told they were granted routinely. Nevertheless, we wanted to give the Soviets plenty of time and applied early. Hardly a week later, our visas arrived in the mail, a full month before we were to leave.

On each of our following trips in June and November 1987, they arrived with similar promptness. Thus it was with some surprise that Bill learned from IREX (the International Research and Exchanges Board, which runs the academic exchange) that his visa for the full four and a half months of our planned stay had not been granted. Instead, the Soviet Academy of Sciences offered him one month in Moscow.

What did it mean? Americans dealing with Soviet officialdom are forever asking themselves that question, forever wondering whether setbacks they encounter are deliberately designed by Big Brother or just the output of standard (or rather, substandard) bureaucratic operating procedures. In this case, both interpretations seemed equally possible. The Academy might simply be saving itself money and trouble, with its target chosen almost at random. On the other hand, it might have sniffed out Bill's interest in Khrushchev.

Bill had worried from the start about the Soviet reaction to a name they had hardly mentioned since Khrushchev was unceremoniously dumped in 1964. To be sure, his name had reappeared in print several times since Gorbachev became General Secretary in 1985. Gorbachev had even praised him in a November 2, 1987, speech commemorating the seventieth anniversary of the Bolshevik Revolution. But by that time, Bill had prepared a summary of his project for the Soviet side which played down his subject.

When the Academy granted him only one month, IREX immediately shot back to Moscow a renewed request for the full four and a half. For several weeks there was silence. At virtually the last minute, the Soviets responded by squeezing out a second month. When IREX forwarded Bill's original one-month visa to the Soviet Embassy in Washington, the embassy at first extended it to one and a half months rather than the promised two. Just a simple mistake? Or yet another bad omen?

By the end of our Moscow Spring, the Academy was offering to let Bill stay for the summer.

GETTING SETTLED

American dog to Russian dog: Tell me about this perestroika *of yours.*

Russian dog: Well, they've made my chain much longer and I can bark all I want, but they've moved the dinner dish farther away.

Our favorite *perestroika* joke, which circulated widely in Moscow, sums up both the achievements and failures of Gorbachev's revolution so far. Easing censorship produces quick results—Russia is full of untold truths, unexpressed ideas, unpublished manuscripts. It is much harder to undo economic patterns and attitudes toward work developed over the past seventy years (or, comparing the work ethic of Russians to their neighbors the Chinese and the Germans, some might say, over centuries). Just as astonishing as the rapid change wrought by *glasnost* is the difficulty of *perestroika:* the tenacity with which most of the economy has so far resisted change.

The system Gorbachev inherited was at a dead end, and three years later key aspects of it still were, despite his ambitious reforms. Living with two children in an ordinary Soviet apartment, we confronted daily the manifestations of a real crisis: the decrepit housing, roads, schools, and hospitals, the abysmally low quality and meager choice of food and consumer goods, the ecological deterioration that is eroding the health of the Soviet population.

The way we lived helped us better understand the paradox that confronts Gorbachev's revolution: the same conditions that make change essential are those that obstruct it. Decades of mismanagement have convinced many Russians, including Gorbachev supporters, that nothing can be changed, while poor health, poor food, and other strains of everyday life sap the energy they might otherwise devote to reform. These conditions are a ticking time bomb. Gorbachev has only so long before they cease to be his justification for the reforms and become his opponents' proof that the reforms have failed. And those opponents are ideally situated to sabotage the reforms: Party and government bureaucrats whose special privileges insulate them from the scarcity they create have strong disincentives for change. They are using their considerable influence to fight tooth and nail against anything that might weaken their power or eliminate their jobs and privileges altogether.

We had never before lived the life of a Soviet family in a regular Soviet apartment building. It is something few Westerners, except those on the academic exchange, ever experience. All foreign journalists and embassy personnel in Moscow, down to the teachers in embassy schools, live in special apartment buildings for foreigners. The space per person far exceeds the Soviet norm; appliances, furniture, electronics, books, and videos are imported from Western Europe. Renovations are done by a special Austrian-run construction firm. Most food is imported from large export firms in Helsinki and Copenhagen.

Foreigners' buildings are "protected" by a twenty-four-hour militia guard posted in a highly visible booth outside the entrance. One taxi driver explained they were there to protect foreign guests from "those of our compatriots" who might try to get their hands on imported goodies. But they are really there, of course, to discourage contact between Russians and foreigners. Soviet guests have to be escorted past them; even in today's atmosphere of *glasnost* this is enough to discourage all but the most dissident, or the most official, of Soviets. The fact that our building had no sentry box amazed our Soviet acquaintances and emboldened several of them to visit us, rather than forcing us always to visit them, as we had in the past.

Our home for nearly five months was a two-room apartment on the fourteenth floor of a brick tower at 7 Gubkin Street, a block from Leninsky Prospekt on the southwest side of Moscow. The building belonged to the Academy of Sciences; though our apartment was reserved for foreign guests of the Academy (several American colleagues had previously lived in it), the other floors were occupied by Soviets, all of whom, presumably, had some connection with the Academy.

The neighborhood was a good one. The university was nearby. So were the new circus, the equally modern Children's Musical Theater, the Central Moscow Pioneer Palace, and the parks and green spaces of Lenin Hills. Streets were wide and pleasantly shaded. Between the buildings were plenty of playgrounds and yards for children. If the buildings had been well built and maintained, the stores stocked, and the air clean, this might have been an urban paradise. It was not.

Our apartment was an average one, by Soviet standards, for a family of four. It had two medium-sized rooms, a kitchen in which four could just squeeze around the table, a balcony, tiny entrance hall, bathroom, and toilet (separate, as in all Soviet housing). Like most new Soviet construction, it was a prefab unit, so the walls under the peeling wallpaper were all solid concrete, making it impossible to hang pictures. But soon after we arrived, Alex and Phoebe had made the painted surfaces their own with posters of White Snake and the Beatles. John Lennon making the V-sign in front of the Statue of Liberty dominated our kitchen all spring, more symbolic than we imagined of what was to come. Surprisingly, we found the apartment had almost everything we needed. For the first month, the refrigerator froze nearly everything we put in it, including milk; the hot water had an annoying tendency to vanish every day for variable periods, usually in the middle of a shower. Every summer it is turned off for a month at a time in various parts of the city for "boiler repair," but our hot water seemed to be on a schedule all its own. There was, however, always plenty of heat.

Our building and its next-door twin were under the command of Valentina Vasilyevna, our *komendantsha* (literally "female commandant," a title that both amused us and suited her personality). She was the one to call for things like refrigerator or plumbing repair, and she usually had the repairman at our door within a day or two. Their repair technique, it turned out, was to rob Peter to pay Paul. When our flimsy plastic toilet seat cracked or the hose to the shower attachment began leaking, her only alternative was to have the repairman cannibalize temporarily vacant apartments in the same building. Spare parts were unavailable, she explained, and besides, all the Academy's resources were going into the new building across the street, in its final stages of completion. During our first months in Moscow, construction brigades of soldiers, many of them with Central Asian features, were brought to work on it in Academy trucks which bore the laconic label "People."

Valentina Vasilyevna proudly told us that when the new building was ready, foreign visitors would have better, three-room apartments in it. A Soviet family would be settled in our apartment. And how long had

they been working on the new building? "Ten years."
Up on the corner of Vavilov and Dimitry Ulyanov
Streets was a large building, evidently under construction, which looked instead as if it were being demolished. The shoddy quality of brickwork and other
construction was evident even to our unprofessional
eyes. Nothing at all seemed to happen at that site during
the five months we were there. We speculated that a
safety inspection had brought construction to a halt and
the responsible bureaucracies hadn't been able to decide what to do with the white elephant. These buildings became symbols for us of the profound problems—
corruption is only one of them, we were told—in the
construction industry, problems that mushroomed in the
Brezhnev years.

Our plumber seemed efficient enough, and we attributed the rapid disintegration of his repair jobs to the
materials he had in hand. The allocation of resources to
repair and maintenance is evidently minuscule. We
were told the story of a Jewish refusenik, a highly
trained computer specialist, who became a handyman
after being dismissed from his institute. The tenants in
the housing unit where he worked adored him, for he
was the only sober workman they had been able to find
in years—which perhaps explains why we found a
wretched state of disrepair in even the newest of buildings. Middle-class Americans, we assured our Soviet
friends, would organize, protest to the landlord, collect
money for repairs themselves. Why didn't that happen
here? A few of our friends recalled episodes when they
had indeed gotten involved in such efforts, but to little
effect.

Some of the scourges of Western urban life have
begun to invade Moscow too. Several years ago we discovered that the entries to friends' apartments, at least
those in better neighborhoods, had acquired door locks
controlled by three-digit code boxes. Our building had

one too, but it didn't prevent neighborhood teenagers
who had no other place to go from hanging out in our
downstairs lobby. Some of them would ride the elevator
to the top-floor balcony and play music or shout down to
their friends below. Then the one piece of flimsy furniture which graced the entryway disappeared; soon the
pay telephone followed. The building administration
evidently tried countermeasures: toward the end of our
stay, we discovered that the door to the fourteenth-floor
balcony had been nailed shut. But since this was the
only access to the fire stairs, and the elevators were less
than reliable, we were not reassured.

Valentina Vasilyevna was down with pneumonia for
the first weeks we were there, so she was only a disem-
bodied voice on the telephone. When she finally re-
covered, she called, nearly two months into our stay, and
announced that she needed to do an inventory of the
apartment's contents. It seemed to make little sense at
this point, but inventory she did. This visit, and the parallel one she made just before we left to make sure all
the things were still there, typified the constant pro-
forma control and verification that goes on in Soviet society. The number of people whose only function is to
check up on others—not counting the KGB—is clearly
far greater than in American society. This overweight
administrative-supervisory structure is what makes Soviet industries and institutions so inefficient; one taxi
driver complained that in his garage there was one bureaucrat (administrator, bookkeeper, or the like) for
every two drivers.

Valentina Vasilyevna turned out to be a stocky, no-
nonsense woman in her sixties, who looked every bit
the *komendantsha*. She clearly approved of our house-
keeping, however, and on her final visit, when we mentioned we'd be leaving behind a few household items
we had bought as "our small contribution to *perestroika*," she positively beamed.

Registration of residence, or *propiska,* is a fundamental fact of life in the Soviet Union. One cannot live in the major cities without it, and once a Moscow *propiska* is in hand, people will do anything to avoid giving it up. Only toward the very end of our stay did the Soviet press begin to question this sacred cow, pointing out that the basis of the residence-permit system was administrative, not legal; there is no justification for it in the Soviet constitution. As temporary residents, we also had to register with the neighborhood *zhek* ("housing space utilization office"), which sent our passports off to the local militia, whence they reappeared in a few days, properly stamped.

While Jane was engaged in this bit of bureaucracy, she found herself alone for a moment in the office with another petitioner, a young man obviously well educated, perhaps a scientist. On discovering she was an American, he launched, with great ironic glee, into a description of all the bureaucratic procedures involved in registration of residence. "See all those forms?" he asked, drawing her attention to a bulletin board full of model forms. He was, he explained, currently engaged in the complex process of apartment exchange. When the clerk returned to the room, however, his momentary frankness ceased, and he fell silent. During the first few months of our stay, people were eager to talk but still careful about where they did so.

Apartment exchange is the way Muscovites manage to move within the city. Each weekend, a tabloid-size advertising supplement appears, full of listings of would-be exchanges. Typed notices frequently appeared on lampposts or the front door of our building. Housing-swap sagas have become legend. We found ourselves reduced to tears of laughter one evening as a good friend explained for half an hour in hilarious detail the steps she had gone through to exchange a two-room cooperative apartment on the edge of the city for her current three-room apartment in a more central neighborhood. The intermediate step had required finding separate one-room apartments for each of the three families who were sharing the apartment as communal housing. The process took a year, lots of negotiation, and a good deal of money changing hands under the table.

We had always assumed that any room assigned to foreigners was equipped with listening devices. On the other hand, our friends almost never seemed to worry about what they said in their own apartments. On rare occasions, if the conversation touched on a particularly ticklish subject, they would unplug the phone or cover it with a pillow. But even such caution had disappeared by the spring of 1988.

Thus we were particularly interested in how our Soviet guests would react in our apartment. In general, those who dared to come didn't seem too cautious, but at certain moments in the conversation they would fall silent and eye the ceiling. For one of our most outspoken visitors, this occurred only once, when instead of uttering aloud the taboo letters KGB, he wrote them on a napkin. Another visitor was quite candid over supper in our kitchen as we discussed Soviet history. But after dinner, he proposed we take a stroll in the neighborhood while escorting him to the bus, and his views took a decidedly more critical turn.

A charming young family in our building had been friends with some of our American predecessors. They seemed eager to get to know us but cautious, at first, about phoning us, and they kept glancing nervously at the ceiling whenever they were in our apartment. They spoke explicitly about their fears and their conscious efforts to overcome them: they'd decided not to let intimidation affect the way they behaved. Yet despite their best intentions and the new winds in the air, it wasn't easy.

One very big change was the willingness of nearly all

our friends and acquaintances to call us on the phone. On previous trips, we had taken pains to contact non-official friends only from pay phones, preferably a good distance away from our hotel, and *never* from the phone in a journalist's or diplomat's apartment. This meant that our friends couldn't call us with last-minute news of an interesting event. Now we began in the old mode, but friends' attitude was usually "So what if they do listen? I'm not going to let fear run my life anymore." We decided that since all our contacts were aboveboard and in some sense professional, it was better for any interested parties to know what we were doing, as long as our friends weren't worried. The phone, which rang constantly, became our lifeline to the world of Moscow Spring.

Vavilov, the main street at our corner, symbolized many of the things both good and still terribly bad about life in the Soviet Union. Traveling one direction on Vavilov was a pleasure. A fast subway ride from the center of town brought us to the University stop, where state-run kiosks sold newspapers, magazines, flowers, and ice cream, and new cooperatives offered waffles stuffed with whipped cream or frozen strawberries. A hundred yards away was the first stop of the tram line; spacious cars, seldom crowded, brought us home in six stops for a cost of five kopeks (eight cents at the official exchange rate of about $1.60 to the ruble). We could stop on the way at the Cheryomushinsky farm market and pick up some fresh food for dinner, then board the next tram and be dropped off right at the corner with our loaded shopping bag.

Vavilov in the other direction was a nightmare. The tram line had been under repair, we were told, for over two years. Because the tracks were ripped up, cars had to make lengthy detours to turn left into or out of our street. Sometimes impatient drivers tried shortcuts across the construction, usually with disastrous conse-

quences. One taxi we were in lost its exhaust pipe. The
driver seemed unconcerned—the car, after all, wasn't
his, and he'd get a breather back at the taxi depot while
it was being repaired.

Vavilov became for us a symbol of the "it doesn't be-
long to me" mentality. Sometime in midwinter, huge
piles of gravel were dumped all along the tracks. They
sat there for months, mountains covered with snow. At
our corner, rebellious drivers gradually knocked over
one of the piles, creating a makeshift road across the
tracks but in the process spilling gravel all over the as-
phalt. Each car that went by ground up the road, and its
own tires, but the spilled gravel stayed there for weeks
—evidently no one thought it his responsibility to clear
it away. In fact, though new sections of the tracks would
be torn up from time to time, and heavy equipment occasionally changed position along the tracks, we had the
feeling that it was being done by phantom workers—we
hardly ever saw anyone actually working on the project.

Litigiousness is not a problem in the USSR. Liability
insurance exists, but people are not used to resorting to
it. One day as we were crossing Vavilov, a woman next
to us tripped on a wire extending from the ripped-up
tracks. She fell hard on her face but fortunately wasn't
seriously injured; she picked herself up, brushed herself
off, and impassively went on her way. Did she, as we
did, blame the authorities for the scandalous conditions?
Did she think of suing? Or was it just another of those
indignities to which she was so accustomed that she
wasn't even conscious of them anymore? We would
have given a lot to be able to ask her, but it hardly
seemed the moment for an interview.

The aptly named temporary "zero" bus replaced the
trams on the line under repair. Some of Moscow's oldest, smallest, and smokiest buses were assigned to the
route, and they ran much less frequently than the roomy
trams they replaced. As a result, a long wait for the zero

bus was rewarded with a crushed, standing-room-only trip and a struggle to get off in which Jane more than once barely escaped with her life and her shopping bag. Several gloves and mittens never made it.

To be fair, Moscow's public transportation is generally good; it transports millions of residents and visitors every day around a very spread-out city with reasonable efficiency. Modern Hungarian-built double buses speed up and down Leninsky Prospekt at frequent intervals. The five-kopek fare for all surface and subway rides seemed a bargain to us, though Soviets on fixed incomes may have spotted inflation when the three- and four-kopek tram and trolley fares were recently raised to equal that of the faster buses and metros.

Snow removal on main roads was remarkably efficient. But pedestrian walks were another issue. Wintertime Moscow is a city of trampled, icy paths, glare ice on sidewalks, slushy gutters, and large piles of snow. It is a nightmare for the elderly. When spring comes, it is a muddy mess for nearly a month. Each year on the Saturday nearest Lenin's birthday, April 22, the whole population is exhorted to turn out for a volunteer work day. In Moscow at least, the 1988 spring cleanup accomplished a lot. But both efficiency and enthusiasm were low; we saw crews of students on the Lenin Hills languidly raking the winter dirt from the sidewalks. The old ritual voluntarism seemed an anachronism in the face of the authentic civic activism we saw growing all around us.

Just beyond our building, tucked away on a dead-end street, was a foreign-currency store that was a beehive of activity all spring. Taxis were constantly pulling into the street, carrying young and fashionably dressed women. This store was not for foreigners but for Soviets who had earned money in foreign currency, usually by working abroad in third-world countries. On their return to the Soviet Union, they were required to turn it in for coupons usable only in these special stores. They carried a selection of imported goods and hard-to-get Soviet products. How much of a selection, we were never to know, for the lines in front of the store were endless, and the militiamen stationed there to keep order admitted only a limited number of shoppers at a time. As part of *perestroika*'s pursuit of social justice, these stores were to close on July 1. The resulting wave of panic buying lasted all spring as Soviets rushed to use up their coupons before, like Cinderella, they turned into ordinary rubles.

We learned what the ruble could buy on Leninsky, which contained some of Moscow's best-stocked shops. Early in our stay, Jane explored those shops for some basic household needs that hadn't been on Valentina Vasilyevna's list. Buying four extra place settings of dishes and flatware became an afternoon's ordeal. By now, most Americans have read of the East European "three line" system: one line to choose the goods, one to pay for them, and one to receive them. In current Soviet practice, the first and third lines end up as an unruly crowd at the same counter, which is invariably understaffed by slow-moving, sullen young female salesclerks. The system seems designed to prevent shoplifting; rarely is merchandise available for consumer examination without the help of a saleswoman, who must be asked to produce the item from a glass case beneath the counter or from shelves behind her. And the division of labor between cash register and merchandise distribution presumably reduces insider pilferage. Questions about the quality of the merchandise or the availability of other sizes or styles are seldom welcome. "You see what we've got. If you don't want it, the next customer will be very happy to buy it, so why should I bother with you" is the unspoken message.

Muscovites were quick to blame the chronic crush in the stores on out-of-towners. As "locals" we constantly

found ourselves giving directions up and down Leninsky to a steady stream of shoppers from all over the Soviet Union. We often encountered Georgians or Central
Asians, the women in colorful native costume, in the taxi
line by the "Moscow" department store, laden down
with huge bundles, probably spending the large sums
they raked in selling their produce at the nearby farm
market. We were told that the city's population of eight
million was increased at least two million every day by
visitors. In lines at the corner produce store, we would
meet women who came into Moscow an hour or two
each week just to buy produce—none at all was available where they lived.

Jane's first stop was "1,000 Knickknacks," one of Moscow's largest housewares stores. The four flatware settings, similar in quality to those sold by American
supermarkets in special promotions, came to twelve rubles—a tidy sum for a Russian whose monthly income
averages slightly more than two hundred rubles.

Compared to the subsidized prices for basic food
items, most manufactured goods, including textiles, are
relatively expensive. In an essay which appeared in the
May issue of *Novy mir,* economics writer Vasily Seliu-
nin traced this arbitrary pricing policy back to the 1920s,
when it was devised as a form of taxation to extract capital for industrialization from the peasants—pay them
low prices for their agricultural products and make them
pay high prices for goods produced by the urban prole-
tariat. Such a pricing system makes little sense anymore.
Self-financing has been introduced to correct such
anomalies by cautious use of market mechanisms: if
overpriced low-quality goods won't sell, factories faced
with taking the losses themselves will presumably alter
production accordingly. The scenario has several obvious problems, the first of which is a managerial caste
trained not in market analysis but in fulfillment of plans
dictated from above. Moreover, until the cooperative

sector and more enlightened factories begin producing better goods at lower cost, consumers will have no alternative except refusing to buy at all.

At the store's only self-service counter, Jane bought a selection of laundry powders and cleaning liquids. Knowing nothing of the various brands, she turned for advice to a woman in line. Most of the products she recommended were produced in the Baltic republics, a significant clue to the backward state of the chemical industry in the Russian republic and the ecological crisis threatening those small, formerly independent nations.

Westerners have read that collectivization was a disaster for Soviet agriculture, that there are long lines for food in the Soviet Union, and that choice is limited. But it's hard for the average American, pampered by California, Florida, and South American produce all winter, to imagine how bad things really are, even in the best sections of Moscow. As emigré writer Vasily Aksyonov put it in his book *In Search of Melancholy Baby*, "When Americans read about food shortages in Russia, they have no clear picture of what is involved. Depending on their political orientation they conjure up either a famine or a late delivery of lobsters." As we often joked to Russian friends, the difference between Soviet and American conversations about food is that, while Soviets share information about what is (or, more often, is not) available to eat, Americans constantly discuss what *not* to eat—less salt, less sugar, less cholesterol, less caffeine. By American standards, the everyday Russian diet is appalling—fatty sausage and milk products, lots of sugar and alcohol, few fresh fruits and vegetables. It is no wonder that heart attacks are common in Soviet men in their fifties or even in their forties.

It's not that there's ever *nothing* to eat. Few people go hungry, which is more than America can boast. It's that the choice of what is available is extremely limited, and even staples can disappear without warning. On previous short visits, we had enjoyed the hospitality of resident Americans, while being a bit snobbish about their reluctance to go native and eat "real Russian food" —after all, we had had many delicious meals at the apartments of Soviet friends who did wonders with available ingredients.

When we stayed in Intourist hotels, we were isolated from the realities of the local food supply. Intourist makes sure that tourists, particularly in prepaid groups, are adequately, if not luxuriously, fed. But on this trip, we were determined to feed ourselves and the children as much as possible from the local economy. For one thing, we received our stipends in rubles, which could not be converted back to dollars or taken out of the country. Except for books, taxis, and internal travel, there was little besides food that we wanted to spend them on.

Feeding our family in Moscow involved balancing three often competing criteria: what was available, what the children would eat, and what would keep as close as possible to the kind of diet we were convinced was essential for our health. About the only thing we found easy to avoid was preservatives—the Soviets are at least twenty-five years behind us in these. It may have been coincidental, but in the first month both of the children came down with Moscow flu, which made them sicker than they'd ever been at home. Phoebe was out of school for two weeks, and Alex developed pleurisy. The experience left us with a new appreciation of the real, immediate connection between nutrition and health, an understanding of the Soviet mother's wolverine-like protectiveness and concern for what her children eat, and an explanation for why Soviets seemed to be ill longer and more frequently than Americans. We brought a generous supply of multivitamins, which we took religiously. To them we attribute our relative good health throughout the spring. Good-quality vitamins are not available to Soviet citizens to make up for deficiencies in diet, and we found ourselves sharing our surplus with friends. We always chuckled to think of one elderly Moscow intellectual taking her Fred Flintstone vitamin each morning.

Actually, we did not do very well in our campaign to feed ourselves from the local economy, but in the process, we got a real understanding of the daily frustrations encountered by Soviet citizens and how quickly and with what resignation they adapt to situations beyond their control. Paradoxically, we also discovered that irregular availability of goods adds a certain *frisson* to the daily grind—each "deficit" item one comes across and manages to bring home is a little victory.

One day Jane noticed the clerk at our neighborhood store doling out half-kilo bags of sugar from a large burlap bag rather than simply taking packages off the shelf. A few days later, she discovered a long line at the usually deserted dry-grocery counter. So we learned firsthand of the sugar shortage, caused by the rise in home brewing. By May sugar rationing had been introduced in most provincial cities; one evening in Odessa, we were at two different homes when someone knocked at the door to deliver "invitations" to buy one and a half kilos of sugar a month. By the time we left, the press was full of articles analyzing the "psychology of scarcity" and trying to understand how one of the few items of which the USSR had always had a surplus could suddenly disappear.

The one item of food in the Soviet Union that was tasty, cheap, and always available was bread. In fact, at twenty kopeks for a one-kilo loaf, farmers were using it to feed their private livestock. Baked without preservatives, it went stale quickly, but was wonderful when fresh. Since it was so cheap, it was easy to throw out stale bread and buy a new loaf nearly every day. We were evidently not the only ones so tempted; posters in every bread store and cafeteria urged customers to "conserve bread." But, as Americans discovered with cheap energy, conscience is far less effective than economics —as long as bread remains cheap, wastage will continue.

Two blocks from our building was the neighborhood fruit and vegetable store, offering a narrow selection of bottled fruit juices and canned fruits, usually in four-liter glass jars that sat on the shelf for weeks, gathering dust. Friends explained that since food processors' output is measured in sheer volume, it is cheaper and easier to bottle one large jar than four or eight small ones. There were one or two kinds of jam, applesauce, and a canned pepper stew. The latter was from Hungary, the former largely from Bulgaria. Occasionally, there would be shipments of Polish frozen foods—mixed vegetables, peas and carrots, once in a while strawberries. Most of the reasonable-quality processed food products available in Moscow stores come from the small countries of Eastern Europe.

As for fresh produce, one could (almost) always rely on five winter vegetables: potatoes, carrots, beets, cabbage, and onions, at subsidized prices that seemed ridiculously low—as did the quality. One night on the news, we saw an exposé of conditions in one of the Moscow "Vegetable Bases," chronically understaffed storage warehouses which supply all the stores in their part of the city. TV cameras panned over a large, unrefrigerated room where a huge delivery of crated cabbages had been ignored since November. By March, the entire stock was rotten, and fetid liquid covered the floor to a depth of several inches. Those responsible had been fired. Such exposés became more frequent, revealing the unbelievable percentage of certain commodities (up to 80 percent, in one account) that spoil in the distribution network. But Soviets are discovering the bitter truth that public exposure of abuses, even by the *glasnost-*

emboldened media, does not immediately eliminate
them. *Glasnost,* again, is far easier than *perestroika.*

We could afford to do much of our shopping in the
nearby Cheryomushinsky farm market. There are several such indoor markets in Moscow, the last vestige of
free enterprise to survive on the margins of the state
system as an outlet for surplus collective-farm produce
or the produce of the tiny private plots collective farmers are allowed for their own use. Prices are two to three
times what the state stores charge for the same commodities—if they have them, which is rare—but the quality
is much higher. We visited Cheryomushinsky at least
once a week for farm-fresh cottage cheese and sour
cream, dill and coriander, apples, carrots, green onions,
tomatoes, cucumbers, radishes, even occasionally eggs
and a chicken. We could never bring ourselves to buy
pork or beef at the marble-topped counters decorated
with grinning pigs' heads and presided over by equally
jovial country folk, though the meat looked appetizing
enough. Nor could we bring ourselves to haggle, as cus-
tom required; and the market's prices were so high that,
even though we could afford them, it went against the
grain to pay them. Ripe tomatoes from the Caucasus and
Central Asia were available all winter—at twenty rubles
a kilo, or about two dollars a tomato. Small wonder that
our fellow shoppers were mostly other foreigners or
very well-dressed Soviets.

Our Soviet friends occasionally splurged at the farm
market, particularly when company was invited. But
they made do in other ways as well. There's more to
Soviet food shopping than what's in the stores and the
farmers' market. Selections of "deficit" items were offered for weekly special orders at many places of work,
and the more prestigious the workplace, the better the
selection. Friends who lived down the road from a Central Committee housing complex luxuriated in weekly
deliveries of scarce dairy products like sweet cream.

Their neighbors got home delivery from special stores, and the surplus (such privileged neighbors were often away on business trips) was delivered to them by the friendly milkman, who undoubtedly got a few extra rubles for his thoughtfulness.

Many grocery stores also had an order department where scarce goods could be ordered in the morning for afternoon pickup, but they usually combined desirable "deficit" products like coffee with a required companion product that was a drug on the market—a way of boosting sales figures and raising the real price of goods. Order departments served different constituencies on different days—the weekly schedule at our neighborhood store included several nearby institutes. "The population" could order only once or twice a week. It helps to have a family member free to get out to the stores in the morning when deliveries are made and to visit several stores "just in case" one happens to have something available.

The phrase "just in case" *(avos')* has lent itself to the handy European string bag, called in Russian an *avoska;* prudent Soviets never leave home without one, or its modern plastic equivalent. The public squares around the entrances to busy subway stations usually have outdoor vendors dispatched by some nearby grocery store, selling whatever happens to be delivered that day. A delivery truck drives right up onto the plaza, and sales continue till the truckload is gone.

For us, all this was a game. We could always fall back on the farm market or the Embassy commissary, where produce arrived from Helsinki every week to ten days. And, like high Party and government officials, we too had our "special store," the "diplomatic gastronome" not far from the American Embassy. The selection of high-quality food and liquor available to diplomats for hard currency probably parallels what is available in "special stores" for the Party and government hierarchy.

The most visible aspect of the much heralded cooperative movement is the wave of new restaurants and
cafés that opened in Moscow in the past few years. By
January 1988 there were already thirty or more, with the
number growing rapidly. There is, of course, no advertising; information about their location and telephone
number circulates by word of mouth. The first to open,
and still the most elegant, was the Kropotkinskaya, located in what was once a private mansion in one of Moscow's few extant old neighborhoods. We ate there twice,
and the food was excellent, the ambience charming, the
service attentive. The prices, however, are nearly twice
that in state-run restaurants, which makes them out of
reach for the man in the street.

The cooperatives are not without other of capitalism's
faults. A young Soviet entrepreneur took Bill to lunch a
few times at "The Stork," located in an old residential
section full of places immortalized in Bulgakov's *The
Master and Margarita*. The building had been newly
landscaped, and an elegant bronze stork decorated the
corner lawn. There was a plush, red-carpeted interior
with heavy red curtains hiding all this luxury from cas-
ual view. Bill noticed that the bill did not come to more
than ten rubles a person; a bit steep for Moscow but,
even when calculated at the official rate ($16), certainly
reasonable by New York standards. We decided to invite
Bill's brother, sister-in-law, and their two boys there for
Easter dinner. In a fit of magnanimity, we included two
of Phil's colleagues who happened to be in town.

When we called to make the reservation, Bill was
asked if we wanted to have the table "set," that is, ready
when we arrived with plates of the traditional cold hors
d'oeuvres or *zakuski* which form an important part of
the Russian meal. "Sure," said Bill. We arrived to find
the large table covered end to end with platters of cold
meats, aspics, tomatoes, spicy Georgian bean salads, etc.
Much of it was too spicy for the children, and there was

a great deal more than even our large group could possibly eat. Still, we went on to order the rest of the meal. When the check arrived, the total came to 260 rubles, or over $400. The *zakuski* alone had come to more than 100 rubles. We found ourselves, in embarrassment, borrowing cash from our guests. We later discovered that this is fairly standard practice; the waitress at another co-op explained that a reservation automatically includes a standard setting of *zakuski*, which becomes, quite literally, a "cover" charge. Still, we think "The Stork" brought much more than we bargained for.

The Atrium, which opened in May on Leninsky, was a marvel of interior design. The designer was an old friend of the poet Andrey Voznesensky from the days when both were students at the architectural institute, and it was Voznesensky who clued us in to the newly opened restaurant, which had no obvious sign. Next to the entrance was a discreet notice with the evidently permanent legend, "Sorry, no free places." But when, with our reservation, we were escorted inside at about seven o'clock on a Friday evening, there were only a few other parties seated in the Italianate, high-ceilinged restaurant, fountains gurgling from its marble walls. The food was quite good, though not Italian, as the name and decor seemed to promise. As at the other cooperatives, liquor was unavailable, though customers could bring their own. The bill this time was less than 80 rubles for five of us. The cooperatives have made life more pleasant for the foreign community and for those few Soviets who can afford them; so far their impact on the life of most Russians has been negligible.

The weekend arts and crafts fair at Moscow's Izmailovsky Park is a new realm of free enterprise with a wider clientele. The site is infamous as the location of a 1970s avant-garde art exhibit which was bulldozed by the authorities. A first-time visitor has only to follow the crowds from the subway station across a field until the

line of artists and craftsmen begins. They display their
wares on homemade portable stands, or simply spread
them out on cloths on the ground. Paintings are propped
against the walls of the magnificent old cathedral that
forms the park's centerpiece. There are copper brace-
lets, popular for their reputed medicinal benefits; cutting boards brightly painted in traditional Russian folk
patterns; painted wooden eggs, many with religious mo-
tifs; handmade *matrioshka* dolls one inside the other,
but very different from the all-alike versions offered in
hard-currency tourist shops; macramé; handmade pot-
holders, aprons, slippers, handkerchiefs; fanciful Plasti-
cine creatures; dancing animal marionettes; handmade
jewelry; and oil paintings of all kinds. Phoebe sat for a
very successful twenty-minute pencil portrait which set
us back all of ten rubles.

One of our favorite entrepreneurs sold glass tumblers
etched with the Moscow skyline and the slogans "Glasnost," "Perestroika," and the ironic "Sobriety—the
Norm of Life." Our least favorite vendor offered a cultural icon for every taste: Stalin, Jesus Christ, poet-bard
Vladimir Vysotsky, or a female nude.

Exhibitors number in the hundreds, shoppers in the
thousands. Visitors make their way along a hilly, wind-
ing path lined on both sides with craftsmen hawking
their wares. The market goes on for nearly a mile. The
crush is such that friends or children can easily get lost
in the crowd. We saw medics remove one woman who
had slipped down a steep bank in the mud of the April
thaw. We briefly wondered if, by closing their eyes to
unsafe conditions rather than trying to alleviate them,
the authorities weren't hoping to discredit the "anarchy" of free enterprise. But the eager crowds of both
shoppers and artisans indicate that the fair meets a need,
if only for something interesting to do on a weekend
afternoon.

The cooperative movement has expanded into education. Jane was invited to observe a cooperative-run English class using intensive oral methods. The students were rank beginners, but their ability to converse, at least within the controlled situation provided, was impressive. The teacher was a talented young woman with nearly flawless American English, dressed in jeans, a T-shirt with a New York Yankees logo, a windbreaker, and running shoes. She even had American body language down to a science. When she switched to Russian later on in the conversation, her whole demeanor changed; the open smile vanished, the face became closed and cautious. The coop, she said, provided her with an up-to-date textbook and methodology, a classful of motivated students, and a place to teach (in one of the local "houses of culture," a kind of community center). They paid her 600 rubles for the month-long course. But she calculated the coop organizers were taking in at least 3,000 rubles from her students alone.

The Soviet-American pizza truck, a joint venture which first appeared in Moscow in the spring of 1988, sold quite acceptable pizza, by the slice or the whole pie, in a variety of locations around town. Some days it was parked on the Arbat pedestrian mall next to the giant Ministry of Foreign Affairs; other days it was in Gorky Park or at the International Hotel, headquarters for foreign firms and businessmen. One sunny May day, pizza-starved Alex made a date with Jane to meet him for lunch at the Arbat location, not far from his job at the Embassy. She had the presence of mind to get there fifteen minutes early, and indeed, there was a long line. But the huge truck's large ovens and energetic young Soviet-American staff kept things moving, and by the time Alex arrived, he was delighted to see Jane near the head of the line. Ten rubles was a bit steep for a cheese pizza, but the wonder was that it was pizza at all. Plenty of Soviets seemed happy to shell out 1.25 rubles for a slice. Both rubles and hard currency are accepted, but there's a catch: for rubles, you get plain cheese. On the days when they work next to the International Hotel, they take hard currency only and offer toppings. At any rate, it was an improvement over the state-run pizza parlor in our neighborhood that often as not was "closed for technical reasons." What, we asked, were the technical reasons? "No cheese."

Another seemingly promising area for newly authorized "individual labor activity" is the taxi business. Here it is really a question of the state regulating, and thereby taxing, an activity that has gone on illegally for years. While high officials sit in endless meetings, the drivers of their official cars pick up extra rubles on the side (*nalevo*) by acting as free-lance taxis. This practice can be curtailed only by cutting down on official cars, a reform both officials and their drivers obviously resist. But there is another class of *chastniki*, or privateers, who use their own cars in their spare time to pick up extra money. In the past, we had been wary of *chastniki*, fearing either provocation or overcharging. This time, when we were in a hurry, we flagged down anyone who would stop and never experienced any unpleasantness. We met some very interesting drivers that way and learned a lot about the limitations of the economic reforms.

Very few if any of our Moscow *chastniki* had registered to become "official." Their reasons were persuasive. Registration required burdensome medical exams, payment of a fee, and of course heavy taxes on the outside income. But most burdensome was the requirement that all individual labor activity be moonlighting; the workers must have primary jobs in the state sector. Several *chastniki*, who drove essentially full time, were understandably reluctant to explain to us how they had worked around this requirement. But the state sees it as essential for its own protection: given the low state salaries and the profits to be made in free enterprise, the labor-poor state sector could quickly be stripped of its most energetic and enterprising workers. Regular taxi drivers often complained that the *chastniki* were taking away many of their most lucrative fares, since they were free to pick and choose their riders. Except in the Baltic republics, where coop taxis now carry removable roof signs, we saw no evidence that the movement to legalize free-lance taxis had gone anywhere.

The real barrier to the cooperative movement lies in the state sector itself. As long as neither its wages nor prices have any relation to reality, the cooperative sector will remain a troublesome exception in a society that has never been comfortable with the entrepreneurial spirit. A professor of law who had been involved in drafting the new law on cooperatives gave a revealing illustration. What would you do, he asked, in the following situation: an entrepreneur buys himself a telescope and sets it up on Lenin Hills at the overlook with a panoramic view of Moscow. In capitalist countries, such sites would have several coin-operated telescopes, but Soviet state enterprise has never thought of installing them. So our entrepreneur has found a need, met it, and takes in up to two hundred rubles a day by charging tourists fifty kopeks a shot for a view of the city. Meanwhile the state employee who works in the park downhill from the parapet earns less than two hundred rubles a *month* for cleaning up trash. How does society cope with this inequality? The obvious American answer, "Encourage competition among telescope operators to bring the price down," is problematic in a society where competition, telescopes, and available labor are all scarce commodities.

GETTING STARTED

As scholars on the academic exchange program, one of our first tasks was getting started professionally. That meant checking in with our official hosts at the Academy of Sciences and at Moscow State University, getting down to work at libraries and archives, and resuming contacts with Soviet colleagues we had met over the years. Even in these initial professional encounters, we hoped to see the beneficent effects of Gorbachev's reforms. But when Bill stopped by the Academy to begin the process of extending his visa, he met the single most unpleasant, unreconstructed, anti-American bureaucrat he had ever encountered.

The administrative offices of the Academy of Sciences are located off Leninsky Prospekt on the grounds of a vast former estate that used to sit at the edge of the city but is now surrounded by it. To reach the faded yellow, colonnaded neoclassical buildings, one passes through

a gate guarded by two statues; the inevitable Soviet po-
licemen are on duty inside the main building. Nikolay
Vasilyevich Belousov, a short, slight man in his sixties
with a fringe of white hair, was in charge of handling
American academic exchangees. Judging by his age and
the size of his office (very big), he had been around for
a long time. We later learned from other Americans that
Belousov had been the bane of their existence. Compared to the average Russian, Belousov did pretty well,
pulling down what must have been a generous salary
and enjoying more than his share of perks. But the
American scholars who paraded through his office over
the years, demanding the kind of access and service the
Soviet system could not or would not provide, outdid
him by far. This must have grated on him even before
perestroika began. When Gorbachev's stress on cordial
relations with Americans threatened to make his brand
of surliness obsolete and deprive him of the good life as
well, his sourness deepened.

Bill knew none of this when he entered Belousov's
office. But Belousov knew all about Bill. He knew Bill's
brother and sister-in-law wrote for *The New York Times*.
That was another reason, it occurred to us later, why the
Soviets might not have wanted Bill around for more than
a month or so. Perhaps Belousov himself had made that
decision, out of fear that he might end up getting unwel-
come publicity if Bill complained to Phil, and Phil chose
to write about it. In fact, Bill and Phil made it a rule to
eschew a correspondent-source relationship. But neither Belousov nor any other official Russian could count
on that. Belousov "knew," or so he informed Bill with a
snide smile, that the main reason we wanted to stay in
Moscow for nearly five months was to make big bucks
renting our house in Amherst.

This didn't bode well for the main item on Bill's
agenda—the matter of extending his visa. "Much too
soon to talk about that," Belousov muttered. If it were

up to him, we thought, the right time would be five minutes before Bill's plane took off for New York. Who had decided how much time to give him? Bill asked. "The institutes with which you sought affiliation," Belousov answered. "They are the ones who know you and are competent to evaluate your work." No one at the institutes in question ever confirmed Belousov's story. We suspected it was made up out of whole cloth. Belousov was the very essence of the bureaucratic bully we had read so many complaints about in the now pro-reform Soviet press—the official who, browbeaten by his superiors, browbeats his subordinates in turn.

Depressed as we were about prospects for extending Bill's visa, we were more distressed about what Belousov's power indicated of the state of affairs in Gorbachev's Russia. With men like him still staffing the bureaucracy, how far could the reforms go? Leaving the office, Bill resolved to do his bit for change by complaining about Belousov to anyone who would listen, asking whether a man like him was representative of the "new thinking" that was supposed to govern relations with Americans. We knew, of course, that Bill's campaign would have absolutely no effect. So we are not about to claim credit for the fact that within three weeks Belousov had been pensioned off and Bill had been granted a visa good for the entire stay he had requested.

Bill never met Belousov's successor. He dealt instead with his former underlings, young men in their thirties who couldn't have been more pleasant and cooperative. They were as caught up in the heady atmosphere of Moscow Spring as we were. One day in early April, Bill dropped by to make arrangements for a trip we were taking to Leningrad and Tallin. What they were preoccupied with that morning was the same daring article we had been reading, which revealed that certain Soviet generals captured by the Germans had been arrested by Stalin after the war, held in captivity until early in the

1950s, and then executed. The young men at the Academy were now asking themselves why even Stalin, a
man of surpassing cruelty, would have done such a
thing. To avoid having to admit, one of them speculated,
that the initial arrests had been a mistake.

For just how many deaths was Stalin responsible? "I
heard that more than ten million died in the course of
collectivization," commented another, as easily and nat-
urally as if he had been repeating a piece of office gos-
sip. Where had he heard that? He had read it in a journal
called *Argumenty i fakty* ("Arguments and Facts"),
which is published for the edification of millions of
Party activists. The figure of ten million deaths from
collectivization is considered too high even by some
Western and Soviet emigré analysts. The fact that it
could appear in an official Party publication and then be
bandied about in an ordinary office was a revelation. We
later learned that similar figures had appeared in other
Soviet journals. But the gruesome calculus of corpses
seemed to have no effect on Gorbachev's second-in-
command, Yegor Ligachev, who continued to insist that
the great achievements of the past were as important, if
not more so, than Stalin's "mistakes." The clear implication of such "balanced" historical appraisals was that
the millions of deaths were in some sense justified, an
acceptable price to pay for past accomplishments. But
the young men at the Academy would have none of that.
Nothing could justify so much killing, said one of them.
Nothing!

So reasonable and accessible were the new men that
Bill dared to ask them about their former boss. They
were suitably diplomatic. He was a man of the old
school, they said; what other people took as nastiness
was his notion of humor. Only body language suggested
that they were as grateful as Bill for his departure.
Where was he now? It turned out he was living in our
apartment house. Bill had complained at home about

him, hoping to convey to the kids, with a personal example, a basic truth about the country they were now
living in. Informed that the "bad guy" lived in our very
own building, they were on the lookout for him. He was
a sad sight when Phoebe finally spotted him opening his
mailbox in the lobby and called to us. Back in his office,
Bill had noticed mainly his arrogance. Now we were
struck by his slight stoop and defeated look. We felt
sorry for him.

That would make a nice ending. We could add a post-
script, reflecting on the complicated human cost of even
the most needed reforms. We could speculate that the
prospect of paying that price greatly intensifies the determination with which older officials resist change. But
the personal sympathy we felt for him vanished in a
surreal coda to the story at a drunken party in our next-
door neighbor's apartment. The neighbor was a visitor
from a Scandinavian country whose citizens are renowned for their ability to outdrink the Russians themselves. He was heading up an Academy construction
project for which Belousov was a consultant. Belousov
turned out to be the soberest man at the party, which
was not saying much. When Bill arrived, he staggered
over, swatted him on the shoulder, and began ribbing
him: "Fancy meeting you here. I thought your visa had
run out by now." Bill toyed with answering that in fact
he was not there, that it was only the vodka that led
Belousov to think so, but before he could, Belousov was
off joshing about Bill's financial situation. "So you're
making big money by renting your Amherst house," he
said again. "And your son must be raking it in working
at the embassy."

Just at this point, Soviet television came to Bill's rescue. Several weeks before, he had taken part in a televised "spacebridge" linking Moscow and Boston. Soviet
television chose to rebroadcast the program that very
evening, and just when Bill was jousting with Belousov,

the one fairly lengthy speech he had made on camera came on the screen. Phoebe, who had been watching TV next door, came running in to tell Bill the news. Emboldened by the coincidence, which seemed to sober up Belousov in a hurry, Bill resolved to find out whether the man was as reactionary politically as he was unpleasant personally. The Soviet press was just then in a tizzy about a conservative manifesto which *Pravda* had lambasted a few days before. We had met plenty of people who were outraged by the manifesto, which among other things condemned Jews as a "reactionary nation," but no one we knew admitted to sharing its sentiments. If anyone did, it would be Belousov. So Bill asked him. And Belousov said that he did, in no uncertain terms. That took guts. Involuntarily, Bill's sympathy for him began to return. But just at that moment, the television screen showed MIT physicist Viktor Weisskopf explaining how he had been allowed to work on the Manhattan Project to develop the atomic bomb even though he had only recently arrived as a Jewish refugee from German-occupied Europe. "Yet again, the damn Jews!" muttered Belousov.

Jane's official contact in the Moscow State University foreign department, in sharp contrast to Belousov, was a pleasant and polite young woman. But Evgenya Stanis-lavovna was limited in the help she could render by the effects of reform in her own bailiwick. The Ministry of Higher Education had just been abolished. In due course, its functions would be transferred to a new State Committee on Higher Education which would undoubt-edly reproduce the same problems under a new name. But in the meantime, Evgenya Stanislavovna had no boss, the worst fate that can befall a bureaucrat. She would have liked to provide authorization and funds for Jane's research trips outside of Moscow, but until the last minute she herself had no permission to do so.

The problems we encountered collecting our stipends

provide a mini-illustration of what *perestroika* is up against. Getting paid by check was impossible; there *are* no checks in the Soviet Union. Sending cash through the mail was obviously out. Computers are still extremely rare in Soviet offices, and it is the advanced office that uses an electronic calculator rather than an abacus.

Bill's monthly obstacle course took him from the Academy's foreign department (which authorized payment) to some kind of comptroller's office (which authorized it again on a different piece of paper) to the cashier who counted it out. When the time came to pay for long-distance telephone calls made on our apartment phone, another Academy office invited us politely to do so in person. Of all the Gogolian clerks' nests we have encountered on our Soviet trips, this was our favorite. Three middle-aged women sat in a row at desks piled high with papers. The clerk closest to the door was a plump but sexy blonde who seemed to be trying to turn a routine transaction into an exciting flirtation with an American. Her colleagues appeared to pay no attention; the only thing that gave them away was their giggles at her sallies. The cashier's office was a mere twenty meters away, but Bill's admirer offered to accompany him. As they strolled across the hall, he could hear her colleagues' giggles turn to guffaws.

Jane's bimonthly stipend trip could consume a frustrating hour and a half. She never went without calling first, to make sure the form was ready, but even this was not foolproof. One day, as luck would have it, Jane had to be back in time for a call we had placed to the States. Since it was Soviet Army Day, she was particularly careful to call first and make sure the office was open as usual. Evgenya Stanislavovna assured her she would be keeping normal office hours. But when Jane arrived, the door was locked, and foreign students waiting there informed her that the whole office had just left "to con-

gratulate the rector and the other men on the occasion
of their holiday." Evgenya Stanislavovna would not be
back for at least forty-five minutes.

Our stipends were paid in whatever denominations
happened to be available that day. Sometimes it was
fifty-ruble bills, a few times it was entirely in fives—our
wallets could hardly hold so many bills. The money was,
more often than not, in brand-new bills. Apparently, the
printing presses were running overtime to cover budget
deficits, producing an inflation Gorbachev only much
later admitted to in public.

On the advice of an American colleague, we decided
to deposit some of our surplus rubles in a bank. On one
of our first days in Moscow, we dropped into a downtown savings bank (*sberkassa*) and asked if we, as Americans, could open an account. The young woman at the
inquiry window looked at us in panic and immediately
referred us to her supervisor, a businesslike older
woman. We repeated our inquiry, and she broke into a
friendly grin. "I don't know," she replied, "but I'll find
out." A quick phone call assured her there was no reason
we couldn't, so we filled out the required forms and got
in line. The forms asked for the usual information:
name, age, address, etc. One question gave us pause:
"To which social group of the population do you be-
long?" A bit embarrassed that our knowledge of Soviet
class definitions did not equal our mastery of Russian,
we quietly inquired what to answer. "We're professors,"
we explained. *Sliuzhiashchie* [white-collar workers] the
girl replied, even more embarrassed than we at the
seeming irrelevance of this outmoded question.

The bank office was definitely low-tech. Account records were maintained in paper files stored on revolving
wooden stands, reminiscent of the dentists' offices of our
childhood. As we were leaving, the supervisor flashed
us another smile and inquired with professional curiosity, "I'll bet things are done rather differently in Amer-

ica." "Yes," we replied, and left. We didn't have the heart to tell her *how* differently.

The Lenin Library offers American academic exchangees a reader's card in ten minutes. All one needs are a passport and two photographs. Soviet citizens do not have it so easy; they must present a special certificate from their place of work. All research, this implies, is for the benefit of the state. Another reason for the limit is that "the largest library in the world" is already overcrowded, and removal of these restrictions would make for chaos. Non-official readers can use their local public libraries, but those are overcrowded too and their collections are much skimpier.

The Lenin Library, an imposing structure only a block from the Kremlin, boasts four huge reading rooms. All are filled soon after the library's 9:00 A.M. opening, and it is common to see would-be readers circling the room, searching for an empty desk. As Westerners, we were assigned to the less crowded Hall No. 1, otherwise reserved for "academicians, professors, and doctors of science."

But under its imposing surface lay a rotting infrastructure, and rather than getting better, it was much worse than when Bill worked there in the 1960s. One warm day in March, Jane was distracted from her reading by an insistent tapping. Could it be that one of the distinguished-looking Soviet scholars who surrounded her was acting up or flipping out? Finally she realized what it was—the ornately carved ceiling of the elegant, two-story-high reading room was leaking, and small plastic wastebaskets had been placed around the room to catch the drips. When we pushed open the heavy, oak doors of the carpeted Hall No. 1, we were hit by a pervasive odor of urine from the corridor, wafting up from the toilets in the basement.

The library cafeteria hadn't improved since the 1960s. Food was relatively cheap, but of soup-kitchen quality or less. Greasy soups, fatty sausage, half-glasses of sour cream, which our fellow readers took straight. Gray, unappetizing cutlets served with soggy macaroni, wallpaper-paste mashed potatoes, or overcooked cabbage. It was a sad sight to observe our fellow diners, all of them, we knew, serious researchers in their own fields, resignedly eating this substandard fare with the bent aluminum forks and spoons that emerged from a cold-water rinse in the dish room.

There are only two microfilm machines at Lenin Library on which one can read back issues of *Pravda* and other newspapers. (Amherst College, with an enrollment of 1,500, has eight.) We were delighted to hear that Xeroxing had at last become possible, but there were no coin-operated, do-it-yourself machines. Our daily routine was conditioned by the ninety-minute slot during which the Xerox window accepted orders from readers in Hall No. 1. The twenty-copy-a-day limit (due, the sign announced, to "a shortage of paper") kept us in line nearly every day. The copies emerged on a coarse yellowish stock reminiscent of construction paper.

The sad state of the Lenin Library shows how the rot that prompted Gorbachev's reforms had reached even the most sacred Soviet institutions. In mid-February 1988, the library of the Academy of Sciences in Leningrad, which dated from the time of Peter the Great, was heavily damaged by fire. Nearly half a million volumes were damaged or destroyed. Investigations revealed that fire-detection systems were primitive or nonexistent. Many of the rare books damaged or lost were undoubtedly never microfilmed because of lack of resources.

Why is such a wealthy country so poor? A major explanation lies in a statistic published in the Soviet press for the first time in 1988: the USSR spends nearly 20 percent of its gross national product on defense, as compared to 6 percent in the United States. (Curiously,

Moscow News felt it could divulge this state secret only in the form of an interview with Zbigniew Brzezinski.) And, as our friends hastened to tell us, that 20 percent was just for the armed forces. What about the cost of the KGB and all the other means of controlling the population?

Late in our stay, in an article by Aleksander Bovin, we came across a phrase that summed up the paradox of power combined with poverty. During the Brezhnev years, Bovin stood out from his peers as a witty, sharp-tongued political observer. One might have expected him to prosper under Gorbachev, but he has not, perhaps because of his association with Brezhnev, or perhaps because in repentance for that association his tongue has become too sharp even for Gorbachev. Bovin was the first to complain of the lack of *glasnost* in foreign affairs. The phrase that struck us occurred in an article in the journal *New Times:* "Some of our enemies abroad," Bovin wrote, "have called our country 'Upper Volta with Rockets.' "

Bovin, of course, went on to deny the allegation, but the very fact that he could mention it was a sign of the times. The device of mentioning and then denying a point has its roots in Old Russian epic poetry ("It is not seven swans descending on the strings of the lyre, it is the talented fingers of Boyan . . ."). It has in fact become a ploy of modern writers bending the censorship. One young scholar explained to us how his book, *Bourgeois Approaches to [his subject],* was far more daring than it appeared at first glance. Though he criticized the writings of Western scholars on the question, he quoted them at length before doing so. Getting those unsayable things before his audience, even though he ostensibly distanced himself from them, was the whole point of the book, and his attentive Soviet reader, he assured us, would understand.

Bovin's phrase continued to haunt us. The evidence

was all around us. What was new was that we did not
have to find it for ourselves—as the spring went on,
more and more of it was published in the Soviet press.
Minister of Health Yevgeny Chazov, joint winner of the
Nobel Peace Prize for founding International Physicians
for the Prevention of Nuclear War, revealed that 30 percent of Soviet hospitals lack indoor plumbing. We had
always felt qualms about complaining to our friends
about Soviet backwardness. But as the months passed,
we became more and more convinced that a country
with the immense natural and human resources of the
Soviet Union no longer has any excuse for the dreadful
conditions in which so many of its citizens live and
work. Before World War II, these conditions were called
"relics of the past." After the war, they were blamed on
"the destruction wrought by the war." The next culprit
was the cold war and the arms race foisted on the USSR
by the West. But nearly forty-five years after the war, in
a world economy where Japan and Germany, which lost
the war, loom so large and even South Korea, Taiwan,
and other small Asian countries put the Soviet economy
to shame, such excuses are no longer viable. And many
Russians now admit it.

In addition to her contact in the foreign department,
Moscow University provided Jane with an academic adviser known as a *konsultant*. Reports from past American exchange participants indicated that this would
probably be a senior, politically reliable scholar who
often dealt with foreigners, probably with no interest
whatsoever in Jane's topic. Instead, her *konsultant*
turned out to be an intelligent and energetic woman in
her thirties with a professional interest, extremely rare
among Soviet scholars, in women's writing. Moreover,
she knew enough about Jane's field to inquire why she
had chosen such a tame topic—"Chukovsky as a scholar
of Nekrasov"—as her formal project for the exchange.
Jane explained that she was actually working on a full-

scale biography, but exchange scholars were careful to avoid stepping on Soviet sensibilities in describing their projects. Nekrasov is canonized as a revolutionary poet for his "sympathy with the people"; Chukovsky had been awarded a Lenin Prize for his book on Nekrasov. In the fall of 1986, when Jane's application was made, discretion seemed the better part of valor. The range of the possible had so expanded since then that Jane's caution now seemed incomprehensible to her adviser.

She invited Jane to her apartment for tea one evening; there, she said, they could conduct their business efficiently. Efficiency was the essence of the woman; she talked fast, thought fast, and wasted no time. The phone rang nonstop, apparently summoning her to all sorts of civic as well as academic activity, but she handled everything with dispatch. Jane was amazed but a bit shaken by her parting comment: "Don't be idle!"

Did Jane want to attend any seminars at the university, her adviser asked. There was one young colleague of hers who was giving a seminar on "contemporary Russian literary criticism." He was very knowledgeable, and the subject should be interesting. "At least," she said, "you'll pick up a few names. And you ought to go to at least one lecture by the chair of our department," she added, naming an older literary scholar whose work Jane knew by reputation as conservative if not reactionary. "You'll find it instructive," she said with a knowing smile. Jane intended to follow her advice. But the senior colleague lectured only twice a month, at very inconvenient times, and those times always turned out to be filled with some more urgent activity.

Jane, however, heard more of him from the junior lecturer on Soviet criticism, who, with his blond beard, long hair, and quiet, otherworldly manner, reminded her of Dostoevski's Prince Myshkin. His course had begun in the fall, and Jane was able to attend only the final two sessions. He had already covered the "left" and the "center," and spent the last two lectures on the "right wing." That was fine, since these were *not* the critics our friends were urging us to read. His survey proved very helpful, letting us know exactly what he thought of the right-wingers and the journals they controlled: *Nash sovremennik* ("Our Contemporary"), *Moskva* ("Moscow"), and *Molodaya gvardiya* ("Young Guard"). Even more interesting, when he came to the work of his department chair, the archconservative, he proceeded for forty-five minutes to give a scathing though perfectly professional critique of his work. His student audience, which had surely been subjected to the old man's lectures, listened with suppressed grins. His lecture, Jane thought, was courageous in a land where academic freedom and tenure are unknown.

Things had also changed at the Academy of Sciences' Institute on the USA and Canada, which was Bill's academic base. The USA Institute (as it is familiarly known by both Russians and Americans) has a mixed reputation in the United States. The director, Georgy Arbatov, is particularly controversial. Arbatov and his colleagues have spread the Soviet gospel on innumerable American TV talk shows. Reacting to this, American commentators sometimes dismiss USA Institute spokesmen as out-and-out propagandists. The truth is more complicated. In the depths of Brezhnev-era stagnation, we once asked a former researcher at the Institute who was intent on emigration to estimate how many of her co-workers secretly shared her views. We were amazed when she answered that a majority had. We were even more amazed in 1988 when what many USA Institute people said confirmed her revelation.

In Bill's application to the Academy, he had been asked to name the Soviet scholar with whom he would like to work. He chose a senior specialist on Soviet-American relations whom we had known for years. But when we arrived, he was in the United States—where

else, doubtless traveling from talk show to talk show—
and was not expected back soon. Bill was disappointed,
but if he had been there, Bill would undoubtedly have
followed a more traditional research strategy. More than
anything else, he wanted to try his hand at oral history,
to find and interview people who had had dealings with
Khrushchev. We suspected, with good reason as it
turned out, that the town was full of such people, ranging from family members to Kremlin aides and assistants
to artists and others who had had run-ins with him. Bill
had brought a few names with him to Moscow. If Bill's
USA Institute host had been around, he might have offered to help arrange interviews. If he didn't succeed,
Bill would have lost valuable time. Without him, Bill
resolved to attempt something truly revolutionary, to act
as if the Soviet Union was a normal country, to proceed
as he would have in the West, to assume that *glasnost*
had brought things to the point where one could simply
call people on the phone and ask to see them. He even
went so far, within a week of our arrival, as to call
Khrushchev's son-in-law, Aleksey Adzhubei, a man who
had been very close to Khrushchev politically as well as
personally.

Bill called Adzhubei's office, and when told he was at
home, asked in his best Russian for Adzhubei's home
number. To call him at all, let alone at home, went
against Bill's every instinct as a Sovietologist. And his
every instinct was right. Adzhubei didn't sound particularly happy to hear from him. When Bill mentioned his
acquaintance with a high-ranking official, thinking the
connection might legitimize the request for an interview, Adzhubei suggested coldly that Bill interview this
high-ranking friend. When Bill had the temerity to press
him further, Adzhubei announced that he was leaving
on vacation—as soon as possible after Bill's phone call,
no doubt—and would not be back for two weeks. When
Bill called then, he declined again on other grounds.

Would he have been more amenable if Bill had gone through channels? Or was it politically risky for him to see Bill? One mutual acquaintance later whispered that Adzhubei had been burned the previous autumn when he discussed his late father-in-law with an American journalist. Another confided that the issue was more proprietary than political; Adzhubei was writing his own account of the Khrushchev era and didn't want to scoop himself by talking to another writer. Though Bill eventually did get to interview Adzhubei, in fact with the help of the USA Institute, most of his interviews were arranged outside of official channels.

With his chosen specialist away, Bill contacted another Americanist, whom he had not previously met. Although promptly invited to come by for a chat, Bill expected his host to be cautious if not standoffish. Instead, they had an exchange of an entirely new sort, a conversation totally devoid of the clichés and awkwardness that had plagued even the most fruitful exchanges with *institutchiki* in the past, a discusson that differed not at all from talks with colleagues back home.

Nor was this first encounter unique. Other researchers Bill had known at the Institute for years seemed to have become new men and women almost overnight. All of them were supposed to be specialists on the United States, but many seemed far more interested in their own country's reforms. Included in this number was the Institute official who is reputed to be a high-ranking officer in the KGB. The only debate among supposedly in-the-know Westerners is whether the man in question is a general or just a colonel in the secret police. Whatever he is, the rank is high enough to justify trying to gauge where he stands, for the fate of Gorbachev's reforms depends in large part on where the KGB stands.

To judge, as Western Kremlinologists are forced to do in the absence of better information, by the tenor of the KGB chief Viktor Chebrikov's speeches, the police were

far from sympathetic with the relative freedom that Gorbachev unleashed. We ourselves heard from a reliable
source that Chebrikov's daughter had quoted her father
referring to the most liberal magazine, *Ogonyok*, as "that
yellow rag." On the other hand, it stands to reason that
the police would not be monolithic on the issue of reform. Those segments of the KGB whose job it is to steal
Western technology know all too well how far behind
the USSR is. Those who keep their ear to the ground
know how alienated the mass of Soviet people really is.
It was precisely KGB like these, led by their then-chief
Yury Andropov, who gave reform its initial impetus. All
this is obviously circumstantial or third-hand evidence.
Whereas the *KGBeshnik* at the USA Institute was, or so
we assumed, the real thing.

It was no surprise that he presented himself as a reformer. A cynic might say that his support was either
phony or a sign that the reforms themselves were. More
significant, he supported efforts by American researchers to open up areas, such as the history of the arms race,
that had been off limits; he expressed impatience verging on outrage when more conservative academics resisted such discussions or tried to turn them into sterile
exchanges; he even tried to help, or so it seemed, to
obtain access to previously unavailable resources.

In a Western country, Bill would have sought from the
start to do research in the archives; here he hadn't even
suggested it. No American we knew of had ever been
granted access to Foreign Ministry archives on a period
as recent as the Khrushchev years, let alone to even
more sensitive Party or police archives. But Bill was
determined to test whether *glasnost* had changed the
rules, and applied for access to Foreign Ministry files. It
was our highly placed friend who promised to try to get
him in. He had Bill write out a formal request specifying
the sort of materials needed, and undertook to press the
case with the Ministry. He suggested Bill call him back

in two weeks. Since there was still no word by then, Bill was reduced to phoning several times a week after that. This, by the way, is standard Soviet procedure. A good Soviet bureaucrat never calls back. Instead, he or she keeps having you call him or her. The procedure doesn't take much time—just long enough for you to be told to call back yet again. Moreover, reaching your man at all can be exhilarating, since next to being told constantly to call back, the most frustrating feature of doing business Soviet-style is trying to get through on the phone in the first place. The problem has something to do with the lack of switchboards or automatic switching systems that can parcel out calls. This means that each official has his own direct line, which none of his co-workers ever answers—whether out of discretion, laziness, or fear, we don't know—and often his secretary doesn't either if she has something better to do.

Nonetheless, Bill's highly placed friend sounded genuinely upset as week followed week and he had no progress to report. According to him, the trouble was an aged official who didn't relish the idea of an American prying into Ministry files. In the previous period we wouldn't have credited this account, especially when our stay in Moscow neared its end and there was still no word from the Ministry. But this time, the man's sincerity made us believe him—almost.

Compared to senior figures at the Institute, younger people there seemed even more emancipated. Still in their early thirties, even younger in some cases, they appeared to be utterly without the ideological blinders or political artifice we had come to associate with politically active Soviets, and they were caught up in *perestroika* in a way that reminded us of our contemporaries during the campus upheavals of the late 1960s in the United States. Suddenly, they saw themselves as citizens trying to remake their country.

Citizens! The very word is revealing. For years the

Russians have seen themselves as subjects, not citizens. A subject suffers what he must; a citizen thinks he doesn't have to. Not all Russians think the time of transition has arrived. The young Americanists aren't sure either. But they have decided to act as if it has. Their decision owes something, we like to think, to the country they have chosen to study. The best aspects of the American example show them not only what they are missing but how to work politically to bring it about.

The task of remaking the USSR is tied to their work in other ways. Unless the country is remade, it will not be safe for them to tell the truth about the United States; the country can be remade only if it reorders its relationship with the West. The effect is strange and wonderful to behold. Not just in the USA Institute, but in every other institution we visited or heard about, people of the most diverse backgrounds and specialties had become not only citizens but "Sovietologists." Sovietology, as practiced in the West, used to be a four- rather than an eleven-letter word in the USSR. Small armies of Soviet "scholars" used to work full time exposing "Western falsifiers of Soviet history." This time, to our amazement, people paid us *more* respect than we deserved. Wrapped up in trying to decipher their own history, intent on working politically to change it, they turned to us for whatever enlightenment we, as longtime students of the USSR, could provide.

Whatever their background, whether they were Americanists or specialists on the third world, they hung on every current political development. Was their institute electing a new scientific council? If so, they gossiped in their offices, politicked in the hallways, attended the meetings, voted and waited impatiently for the votes to be counted, relished the defeat of the long undeserving and the victory, if not of the good and the pure, then at least of the better and the less unclean. Their activities extended beyond their own institutes. One of the most fascinating features of the age was the exfoliation of "informal groups" devoted to all manner of issues but having in common the kind of fledgling independence from Party or state control that was anathema a mere three or four years ago. Among these groups were "discussion clubs," most of which seemed to name themselves after *perestroika* or *glasnost* as protective coloration.

A discussion club that Bill attended early on at the invitation of a young Americanist seemed an unlikely setting for fireworks. It snuggled safely under the wing of one of the most establishment of all Soviet institutions, the Soviet Committee for the Defense of Peace. Located in a posh townhouse on *Prospekt Mira* (Peace Avenue), the committee boasts a big, elegantly appointed conference room in which members of the club and their guests were invited to gather once a month to discuss a subject chosen by the club's board.

Bill's friend was not on the board, but another young Americanist was. Both apologized for the fact that the day's subject, "The International Right to Peace," sounded old-fashioned. But talk around the table had a way of getting interesting, they assured Bill, even when the official subject wasn't. The setting itself seemed to be an obstacle to the kind of discussion advertised. The table was actually a series of tables, arranged in a huge square with an open space in the middle. Comfortable chairs with individual microphones in front of them were ranged alongside. But the microphones allowed only one person to speak at a time. When your turn came, you pressed a button and spoke. Before anyone else could speak, you had to press your button again. On the walls were large posters, with doves of peace in all the right places, announcing both the formal name of the club—"The Peace and Human Rights Discussion Club"—and the theme of the day. The chairman sat at the head of the table, flanked by a panel of experts, and announced that once the experts had had their say, everyone in the room was invited to address the group. There was no constraint on what could be said; the only limit was that it not take more than seven minutes to say it.

The first expert began to drone on about how the United States showed its true colors by refusing to pass a law prohibiting "warlike propaganda" in American media. Suddenly a gong rang, indicating his seven minutes were up. He was immediately attacked by the next speaker, an older Americanist, who insisted in what seemed to be high dudgeon that the United States could not possibly pass such a law because the First Amendment prohibited it.

Unfortunately, Bill had to leave to keep an appointment before many more minutes had passed. He would return later in the spring to a more tumultuous meeting, but as he pulled away from the table this time, he caught a glimpse of things to come. The young USA Institute man on the club board was blasting excessive Soviet secrecy in the field of international affairs, calling it a "national shame" that the Soviets used American nomenclature to designate the USSR's own weaponry, demanding that if secrecy must be preserved at least the criteria be opened up for public scrutiny and debate.

STEPPING OUT

We first encountered the name of Yury N. Afanasyev a couple of years ago in the Soviet press. The rector of the Historical Archives Institute (which trains archivists), he gave an interview in which he called for a radical reevaluation of the Soviet past, not another exercise in rewriting history so as to glorify those in power but an attempt to tell the whole truth for the first time in decades. Even by the standards of 1988, when Afanasyev had been joined by others making the same demand, his interview was stunning; so were other pieces he published, beginning in 1986.

Bill first met Afanasyev in the summer of 1987 when he co-chaired a delegation of American historians and political scientists that was meeting in Moscow with a counterpart Soviet group. Afanasyev was not a member of the Soviet delegation. The conference subject, the origins of the cold war, was far from his academic expertise, the history of France, and his institute was outside the Academy of Sciences, which had co-organized the meeting. In fact, he was anathema to many Academy historians, who resented the sharp language with which he dismissed so much of their work.

When Bill met him at a reception at Spaso House, the American ambassador's residence, Afanasyev was standing alone in a corner. Unlike his compatriots, he didn't speak much English. He didn't look like them either; he looked like a vigorous young Soviet engineer, strong and robust, with chiseled features, a square jaw, and a full head of hair.

Afanasyev had previously worked for *Kommunist*, the theoretical journal of the Party Central Committee, and for the Higher School of the Komsomol (Young Communist League). It was rumored that he had been dismissed from the same institute that was sponsoring Bill's delegation's visit for his unorthodox views. He struck Bill on that first meeting as embattled.

And he still did in early February 1988 when Bill entered the rector's office of his institute, in a historic nineteenth-century building just a few blocks from Red Square. Bill had called Afanasyev to arrange the appointment. Not only had he invited Bill to come by, he urged him to think of the institute as a kind of base, to stop in whenever he wanted to, to attend public lectures and generally consider himself at home.

It was the determined way he expressed his own ideas, the way he seized and held the floor, even though Bill was hardly about to take it from him, that made him seem embattled. Bill raised the issue of foreign policy, not one on which many Soviets permitted themselves to speak freely. Most of the revelations that had gushed out under *glasnost* concerned Soviet domestic politics. But Afanasyev launched into a thoughtful analysis. Khrushchev's famous boast, "We will bury you," was not meant literally, he said; it reflected Khrushchev's deep belief that Communism would inherit the earth, a belief that still influenced Soviet policy, even though few people believed it anymore. Afanasyev pulled a coin from his pocket and pointed out something Bill had never noticed: the coin showed the earth overarched by the hammer and sickle. "We don't even think about such symbols," said Afanasyev, "but they affect us." What the Soviet Union needed was to replace outdated ideology with common sense. An example: the hallowed conviction that capitalism has passed its peak. "Some peak, some pass," he said dryly, pointing out that capitalism was forever reaching new peaks in the form of electronics, computers, and so on.

This was pretty strong language in a country where Marxist-Leninist ideology is still taken seriously. We wondered whether similar language could be heard on public occasions from others less notoriously bold than Afanasyev. The place to test the question was at one of the public lectures Afanasyev had invited Bill to attend.

We should have suspected the audience would be the main attraction when Afanasyev suggested that Bill drop by his office fifteen minutes early so that he could escort him into the hall and get him a seat. Entering the building, Bill passed a bulletin board announcing the activities of the local Communist Party cell and Komsomol. There was also an honor roll celebrating the achievements of the most active young politicos. In the lecture hall was an immense portrait of Lenin and posters proclaiming in huge letters GLORY TO GREAT OCTOBER and " THE PARTY IS THE MIND AND CONSCIENCE OF OUR ERA" —LENIN. There were photographs of Institute students marching in the anniversary of the Revolution and May Day parades. In past years, ideological or patriotic displays of this kind had always turned our stomachs. This time, the propaganda seemed strangely out of place and yet comforting. Clearly, Afanasyev and his students had gone beyond it, or perhaps we should say filled it with

new and more meaningful content, but the display gave
them a certain protection from ideological watchdogs
who still patrolled the borders of speech and behavior.

The lecture hall was on the first floor, with windows
facing onto 25th of October Street. In early February
they were closed, of course; in the spring one could see
and hear pedestrians tramping to and from Red Square.
When Afanasyev's speakers were at their most radical,
Bill found himself wondering what the passersby would
think if they could hear. He imagined them clambering
through the windows into the hall—but whether to join
the celebration of *glasnost* or to crush it, he wasn't sure.
In the tradition of Russian public events, the speaker
stood at a lectern several feet in front of a long table
reserved for the "presidium" of the meeting. Traditionally, the presidium marches in to predictable applause
as the session begins, and the orator speaks with his
back to them, blessedly unable to see their reaction,
which often consists of chattering among themselves or
nodding off. There were none of these formalities at
Afanasyev's institute. The only people at the presidium
table were he and a student who introduced the speaker,
moved deftly to questions and answers when the lecture
was over, and thanked the guest at the end.

The loudspeaker system in the hall left something to
be desired. Every now and again the lecturer's voice
would fade away and be replaced by what sounded like
local militiamen barking orders to each other on a police
radio. When this happened, the audience would laugh
nervously, especially later in the spring when conservatives were on the rise in the Party and people like
Afanasyev were likely targets.

Bill was glad to be escorted into the hall, for although
it was filled to overflowing, the sea of people parted
before Afanasyev. The speaker was a philosopher
named Kapustin. His talk, which took about an hour, was
good, tracing the destructive impact of Stalinism

on culture decade by decade and coining such phrases
as "bureaucratic authoritarianism" (for Stalinism) and
"authoritarian bureaucracy" (for Brezhnevism). But it
paled in comparison with the question period that
followed and continued without a break for another
two and a half hours. The questions were sometimes
shouted out; mostly they were passed forward on slips
of paper, a traditional Russian form that at first seemed
likely to stultify the exchange but instead intensified it.
The anonymity of the written questions emboldened
their authors. The discipline of writing them down con-
centrated their minds and their prose. Kapustin responded with a forthrightness exceeding that of his own
lecture. The only person who suffered from the system
was the poor soul in the first-row seat on whom the various rivulets of written questions converged. Throughout the talk itself and even more often afterward, he
served as the conduit, passing slips of paper to the
speaker, who carefully read out and answered each one
of them.

The audience consisted in approximately equal measure of students and others; many, Bill later learned,
were from other institutes around town, still others were
the kind of unaffiliated intelligentsia in which Moscow
abounds. Their questions and comments took Bill's
breath away. The first shock was to learn that no one in
the hall had anything good to say about Stalin. Back in
New York in November, he had carefully read Gorbachev's major speech on the seventieth anniversary of the
Bolshevik Revoluton and written about it on *The New
York Times'* Op-Ed page. When it came to the Stalin era,
the speech was delicately balanced. Gorbachev went
farther than Khrushchev in condemning Stalin's great
terror of the late thirties and in implying that a lack of
democracy in the Party had allowed Stalin to come to
power. But he carefully avoided condemning outright
the forced collectivization of agriculture that destroyed

millions of innocent peasants, or the devil's pact that
Stalin signed with Hitler in 1939. We had assumed that
Gorbachev's version constituted the new Party line, to
be breached at one's peril.

Obviously the institute audience had concluded otherwise. Either that, or they were determined to press
the limits anyway. Nikolay Bukharin, a colleague of
Lenin's whom Stalin had liquidated, was about to be
rehabilitated, partly in an effort to find some Soviet
leader between Lenin and Gorbachev in whom to believe. Several members of the audience were critical of
him, not as an enemy of the people but as someone who
had helped Stalin to power and betrayed others by confessing in the end to crimes he never committed. Stalinism was a political tendency, Kapustin replied, not the
creation of one man or group of men. Bukharin may have
aided and abetted that tendency, but at least he remained a living, breathing human being, which his exe-
cutioner did not. What about Trotsky? It was his
program that Stalin carried out, replied Kapustin. "Not
so," said a voice. "At any rate, Trotsky was honest." At
this point, Kapustin did something really revolutionary;
he admitted, in the heat of the battle, that he did not
know enough, had not read enough Trotsky, to know for
sure.

Collectivization, said a note passed up to the lectern,
had been an unmitigated catastrophe resulting in at least
five million deaths. Kapustin did not disagree. Bill could
hardly believe his ears when the next questioner politely inquired whether Stalinism wasn't a species of
totalitarianism on a par with Hitler's. There was indeed
"a basis for such a view," Kapustin answered carefully,
but there were those who disagreed with it. Why had
not even one of the old-guard Leninists spoken out
against the terror before being destroyed by it? Were
the people gathered in this hall any braver themselves?
"What are *you* doing to prevent a reversion to the past?"

a note asked. He was doing, or at least trying to do, philosophy, Kapustin answered, adding that what had passed for years as "Marxist-Leninist philosophy" was neither Marxist nor Leninist nor philosophy. "What are *we* doing?" someone shouted out. "Are we doing enough?"

The last remark brought to the surface an unspoken fear that many in the hall seemed to share, fear for the future. "There's plenty to be afraid of," said Kapustin, catching the implication. "We must all take risks."

The questions and comments that came cascading forth touched on almost every taboo one could think of. Didn't the Revolution's attack on religion invite the evil that came later? The author of this question chose to identify himself as a first-year student at the institute. Had violent revolution ever done a people more good than harm? Wasn't the emigration of so many intellectuals understandable, if they couldn't breathe in the Soviet Union? Kapustin praised the early works of Solzhenitsyn. Of Andrey Sakharov he said, "I take my hat off to him; he stood alone against the system." "What are dissidents," someone shouted out, "except people who dared to speak the truth to the end?" If Brezhnevism was another word for rule by the bureaucratic machine, what was new about the machine now except the man at the wheel? It will take time and struggle to change things, Kapustin replied.

Bill couldn't help thinking of a scene he had witnessed twenty-two years before at Moscow University. He had been stunned by the way a student audience bombarded a Party speaker with skeptical questions, and he began his first book with that event. It was not atypical, but in the end what had come of it? The rebellious students had accommodated themselves to the Brezhnev era.

A few days after the Kapustin lecture, Bill was invited to an informal interdisciplinary seminar attended by young scholars from various Academy and pedagogical institutes around town. Its members had held at least one previous session on alternatives to Stalin, or rather on the question of whether there had been any. The subject this evening was the origins of the cold war. As the author of *Stalin's American Policy*, Bill had been asked to talk about Stalin's role.

Bill had given presentations to Soviet scholars before, occasions which all too often turned out to be frustratingly sterile. As a guest of the Soviet Union and a Sovietologist who depended on frequent trips to the USSR for access to key sources, he had gone out of his way to be polite. He had never said anything he did not believe, but he had not said everything he did. Occasionally he had resorted to euphemisms.

The Soviets had been even more predictable. No matter how bold and unorthodox they could be in private, there were sharp limits to what could be said in the presence of other Russians, and the same person could be considerably more forthcoming in the U.S. than in the USSR. Perhaps the most dramatic example of this occurred in Amherst, where we had a visiting Soviet scholar staying with us for nearly a week a few years ago. We had known him for some time; sitting around the breakfast table, he took us more into his confidence than ever before. At a dinner party in his honor, just before a lecture he was to give, he joined in a scintillating no-holds-barred argument on the virtues and vices of democracy. Yet when we adjourned to the lecture hall, and especially after he caught sight of a local newsman in the audience, he became a changed man. The talk that followed was standard anti-American boilerplate, in no way different from innumerable diatribes we had heard over the years.

Yet now in Moscow, in February 1988, Bill felt himself getting carried away. If *glasnost* was what they wanted, *glasnost* was what they would get. He resolved to give the most candid, hard-hitting talk he had ever heard, let alone given, in Moscow. To do it right, especially in Russian, he set aside the whole day before the seminar to prepare. He carefully wrote out his talk on six legal-size pages, and even rehearsed it out loud before taking the subway. The participants gathered in a small but quite pleasant hall decorated with photos of a workers' uprising in 1905. They were met at the door by a representative of the district Party committee, which had apparently given the group its blessing. The sight of this Party official sobered Bill. If the Party was involved, however indirectly, surely the occasion could not be as open and candid as he had imagined. But it was too late to turn back. His Russian text was prepared.

Read several months later in the quiet of Amherst, the text didn't seem as tough as it did then. But it still seems strong enough. "You Soviets are full of praise for Gorbachev's so-called 'new thinking,' " he said, "but all the praise for new thinking implies that there once was 'old thinking' that wasn't so sound. And yet you say little if anything about that except to praise it as well. The fact is, Stalin's way of thinking largely caused the cold war. True enough, we Americans contributed. For example, we led Stalin to believe he could grab Eastern Europe and get away with it, and then reacted as if the seizure meant a new world war. But whatever we did, Stalin would see us as a mortal enemy and treat us accordingly. That way of seeing the world was rooted partly in his ideology, partly in his experience in the dog-eat-dog world of Kremlin politics, but mostly in his warped, paranoid mind." Toward the end of his talk, Bill reached shamelessly for a Kennedyesque climax: "If Stalin was so suspicious as to conclude that his closest comrades in arms, not to mention millions of ordinary Russians, were enemies of the people, how could we have ever persuaded him that our people were not his enemy?"

The Soviet historian who had been invited to serve as

commentator started out by refuting what Bill *hadn't* said—that Stalin had aspired to conquer Western Europe and then the whole world—and went on to quibble with several secondary points instead of confronting the main ones. "Unfortunately," said the first speaker from the floor, with a nervous glance at the commentator, "I agree almost one hundred percent with Professor Taubman." Actually, he didn't. With one interesting exception, all the speakers insisted that Bill's criticism of Soviet policy hadn't gone nearly far enough. His stress on Stalin's paranoia was misleading, said one, as was his argument that American policy tempted Stalin to overreach himself. The cold war was neither a projection of Stalin's personality nor a Soviet reaction to American behavior. It was cold-bloodedly employed to justify repression at home. Bill had conceded in passing that Stalin might have sincerely feared the United States. "Not at all," objected one participant, "it was the United States that feared us, and well it might have. Looking back now at the Stalin era, we fear *ourselves* in retrospect. If the United States knew then what we are finding out now about our own history, then it is understandable that they saw in us a mortal threat."

One young man cited Stalin's demands on Turkey and Iran in 1945 and 1946 and the Berlin blockade of 1948 as reasons for the West to beware. He refuted in detail the still standard Soviet argument (which Bill had been shocked to hear from established scholars at the U.S.–Soviet conference the previous summer) that South Korea started the Korean War by invading the North. He quoted from Czech documents released during the Prague Spring to suggest that Stalin was seriously contemplating an attack on Western Europe in 1952, when he was reported to have said, "The United States demonstrated weakness in Korea, and now we have the bomb."

Most of these points have long been debated in the

West. But few if any of the arguments Bill heard at the seminar had seen the light of day in the USSR. "It's not fair," one participant said, "that we get all the details of your secret decisions from your archives, whereas you know so little of our policy-making process." The real shame, in fact, is that Soviet scholars know so little about their own government's decisions.

At least one speaker vigorously disagreed with the whole discussion. He contended that neither super-power was responsible for the cold war. The conflict had been a clash between great powers, the kind of confrontation with which history is replete. It made no sense to place blame when what had happened was simply the way of the world.

Throughout the evening, Bill's commentator sat silent and stony-faced. Given the chance to say the last word, he mixed an attack on the Soviet participants with self-pity. He regretted, he said in what seemed almost a whine, that Soviet public opinion, at least as represented by those in this room, was now unanimously 180 degrees from where it had been a mere three years before. The implication was clear. It was his young critics who were the conformists. It was they who were rushing along with the mob, while people like him stood up for the high standards of scholarly discourse.

In fact, establishment historians of the Soviet period had entered their field at a time when neither truth nor talent was rewarded, but rather orthodoxy and circum-spection. They knew what they were getting into. Some of them may have genuinely craved access to archives that were denied them, but others couldn't have cared less. The commentator was a fairly recent convert from a diplomatic career. He might develop into a distin-guished historian, but not by questioning the motives of talented people who, taking advantage of *glasnost*, were genuinely in search of truth.

Bill was eager to learn more about the seminar participants. Their first instinct seemed to be to gather around him at the close of the meeting, but soon they began to disperse. Bill found several who were willing to chat, but only for a moment. One said she worked for a youth magazine and would call Bill for an interview. She never did. Another wanted to introduce Bill to his family. He never did either. And so, despite its revelations, the seminar left key questions unanswered. Why did some participants speak so boldly during the meeting, yet turn and flee at the end? Why would others commit themselves to future contacts and then not follow through?

Bill's next experience was on television. "Space-bridges" are what the Soviets call television programs that link audiences in different countries. Soviet authorities love them, because they vividly display the Soviet Union's dedication to peace and friendship; so do the people because, however structured and stilted the format, they can still glimpse countries to which most Russians do not travel.

Though the American public has shown far less interest, several U.S.–Soviet spacebridges have been broadcast in the United States. A few years ago Bill flew to San Diego to hold forth for two minutes on a spacebridge devoted to "Remembering War." Apart from the technical miracle involved in creating a live conversation between San Diego and Moscow, he was most impressed by how little of substance got said. There was the usual tendency to be diplomatic and avoid controversy. Russians and Americans congratulated each other on their wartime cooperation. When Bill reminded viewers how those good times ended and why, a Party official in Moscow replied with what the Soviets like to call a "resolute rebuff." Later spacebridges have been more frank, and even abrasive. And Phil Donahue together with his Soviet sidekick Vladimir Pozner have popularized the form still more.

The prospect of Bill's appearance on a spacebridge in Moscow appeared on the horizon along with Tufts University professor Martin Sherwin. Sherwin, who wrote a major work on the American decision to bomb Hiroshima, was involved in an ambitious project with Academy of Sciences vice president Yevgeny Velikhov, who doubles as Gorbachev's science adviser. Together they were teaching a "joint course" on the history of the arms race. For most of the spring semester Sherwin met his American students in Medford, Massachusetts, while Velikhov lectured at Moscow University. Several spacebridges were planned to link the two classrooms. Just after Sherwin had been in Moscow making final arrangements for the telecasts, he suddenly returned for a flying one-day visit. The overburdened Soviet television people had cabled that they could not do the telecasts after all. With Velikhov's help, the bridges were rebuilt. Bill took part in the day's frantic negotiations at the Academy and at Gostelradio, and by day's end he was slated to participate in the first spacebridge on the Soviet side.

The telecast would address the first five years of the arms race (1945–50); panels of experts on both sides would exchange views, followed by questions and comments from students in Moscow and Medford. Someone on the Soviet side, apparently the deputy director of the USA Institute, Andrey Kokoshin, had the bright idea of breaking down the us-versus-them appearance of the two panels by including an American on the Soviet panel and a Soviet on the American side. Given Bill's book on the period, plus the fact he was on the spot, he got the nod in Moscow. A visiting Soviet physicist would join his American colleagues at Tufts.

This was the first time Bill had appeared on Soviet television, and he was more than a little uptight. He would have wanted to speak Russian anyway, but the technical arrangements left him no choice. Interpreters would be standing by to translate what was said in Moscow into English, and in Medford into Russian. Bill's linguistic success at the seminar had been encouraging. But this challenge would be entirely different. Anything he got to say would get said in the course of an ongoing interchange. In English, he would have been glad to go with the flow, but not in Russian with the whole USSR watching. He couldn't predict what would fit into the conversation, so he set out to prepare five or six "spontaneous" comments that might be relevant. He needed to check several facts in recent American books. Neither the American Embassy nor *The New York Times* Moscow bureau had them in their libraries, nor did the USA Institute. Bill finally found them at INION, the modern, well-maintained library of the Scientific Institute for Information in the Social Sciences. A helpful librarian brought them to his desk in ten minutes; in the old days, they wouldn't have reached a Soviet reader in ten years. Books like these had traditionally been kept under guard in "special collections," access to which required special authorization based on "the need to know." As part of *glasnost*, Western publications are being made available to specialists.

Arriving at the television studio, Bill found it full of cheerful, bright-eyed Soviet students. On a large screen at one end of the room, their Tufts counterparts could be seen gathering in Medford. Besides Velikhov and Kokoshin, Bill's fellow Soviet panelists included two aged atomic scientists who had long been kept hidden from the world for "security reasons" and were now appearing in public for the first time. While makeup was being applied to his face, and with show time a mere five minutes away, Bill learned that he was expected to deliver a ten-minute comment at some point during the proceedings. While panelists on both sides gossiped and greeted each other via the cosmos, Bill hunched over his notes trying desperately to turn five disjointed com-

ments into a single coherent one. He was still at work
when the program began; the videotape shows the other
experts calmly watching one another on the big screen
and Bill bent over his papers.

Fortunately, the elderly scientists relished their first
taste of the limelight. They held forth at great length,
and suddenly the hour alloted for initial expert discussion had gone by. It was time for the students' questions,
and Bill had yet to utter a peep. It dawned on him that
his freshly crafted ten-minute speech would not do after
all; he would be lucky to get a word in edgewise. So
once again he set to work frantically, trying to look cool
and relaxed in case the camera happened to focus on
him, to reduce his remarks to three minutes or so. Meanwhile, all the remaining panelists, except the Russian in
Medford, who seemed to share Bill's fate, managed to
get the floor. With time running out, Bill had to decide
whether to force his way into the discussion or let the
program end without saying a word. After his day-long
preparation he was determined to be heard, the more so
since he thought he had something to say.

All the other panelists seemed to agree that the arms
race might well have been avoided, especially if the
United States, which was first with the bomb, had informed Stalin of its development at an earlier stage. Bill
strongly disagreed—and said so. It was ironic but true,
he continued, that the arms race was harder to stop before it began than to slow down in 1988. The most important reason was Stalin's deep distrust of the capitalist
West. Would informing our wartime ally of the Manhattan Project have convinced him of our good intentions?
Bill thought not. He coupled this criticism of Stalin with
praise of Gorbachev. The latter's "new thinking" included the notion that "the security of the USSR depends on the United States not feeling insecure." But
Stalin hadn't seen things that way. In his view there
could never be truly mutual, long-lasting, peaceful co-

existence between capitalism and communism. In the
long run, war was inevitable. To speak, as Gorbachev
now did, of guaranteeing American as well as Soviet
security would have been absurd to Stalin.

When Bill finished his brief oration, the Soviet students in the studio broke into loud applause. But a co-
panelist, reacted as if stung—the way the Party official
had on the San Diego–Moscow spacebridge five years
before—and launched into the obligatory rebuff: Harry
Truman had been distrustful too; postwar American war
plans envisaged the atomic destruction of the USSR; all
that the innocent Soviets had done was respond to the
"American threat." Yet, a few moments later, with the
camera pointing elsewhere, he whispered sheepishly,
"Sorry, I didn't mean to defend Stalin."

When the telecast ended, Soviet students crowded
around Bill, firing questions at him. What were American Sovietologists studying these days? The same questions you are, he answered. Did Bill think there had
been any viable alternative to Stalinism? Too complicated for a short answer, but probably not. Nods of
agreement from some students. Had *Stalin's American
Policy* (which Bill had brought with him to refer to) been
published in the USSR? Are you kidding, responded
another student. Would Bill agree to be interviewed by
a student newspaper? Yes, of course. (But like the journalist who requested an interview after Bill's seminar
appearance, this one, too, was never heard from again.)

By the time Bill broke away from the students, his
fellow panelists had left the studio. He found them
again in the lobby, engaged in a spirited discussion of
the very issue he had raised. "I was just defending your
position," said a young USA Institute staffer who had
been in the audience. "I don't think informing Stalin of
the American bomb project would have made any difference." Velikhov, who had disagreed with Bill on camera, remained silent this time. But he offered Bill

something more valuable than agreement—a ride home
in his mammoth chauffeured limousine. The ride was a
symbol. It seemed to say that if anything needed to be
forgiven, it was. Since the size of a Soviet official's limo
varies directly with his power and influence, the gesture
wasn't lost on the others waiting at the curb.

Several days before, another Soviet official had urged
us to accept any and all media exposure we were offered. It almost didn't matter what we said or were
quoted as saying. The very fact that the media judged us
worthy of their attention signaled to the lower-level bureaucrats with whom we dealt every day that they
should do the same. Several days later, Velikhov confirmed his good will by inviting Bill to address his class
at Moscow University. Twenty-two years before, Bill
had sat in the back of the same Moscow University lecture hall, trying not to nod off during the dry, long-
winded lecture. Now he found himself debating the
arms race with Gorbachev's science adviser before some
three hundred students and faculty. Velikhov asked Bill
to elaborate on his televised comments. This time, with
no cameras around, they provoked not a slashing rebuff
but some thoughtful reflections from his host.

Standing by Velikhov's side in the well of the lecture
hall, before row upon row of steeply rising seats, Bill
had to remind himself of how rare and wonderful the
occasion really was. By American standards, the scene
was utterly normal: a busy prof enlightens his students
and saves his own valuable time by inviting a visiting
fireman in to chat. Velikhov even showed his students a
film (an American documentary about the decision to
drop the bomb on Hiroshima), another classic way to fill
the students' time without taking too much of the faculty's. Yet what was ordinary in America was extraordinary at Moscow University. Once again, students
surrounded Bill afterward as if he had come from another planet. They peppered him with questions not

only about the arms race but about the upcoming American election. The by-now-familiar invitations to get together began, only to be interrupted this time when one student warned the others that arranging an unauthorized meeting with an American professor was still beyond the pale. Later in the year, when Professor Sherwin brought nearly seventy Tufts students to town, their Soviet counterparts demonstrated no such hesitation. But getting together with a professional Sovietologist was evidently different.

Despite Bill's appearance in Velikhov's class, we still wondered what would happen when the spacebridge was edited for broadcast in the USSR a month or so later. Well disposed as Velikhov was, it was not he who decided what tens of millions of Soviet viewers could see. It was hard to believe Gostelradio would ax Bill's remarks, inviting the charge that they had censored the only quasi-critical comments on the program. Most likely they would leave Bill in but "smash" him with his co-panelist's rebuff. Early in April the answer came in the Soviet version of *TV Guide*. The spacebridge was to be shown on Easter Sunday afternoon at two o'clock, not exactly prime time, even in a militantly atheist state, but at least on the main Soviet channel. Along with a blurb, the guide printed a large picture of the Soviet panel, including Bill. We gathered with Soviet friends to see the program. Bill's speech was left in and the rebuff was out. The only thing that marred the occasion was that our friends didn't like the show. It was, they said, dull. What was the use of bringing Soviets and Americans together if all they did was smile and agree? Only Bill, they said, dared to be controversial. But even he, they added gently, was not as daring as he should have been.

THE CULTURAL

HERITAGE

*Let us look back, let us look carefully into
the past (for it is in us today), not for self-
denigration or self-glorification, but for the
honest labor of self-knowledge, in order to
work out, at last, a sober, adequate self-
consciousness: who we are, what we are
capable of, what we must do.*
    YURY KARYAKIN

"Americans are so totally free that they are free
of culture as well," declared Tatyana Tolstaya, one of Russia's most talented young writers, after
her first visit to New York. What, exactly, did she mean
by this Delphic remark?

World-famous literary scholar and semiotician Yury
Lotman, speaking to a packed hall at Afanasyev's Historical Archives Institute, theorized that it is "culture" that
enables individuals to weather social change, but if
change is too sudden, culture cannot fulfill its mission
and civil horrors like witch trials, civil war, and purges
result. Lotman's announced topic, "Mass Behavior in
Conditions of Mass Emotions," sounded abstruse
enough, but Soviets are expert at reading between the
lines. As he talked for an hour about the paradoxes of
sixteenth-century witch hunts ("We think of the phe-
nomenon as medieval, but we overlook the fact that it

was contemporary with the Renaissance"), even we saw
the clear parallels in recent Soviet history. The implica-
tions of his hypothesis about "too sudden" social change
were clearly applicable to the Revolution, to the rapid
industrialization of the 1930s, and, ominously, to the
breathtaking changes occurring under *perestroika*. Was
Lotman warning his young audience of the dangers that
lay ahead if change moved too fast and their generation
was not sufficiently armed with its own culture to
weather the storm?

Culture for Russians, at least for those in the intelligentsia, means a body of literature, art, music, and other
creative arts that transmits moral values. "Art for art's
sake," though it has flourished for brief periods, has always been suspect. Russian writers accept a burden of
responsibility for their society and its moral health quite
different from that customary in the West. Russian literature has always served the nation as the kind of public
forum that the political culture and government censorship have made otherwise impossible. Literary works
have become touchstones, ways of crystallizing and analyzing factors in the nation's social fabric that are otherwise amorphous or unspeakable. The Russian reader is
a special breed, schooled by generations of censorship
to Aesopian readings.

Culture is historical memory as well, and a great struggle is being waged in the USSR right now for the own-
ership of historical memory. It is ironically fitting that
the archnationalist, anti-Semitic fringe group *Pamyat*
(Memory) should have usurped precisely this word for
its title. Its interest in Russia's pre-revolutionary national heritage overlaps with a more widespread concern for preservation of Russia's architectural legacy and
a revived curiosity about the heritage of Russian Orthodoxy. Soviet society has literally had its recent history
stolen from it—and not only the history itself but the
important works of creative imagination that were meant

to help the society make sense of that history. One great gift of *glasnost* is the stream of suppressed works that are now being given back to their rightful owners, after decades when only foreigners and emigrés had access to them.

The recovery of historical memory and the publication of suppressed works go hand in hand: until the event they treat is admitted, the books cannot be published. On the other hand, their publication often serves as a way to reopen a painful subject. Long-suppressed tales, both personal and national, are being told. Westerners would see it as a process of national psychoanalysis; Soviets, among whom Freud has long been nearly unmentionable, would speak of it as the tales of a haunted collective conscience. A typical reader's letter in response to Mikhail Shatrov's historical play *Further, Further, Further* illustrates the way in which Russians are accustomed to see their society as an interrelated organism, and memory a crucial part of its health:

> We want to change our economy, we are fighting for the renewal of society, but until our conscience is clear there will be no successes in any sphere. Doctors have a phrase—"slumbering infection." . . . While its source still exists, the health of the organism is constantly under threat. Thus it is with memory.

To an American, Russian literature presents an unusual picture of national unity. The collective ethic runs deep in Russian society—it far predates Communism. More than that, Soviet history, usually in a tragic fashion, has imposed itself far more intimately on the lives of individuals than has generally been the case for Americans. No Soviet family escaped the consequences of the Revolution, collectivization, the purges, the war, the Khrushchev thaw, or the Brezhnev stagnation. The classics of Soviet literature to some degree all deal with experiences shared by society as a whole.

Moscow in the spring of 1988 was like one large seminar where, miracle of miracles, everyone had done the reading. Conversations very quickly got down to the big questions about what ails Soviet society and how to cure it. Our friends claimed that our presence encouraged such discussions, but we saw it as a society once again going through a unified experience of social change, with its culture serving as the glue to hold it together. We finally understood that this was what both Lotman and Tolstaya were talking about.

Since the nineteenth century, the common ground for Russia's debates has been the "fat" journal, issued monthly with two hundred or more pages of prose, poetry, literary criticism, and *publitsistika,* the Russian term for the socially conscious essay or opinion piece that explores the roots or seeks the solution to one of Russia's many problems. Most of the nineteenth-century classics of Russian literature first appeared in such fat journals, particularly in Nikolay Nekrasov's crusading *Contemporary,* which was finally closed down during the reaction of 1866. During the Khrushchev thaw, this social role was filled mainly by *Novy mir,* under the editorship of Aleksander Tvardovsky. Under *perestroika,* there are many bold journals and magazines rather than just one. Interesting and provocative pieces appear in the most unexpected places. But certain publications—*Novy mir, Znamya, Ogonyok, Literaturnaya gazeta, Moscow News, Sovetskaya kultura*—took the lead in probing and expanding the boundaries of *glasnost.*

Though the number of leading fat journals is relatively small—about ten are published in Moscow and Leningrad, others in provincial cities—few families can afford to subscribe to them all. Households divide up the subscriptions and circulate each issue among themselves and their friends. Thus, hiding behind the circulation figures of these journals is at least a four- or fivefold number of readers. Under self-financing, journals must now compete for subscribers, a development that clearly propels their editors in the direction of ever more controversial publications. In 1988 subscriptions to *Novy mir,* which began the year by publishing *Dr. Zhivago,* were up 132 percent to 1,150,000. *Druzhba narodov,* which in 1987 published Anatoly Rybakov's *Children of the Arbat,* was up an incredible 443 percent. Reader interest is so high that even the conservative *Moskva* and *Molodaya gvardiya* scored modest, though much smaller, gains. *Pravda,* down by 3.6 percent, was one of the few Soviet periodicals that actually lost readers.

By the time Stalin died in 1953, the realm of the permissible had been narrowed to the choking point by political, stylistic, and puritanical taboos. Literature was locked into the straitjacket of Socialist Realism. Forced to work within Stalin's restrictions, the Soviet film industry managed to turn out only a few films a year. The Khrushchev thaw of the 1950s and 1960s made it possible once again to publish many formerly repressed writers, particularly the quartet of poetic giants born at the beginning of the 1890s: Anna Akhmatova, Boris Pasternak, Marina Tsvetayeva and, a bit more cautiously, Osip Mandelstam. Many politically sensitive works, like Akhmatova's *Requiem* or Pasternak's *Dr. Zhivago,* remained unpublished; awkward aspects of their biographies, like Mandelstam's death in a Siberian transit camp, were avoided, but their poetry, more and more with each edition, became available to the Soviet reader. Isaac Babel, shot in the purges, was rehabilitated, along with other prose writers from the relatively permissive 1920s. In a final, belated gesture of the Khrushchev thaw, Mikhail Bulgakov's *The Master and Margarita* was published in 1966.

These works, and the generation of talented writers who made their debuts after Stalin's death, nourished the intelligentsia through the Brezhnev years of increased cultural and political repression. Their authors became cult figures: every Moscow apartment we visited in those years had their photographs displayed on a bookshelf, and particularly treasured books would be displayed face outward. Most of what was not published circulated in *samizdat* or was published abroad and smuggled into the Soviet Union *(tamizdat)*. Readers with the desire, and the connections, could get access to almost anything. Given a book or a manuscript for twenty-four hours, they would think nothing of staying up all night to read it. A joke circulated about the mother who typed out *War and Peace* in a carbon copy on onionskin, so that her daughter, thinking it was *samizdat*, would read it. Now hardly anyone thinks of *samizdat* any more and even *tamizdat* is less interesting; most of the "forbidden" classics have been published in Soviet journals within the last two years.

The writers who emerged in the fifties and sixties eventually chose one of three paths: emigration, co-optation, or marginalization. Many of the most talented were forced into emigration because they could not be silent or mince their words, or because the mediocrities who controlled official culture felt threatened by their talent. Other young Turks of the sixties, most notably Yevgeny Yevtushenko, Andrey Voznesensky, and Chingiz Aitmatov, made an uneasy peace with the literary establishment, whose perks, including country dachas and Writers' Union posts, they now enjoy. Still others maintained an uneasy truce; while not emigrating, they managed to maintain most of their creative independence, for which they suffered frequent clashes with the cultural bureaucracy. Several of them—Yury Trifonov, Vasily Shukshin, Vladimir Vysotsky—died prematurely, perhaps from the strain. Among the most talented to survive was Fazil Iskander.

In the new age, the co-opted have emerged as defenders of *glasnost*, using their positions to support good causes, like Voznesensky's fight for the establishment of a Pasternak museum. Those formerly marginalized, particularly the dead ones, have become heroes, and by the spring of 1988 even the emigrés were being welcomed back into the fold of Soviet literature.

The landmark cultural event of *glasnost* between Gorbachev's accession to power in 1985 and the end of 1987 was not a work of prose or poetry but Georgian director Tengiz Abuladze's film *Repentance*. Like many of the most talked-about publications of 1987, the film had waited several years. It was made in 1983, when the brief Andropov regime gave some hint of the changes that would be possible under Gorbachev, and when the current Foreign Minister, Eduard Shevardnadze, was Party boss of Georgia. Under Chernenko, the film went on the shelf, to be released at the very end of 1986 only through Shevardnadze's personal intervention. With its intentional anachronisms—secret police arrive to arrest their victims riding in eighteenth-century carriages and dressed in medieval armor—and layers of symbolic meaning, *Repentance* is an examination not just of Stalinism but of totalitarian dictatorship in general, and of those qualities in the human soul that allow it to flourish. The film's impact on Soviet audiences was immense; by the following June almost everyone had seen it, many more than once. It has become a milestone in the history of *glasnost*, and its final line, "What good is a road that does not lead to a church?" has become proverbial. In April 1988, Abuladze won the Lenin Prize, the Soviet Union's highest honor for creative work, for the film and the two earlier parts of the trilogy it concludes.

In the major journal publications of 1987, the nation struggled to recapture its historical memory from those who had not only stolen but disguised or deformed it. Each of these works touched a particular blank spot in

Soviet history: collectivization (Boris Mozhaev's *Peasant Men and Women*), the beginning of the purges (Anatoly Rybakov's *Children of the Arbat*), the wartime deportation of entire minority nations (Anatoly Pristavkin's *A Little Golden Cloud Spent the Night*), the rise of the Stalinist bureaucracy (Aleksander Bek's *A New Assignment*), the destruction of Soviet genetics (Vladimir Dudintsev's *White Garments* and Daniil Granin's *Zubr*). Two long-suppressed narrative poems by beloved poets, Anna Akhmatova's *Requiem* and Aleksander Tvardovsky's *By Right of Memory*, treated the purges of the thirties from the viewpoints of the mother and son of victims. Bulgakov's *Heart of a Dog* took a fantastic and satirical look at the politically complex 1920s and ridiculed revolutionary hopes to create a "new Soviet man." With the exception of Akhmatova's poem and perhaps Bulgakov's short novel, none of these works is a literary masterpiece. But their importance as social documents is clear: each became the text for analysis and debate in *publitsistika*, and each generated masses of reader letters, which were published in turn as part of the ongoing discussion.

Throughout 1987 literature kept its lead in treating historical blank spots that historians and politicians still feared to touch. But Gorbachev's November speech on the seventieth anniversary of the Revolution seemed to shift the balance toward history and economics. Literature in 1988 was freer to be literature. The fat journals began publishing a series of major masterpieces suppressed only because they treated then untouchable themes: Pasternak's *Dr. Zhivago*, Zamyatin's *We*, Grossman's *Life and Fate*. Nabokov, Kafka, and even, incredibly, the long-taboo *1984*, *Brave New World*, *Animal Farm*, and *Darkness at Noon*, have now been made available to the Soviet reader. We saw plenty of straphangers on the subways absorbed in *Dr. Zhivago* or Nabokov's *The Gift*. But most of our friends had read these works long ago, in emigré editions, *samizdat,* or even in manuscript. In 1988 the center of their attention and ours shifted away from literature to *publitsistika* itself.

For Jane, the most astonishing development of Moscow Spring was the resurrection and legitimation of the Russian literary emigration. Previously unspeakable names—Brodsky, Sinyavsky, Voinovich, Aksyonov, Galich, even Solzhenitsyn—were spoken aloud from public stages and found their way into print. On previous trips, friends had quietly pressed us for information about favorite writers who had vanished from sight after their emigration: What were they doing? How did life "over there" affect their writing? Their books were likely to be confiscated if customs discovered them; what little did get through was passed from hand to hand by eager readers.

In the spring of 1987, seven emigré cultural figures, including writer Vasily Aksyonov, signed an open letter in the Western press expressing doubts about the true extent of *glasnost. Moscow News* stunned its readers East and West by publishing the letter—balancing it, however, with a critical rebuff. By the spring of 1988, major journals were scrambling to publish something by or about Joseph Brodsky; establishment film director Eldar Ryazanov talked of making a film from Vladimir Voinovich's *Adventures of Private Ivan Chonkin,* and the triumphal return visit of Yury Liubimov, former director of the Taganka theater, was covered by the press in sentimental detail. A long article in the leading theater journal recounted details of the petty bureaucratic harassment that had eventually led him to stay abroad. In June, there were even rumors (premature, it seems) that Grigory Baklanov, the editor of *Znamya,* was negotiating to publish Solzhenitsyn's *Cancer Ward.*

While we were in Moscow, two major conferences took place, one in Denmark, one in Portugal, at which delegations of Soviet writers, critics, and editors met

with emigré writers, many of them old friends and colleagues, on an equal footing. If such meetings took place
before when Soviet writers made rare visits to the West,
they happened privately, almost surreptitiously, and, for
the protection of the Soviets involved, no one talked
much about them. Now the situation had changed entirely. Soviet customs were doing only cursory checks of
incoming baggage, and their concern with protecting
their countrymen from "subversive" literature had
considerably lessened. Editions of Brodsky and other
relatively apolitical emigré writers were seldom confiscated. The writers' conferences in Europe were the object of great curiosity, and reports by their Soviet
participants were given wide circulation.

As Tatyana Tolstaya put it at a public lecture after the
PEN conference in Lisbon, "There were all the writers
whose names had been relegated to silence in the ten or
fifteen years since their emigration. It was as if they had
been resurrected from the dead. The wild thought
struck me that if they could reappear, perhaps even Akhmatova and Pasternak might come back to life, too."

Basing her remarks on her two recent trips abroad,
Tolstaya patiently, even enthusiastically, answered her
audience's endless questions. To those who inquired
hopefully about the possibility that one or more of their
favorites would return for good, she replied with a realistic survey of the legal, economic, and practical barriers
that remained to be overcome. So far, the only emigré
writer to return for good was the nonagenarian poet
Irina Odoevtseva; her arrival in Leningrad in 1987 was
triumphantly chronicled in the Soviet press.

In the Soviet Union, there is culture and a cultural
bureaucracy—and the two do not coexist happily. Each
of the creative professions—writers, artists, composers,
actors, architects, filmmakers—has a union with its own
comfortable club building and provides a wide variety
of perks, ranging from vacation trips to dachas to special

bookstores. Though the leadership of some of these
unions has been replaced in the last few years, the sur-
vival of the entrenched establishment in several others,
notably the composers' and writers' unions, is so notice-
able as to cause bewilderment in the West. What is the
source of these men's power, and how have they managed to hold on to it for so long? Just before we arrived,
two bold challenges to these cultural bureaucrats appeared in the press.

Natalya Ilina is a forceful and vigorous woman who
looks nowhere near the age—early seventies—her official biography indicates. Her sharp wit and sharper pen
have made her one of Russia's masters of the literary
feuilleton. In a January 1988 article in *Ogonyok*, she
took on the entrenched oligarchy that controls the Writers' Union secretariat, accusing them not simply of lack
of talent—that would surprise no one—but of fraud
and embezzlement. She detailed the system by which
they arranged mammoth editions of their own works,
for which they received equally mammoth royalties.
(Under the quaint system of Soviet publishing, royalties
depend on print runs, not on sales.) The editions decorated shelves in bookstores, libraries, and warehouses
for a while before being shipped off for paper recycling.
She pointedly compared the impunity with which they
carried on their fraud with the stiff punishment meted
out to hapless workers arrested for carrying off a few
boxes of chocolates from the assembly line. She outlined
the pattern whereby publishing-house executives had
relatives or in-laws in literary journals, which, not coincidentally, often published their work; journal editors,
also "by chance," had family connections at publishing
houses. These same literary fat cats were publishing articles lamenting the fact that there was no room for talented young authors because the journals were filled
with "necrophilia," a fascination with the works of dead
authors like Akhmatova, Pasternak, Zamyatin, Gross-

man. The real "dead authors," Ilina demonstrated, were those who still controlled the Writers' Union apparatus.

An object of Ilina's particular scorn was Georgy Markov, longtime first secretary of the Writer's Union and member of the Central Committee, who had been recently kicked upstairs to a cushy post in which he can continue to draw perquisites in his sunset years. Markov's slender output is known by few and read by fewer, but in 1986 *Pravda* published a glowing article about the opening of a Georgy Markov literary museum in his native village in Siberia. "When," asked Ilina in high dudgeon, "has Russia ever had museums in honor of *living* writers?" And this in a country where the Pasternak museum was still an unfulfilled promise, where there were yet no museums of Akhmatova, Tsvetayeva, Mandelstam, Bulgakov!

Yury Karyakin, the philosopher, was disciplined by the party for pursuing his own personal de-Stalinization campaign after Khrushchev's fall. More recently employed at the Institute of the International Workers' Movement, he has become one of the intelligentsia's heroes. He was asked by *Znamya* to reply in print to an open letter which attacked Mozhaev's novel on collectivization from a classic Stalinist position. The letter writer was the son of Stalin's notorious ideological hatchet-man Andrey Zhdanov. Yury Zhdanov, a chemist by profession, is living out his years as rector of Rostov University. He later decided to withdraw his broadside ("This is not the proper time to hit back"), but Karyakin published his answer, "To a Certain Incognito," anyway, unmasking the classic Stalinist philosophical and critical moves in Zhdanov's letter. All our friends knew who the target was and delighted in the skill with which Karyakin demolished his target. In May 1988, Karyakin published an even bolder attack on the senior Zhdanov in *Ogonyok*, pointing out that despite protests and articles in the press, his name still "graced" Leningrad

University and his vicious 1946 denunciations of Akhmatova and Zoshchenko, never retracted, were still official Party policy.

Ilina and Karyakin made overwhelming cases, but they had chosen formidable opponents. They were still flourishing, but the continued strength of the conservatives and the tentativeness of reformers less combative than they help to explain what we came to call the "Yes, but" character of many cultural events we attended between January and March.

THE

CULTURAL SCENE

C ultural events during our first few months in
Moscow often broke taboos of one sort or another. But the taboo-breakers seemed to feel they had to
leaven their daring with dullness. Were they afraid to
upset cultural watchdogs? Or were old habits of ritual
utterance and longwindedness harder to overcome than
the taboos themselves?

As we arrived, the country was launching into an all-
out observance of Vladimir Vysotsky's fiftieth birthday
which nearly rivaled the 1987 sesquicentennial celebration of Pushkin's death. Vysotsky, a multitalented artistic rebel who died in 1980 of a heart attack at the age of
forty-two, has come to symbolize the Russian soul and
its repression under the "period of stagnation." The
change in official attitudes toward him in the last year or
two had been the most dramatic shift in cultural policy
for the average Russian who doesn't subscribe to *Novy
mir* or read Pasternak.

Officially, Vysotsky was an actor at Yury Liubimov's Taganka theater and occasionally appeared in films. Jane saw him play Hamlet in Liubimov's memorable staging fifteen years ago and will never forget his entrance from the back of an empty stage. Sitting down on the edge with his guitar, he sang Pasternak's Hamlet poem from *Dr. Zhivago*, which was then, of course, unpublished in the USSR. His acting, seething with repressed rebellion, made Hamlet uniquely relevant to the frustrations of his generation. A single woven curtain, the only scenery, served as the arras, and the metaphor of being overheard emerged from the text to make this a very contemporary *Hamlet* indeed.

The other side of Vysotsky was the poet-bard who sang his bitter, satirical ballads in an unmistakable husky voice to the accompaniment of his guitar. Vysotsky's songs were immensely popular with not only the intelligentsia but the working class and, it was persistently rumored, the higher-ups as well. They circulated widely in *magnitizdat*, homemade, often crude recordings of his concerts. One was as likely to hear him playing from a cab driver's tape recorder as in the background of one of those crowded, talk-filled evenings at the homes of the intelligentsia. The only official acknowledgments of his work were two rather tame records, sold largely in foreign-currency stores, and a small volume of his song-poems published shortly after his death. But the legend grew. A twelve-tape "collected songs" that sold in New York for nearly $100 was a hot item, its emigré publisher said, among Soviet diplomats, who probably resold it for much more when they got home. Vysotsky's marriage to the French actress Marina Vlady, a descendant of White Russian emigrés, added to his legend, as did his hard drinking and fast driving. Here was a man defying all the rules and getting away with it.

Russians tend to extremes in either vilifying or deifying their literary figures. They idolize their poets, particularly dead ones, the way Americans idolize rock stars. Joseph Brodsky once ventured the hypothesis that, after the Church lost moral authority at the beginning of this century, Russians looked to their poets for the moral guidance they had formerly sought in saints' lives. The Russian penchant for literary museums far exceeds anything in America. For instance, Jane signed up for a four-hour bus tour of "Moscow places connected with the life of Marina Tsvetayeva." The bus was at least three-quarters full of Soviet tourists, and similar tours were scheduled eight to ten times a week. Fifteen different guides ran the tours; Jane's recited lengthy passages of Tsvetayeva's poetry by heart. Jane later wondered aloud to an American audience whether there was any equivalent in America. Someone instantly came up with the answer —Graceland, Elvis Presley's Nashville home.

During Vysotsky's jubilee, an entire issue of the popular film magazine *Soviet Screen* was devoted to him. Monuments were unveiled in front of his apartment building on Malaya Gruzinskaya and in the courtyard of the Taganka theater; there were always fresh flowers at both locations and on his grave, a site of frequent pilgrimages. The fat journals published his song-poems and articles about him. A relatively expensive illustrated collection of his poems and prose, with memoirs of him by his contemporaries, was issued in an edition of 200,000. But the greatest memorial was a documentary tribute spread over four nights of prime-time TV. Eldar Ryazanov, the moderator, reverently traced the story of Vysotsky's life, interviewing at length his old friends, his widow, father, stepmother, and mother, who lives on in his apartment.

We had to catch the second episode at its repeat showing the next morning, for that night we were invited to Spaso House, the American ambassador's residence, for an evening to honor visiting American poet William Jay Smith. For many years, Smith has been translating major Soviet poets, particularly Bella Akhmadulina and Andrey Voznesensky. The evening was a love fest of American/Soviet poetic ties. Three Soviet poets shared the stage with Smith: Voznesensky, Boris Zakhoder, writer of children's and satirical verse and well known for his brilliant translation of *Winnie-the-Pooh,* and Vitaly Korotich, the Ukrainian poet better known in the West as editor of the magazine *Ogonyok.* Smith read his translations of Voznesensky and Zakhoder, Voznesensky and Zakhoder their own verse and translations of Smith. It was all very cordial; a far cry, Smith recalled, from an earlier reading at Spaso just after the invasion of Afghanistan and the imposition of trade sanctions, when most of the invited Soviet guests suddenly developed sick children or dying parents.

At cocktails preceding the reading and at the buffet dinner that followed, Soviet editors, critics, and cultural bureaucrats circulated pleasantly, if a bit awkwardly, with the American guests. One sign of change was the presence of Maya Aksyonova, wife of the emigré writer. The fact that she could mix and mingle with the assembled Soviet litterateurs, many of whom were old friends (or enemies), was evidence of the major shift in official attitude toward the emigration.

For us, the surprise of the evening came from Korotich, who read in a beautiful, sonorous Ukrainian, a language we had seldom heard in its literary form. An even more pleasant surprise was the translation, the equal of those produced by the evening's honored poets. The translator was Jack F. Matlock—our evening's host, the American ambassador. Matlock was trained as a Slavist. He prides himself on making speeches in the native languages of the republics, even the non-Slavic ones. Matlock's ability to appear on Soviet media without a translator is a great asset in the *glasnost* era, when he is given the opportunity to do so.

Both poems Korotich chose to read can be read as parables of his crusading work on *Ogonyok.* We found "The Mirror" particularly meaningful and, in light of the

severe criticism he would attract during the June Party
conference, prophetic as well:

> I am a mirror.
> People undress before me
> And try on new clothes as I watch.
> I can see
> Even the noblest unclothed.
> I see how folks pretend they're wearing medals,
> Though none had ever been awarded.
> I don't know
> what you think of your reflection.
> I am deaf.
> I hear nothing.
> I know
> sometimes you don't care for
> My work.
> Only, for goodness sake, don't get mad.
> I've always been honest.
> Even when you put me
> In a gilded frame,
> Even when you squeeze me
> into ornate millwork
> I'm still behind a gate
> Through which you must pass
> to enter your own souls.
> . . . .
> When you see the truth,
> Searing like a flame,
> And find it unbearable,
> You break me to pieces.
> So go about your business without me.
> But then failure will be lurking there for you.
> For this world, after all
> needs someone
> With a straight and honest gaze,
> To tell it like it is, and was, and will be.

Cultural evenings at the Embassy, though, were never as exciting as those held in the auditoriums of the cultural union clubs or factory-affiliated "houses of culture." These occasions held large Soviet audiences rapt for up to five hours. The first one we went to, in late January, was the only disappointment, an indication in retrospect of how far and how fast things moved. It was billed as a round-table discussion on the upcoming millennium of the Russian Orthodox Church. By the time of the actual celebration, which began just as we left in June, media treatment of the Church had changed dramatically, reflecting equally dramatic changes on the part of the political leadership. For the first time ever, part of the Easter service was broadcast on Soviet television. In late April, *Vremya* and the central newspapers featured pictures of Gorbachev meeting cordially with the metropolitan and other church leaders. A feature-length documentary film on the Kiev cave monastery and its traditions was released in honor of the occasion. *Moscow News* and other media gave extensive coverage to the millennium celebrations with articles on such topics as bell ringing in Moscow monasteries or profiles of the nine new saints canonized for the occasion.

But in January, it was still startling to see Russian churchmen in their black robes and miters sharing the stage with scholars from various research institutes, including, for some reason, the USA Institute. Historian Yury Afanasyev's role as moderator seemed to promise frankness, and perhaps a few fireworks. The crowd was full of serious young people and bearded, distinguished-looking professorial types.

World-renowned literary scholar V. V. Ivanov led off with a lecture on the state of pagan religion among Slavic tribes at the time of Christianization. Ivanov argued that there were well-developed extant cultures and belief systems that scholars have neglected but which clearly left their mark on the Christianity that developed on Russian soil. It was an important theme, but not one in which the audience saw much contemporary political relevance. Ivanov went on well beyond his appointed time, and the audience broke into the rhythmic applause that tells the speaker it's time to quit. It was the only occasion all spring when we heard it; news reports tell us it was used on several speakers at the Party conference in June.

Another disappointment was the leading churchman, whose clichéd vocabulary seemed more that of a Komsomol organizer than of a man of God. The Church representatives were circumspect to the point of boredom, indicating exactly how far the Church had adapted to the powers that be. Only the junior member of the delegation, a teacher at the theological academy, stood out. Judging by his surname (Asmus), he was probably the grandson of a distinguished scholar of German philosophy, a lifelong friend of Boris Pasternak. It was clear that he had entered the Church for reasons of faith rather than career, and his presence hinted at a hope for the intellectual rebirth of Russian Orthodoxy in what promised to be very different times.

The sheer number of people on stage, nearly twenty, meant each speaker was lucky to be heard once, and no "round-table" ever developed. The audience soon began to get restless, and when they got hold of the microphone, complained about the lack of a real exchange on stage. They were clearly already used to one.

Publicity for most of these meetings was by word of mouth. It was a while before we plugged into the information network, but once we did, we quickly learned to rely on our friends for a sense of what was worth going to. Events we learned of on our own, from newspaper or other publicity, were frequently disappointing.

The same went for the theater. Our friends taught us to choose a theater, not a play. All Soviet theaters are permanent repertory companies, with their own staff of actors and their own artistic traditions. Despite the spate of small "theater studios" that had blossomed in the last year, there were still only a few interesting theaters in Moscow. Whatever they do, we were told, is likely to be good. No matter what play other theaters are putting on, it's unlikely to be worth seeing.

Jane learned this the hard way. In *Leisure in Moscow*, the weekly guide to theater, films, concerts, exhibitions, and other cultural events, she saw an announcement of two plays: "The Poet Marina Tsvetayeva" and "Boris Pasternak and Marina Tsvetayeva." Jane had spent twenty years of her life studying and writing about Tsvetayeva, particularly about her complicated epistolary romance with Pasternak. Tsvetayeva had been rehabilitated during the Khrushchev thaw; in fact, as the bus tour testified, she had become a kind of cult figure. A play devoted to her seemed promising; a play about the Tsvetayeva/Pasternak relationship even more exciting.

Jane began to be suspicious when the tiny theater was less than half full before the performance; Russians are so starved for theater that even mediocre performances are fairly well attended. Then a single actress, dressed in black, emerged and began reciting Tsvetayeva's poems in an artificial, overemotional voice. Jane and the friend she had brought along could hardly wait for the intermission, when they—and most of the rest of the audience—headed for the exits. "Come back when we have a better play," the coatroom attendant urged. "I could have told you," Jane's friend said, "but I thought you'd better learn for yourself." From then on we followed the rule: if tickets are on sale, it's probably not worth going to.

Tsvetayeva's rehabilitation was easier than Mandelstam's. She had, after all, voluntarily returned to the Soviet Union from France in 1939, if only to commit suicide two years later. Much of what she wrote while she was an emigré is extremely difficult, but it is her more accessible romantic poetry, written just before and after the Revolution, that makes her so popular in Russia today. Mandelstam, on the other hand, is a difficult poet who was exiled for an anti-Stalin poem and died in 1938 in a Siberian transit camp. He has been published in Russia since the 1960s, but much more selectively than the other members of the "great quartet." It was therefore another sign of the times when *Moscow News* noted plans for the first-ever Soviet scholarly conference on Mandelstam.

Held at the prestigious Gorky Literary Institute, the three-day conference featured more than fifty papers read by luminaries of Soviet literary scholarship and criticism from all over the USSR—some who had long been authorized to work on Mandelstam, others whose devotion could finally receive recognition. Much was publicly revealed about Mandelstam's life and work that had never before been officially uttered in the USSR. One distinguished critic spoke on Mandelstam's "Ode to Stalin," a bizarre work produced when Mandelstam, desperate to save his life and that of his wife, tried to put his muse at the service of the dictator, and found that she rebelled. Jane later passed the speaker a note, asking if he knew of Mandelstam scholar Clarence Brown's twenty-year-old article on the subject. No, he replied, but his own article had been written eighteen years before and had sat "in the drawer" until now.

One February night, Jane was invited to Moscow's only jazz club, the Blue Bird, located in a basement near the center of town. Her hosts, longtime refuseniks in their fifties, reminisced about the high Stalinist days when playing or listening to jazz was a state crime. They themselves were not jazz aficionados but had obtained tickets through friends of their son and wanted to share the treat with Jane. The club was a labor of love; both the organizers and the musicians had full-time regular jobs. This particular evening was a special testimony to Moscow's new romance with the West. Sir Geoffrey Howe, Great Britain's foreign minister, was in town for a few days of negotiations with Shevardnadze. Howe was a great jazz fan and made known his interest in hearing some of the Moscow variety. So this jam session was scheduled for Monday night at nine thirty, the only time Howe was available, rather than the usual Wednesday at eight. The crowd was heavily laced with foreigners, mostly British diplomats and Western journalists. It was an odd scene: Jane felt more like a Muscovite than an American as she and her friends watched the social mores of the British maneuvering for seats at Sir Geoffrey's table and the chance to exchange a few pleasantries with him. The highlight of the evening was a young pianist named Misha Altman, whose improvisations combined classical jazz technique with strong hints of the Klezmer melodies of his native Kishinev.

Soviet film was one of the first cultural fields to show signs of *perestroika*. Elem Klimov, the new head of the Cinematographers' Union, knew censorship firsthand. His own *Agony*, released in the West as *Rasputin*, was banned for years because its depiction of a weak, family-loving Nicholas II was regarded as too sympathetic. Klimov was instrumental in setting up a review commission to assure the release of films—by one estimate, as many as two hundred of them—that were sitting on the shelf when *perestroika* began.

This flood of repressed films, many of them of high quality, had given the Soviet screen a deceptive glow which was beginning to wear off when we arrived. With most of those films now released, the industry had to confront the realities of *perestroika*. In a period of rapid change, filmmaking is hampered by long production times—it takes nearly two years, even in the best of circumstances, to get a film from idea through scenario to distribution. This means that films hitting the screen in 1988 were conceived in the first year or two of Gorbachev's rule. Though they may then have pushed the frontiers of the possible, they now seemed almost passé, and Soviet viewers preferred to stay home and watch television, which was often more daring.

Another new problem for the film industry is self-financing, which means that studios have to worry about the profitability of a film. This wreaked havoc with the traditional studio system, founded on large state subsidies, and new film production was down. Soviets have often boasted that their film, theater, and literature, unlike those in the West, are not subject to the censorship of the marketplace. It now appears that they may have substituted one form of censorship for the other. Some of the most interesting films we saw seemed to have made serious artistic compromises in order to draw viewers.

Eldar Ryzanov's *Forgotten Melody for Flute*, one of the most popular movies of the winter, was billed as "the first *perestroika* comedy." It got mixed reviews, and we discovered why. The film's hero, or rather anti-hero, works in the "Main Administration for Leisure Time," an agency that does little but issue endless directives interfering in the cultural life of the citizenry. In this capacity, he visits an amateur production of Gogol's *The Inspector General*, whose modern staging indicates only too clearly that the bureaucratic scourge Gogol satirized is still as dangerous as ever. In a show of magnanimity ("These are new times") he ostensibly approves the show, then tells his subordinate to make sure "higher-ups" forbid it after all.

The first sections of the film contain some marvelous if heavy-handed jabs at the bureaucratic mentality and a few lines that, at least at the time, were regarded as daring. For example, in the opening sequence, Muscovites on their way to work read newspaper articles on "acceleration" and *perestroika* as they sit, stopped in traffic, so that a large black limousine can speed by. But the movie loses its direction in pseudo-Fellini dream sequences and a romance between the bureaucrat, who owes his career to his father-in-law's eminence, and a poor-but-honest nurse. He betrays her time and again, unable to break with his wife and comfortable life, while she, implausibly, takes him back every time. We thought their relationship perhaps symbolized that between the people and the bureaucracy—though they get screwed time and again, it's they who keep it alive. The irony of *glasnost* is that such seemingly daring satire is actually fulfilling a mandate from above, as Gorbachev appeals to the creative intelligentsia in his struggle against the entrenched bureaucracy.

Friends invited us to a screening of a new documentary called *More Light*, at which one of the two filmmakers would speak. We had heard that documentary films even more than art films had become a path-breaking medium. The screening was to be held at the Composers' Union, a building in central Moscow just off Gorky Street. The filmmaker, Igor Itzkoff, had recently won the Lenin Prize for his work on a documentary about Marshal Georgy Zhukov, the World War II hero who was later shunted aside by Stalin, raised up and then fired again by Khrushchev. *More Light* had been made for the seventieth anniversary of the Revolution. It took its name from the demand of *glasnost* for more light on the so-called "blank pages" of history and other hitherto proscribed subjects and featured highlights of the entire seventy years since 1917, including remarkable, previously unseen footage from police archives.

In the tradition of such evenings, the filmmaker was to introduce the film before it was shown and then comment and answer questions. Burly and bearded, Itzkoff turned out to be a wonderfully informed, hugely entertaining host, a kind of "stand-up historian" who combined a scholar's knowledge and acumen with a comedian's nonstop wit. He explained in his prefilm talk that key footage, including never-before-shown shots of Trotsky and Bukharin, came from the KGB. The KGB's predecessors, the dreaded OGPU and NKVD, had seized the film and squirreled it away in their archives ("Everything in its proper place at the secret police," joked Itzkoff), never dreaming that it would ever see the light of day. But the KGB itself had been helpful in retrieving it, and even though the film was made before Gorbachev's November 2, 1987, speech, the censors had posed no obstacles. Nor had the top political leaders, who, in traditional Soviet fashion, had not been too busy with affairs of state to check out *More Light* for themselves.

All art has been of interest to Russian rulers since long before 1917. Soviet rulers have paid particular attention to film, which Lenin once proclaimed "the most important medium"—words that are printed in huge letters on the wall of the auditorium at the Cinematographers' Union. Given the Politburo's concern with historical revisionism, particularly on the eve of the seventieth anniversary, one can understand why they scrutinized this documentary. But Gorbachev asked only that the film not be released until after the November 7 celebrations. And Yegor Ligachev, the Politburo member reportedly most averse to critical coverage of the past, sent word, according to Itzkoff, that he liked it.

Once the lights dimmed and the film came on, we could see why both *Moscow News*, which had given it a rave review, and Ligachev had liked it. It was carefully, exquisitely—excessively, it seemed to us—balanced. Triumphs and tragedies flitted across the screen in regular alternation. Both got almost exactly equal time. There was Trotsky, shown for the first time in decades, looking dashing and arrogant as he mobilized Red Army

troops during the Civil War. There was Bukharin, looking like, as Lenin once described him, "the favorite of
the entire Party." There was Lenin himself, shown not
as a revolutionary demigod but in repose, leaning
against his limo in Red Square, even hamming it up a
bit for the camera. Most of the old Bolsheviks, the men
Stalin exterminated in the thirties, passed in review.
The film lamented their fate. It offered a few harrowing
scenes of the forced collectivization of agriculture and
even a passing glimpse of cattle cars taking prisoners off
to concentration camps. Its single most dramatic shot,
which absolutely stuns Russian audiences in an era of
growing official respect for religion, was of the vast Cathedral of the Saviour being blown up. Built on a site
where Stalin planned to put one of his huge wedding-
cake skyscrapers—but where he ended up with a swim-
ming pool instead when the ground turned out to be too
swampy—the church was dynamited in the thirties. Re-
corded by a contemporary newsreel, the scene was
shown in slow motion—the splendid edifice surrounded
by ominously empty streets, several small puffs of
smoke accompanied by flying bricks, and then, in ever
so stately a fashion, the crumbling and final collapse of
the majestic cathedral built by public subscription to
commemorate the national victory over Napoleon in
1812.

But alongside all this were the glorious victories—the
Revolution itself with workers and peasants marching
off to do battle with the class enemy, the triumphant
industrialization campaign with new factories belching
smoke and turning out tanks, the incredibly costly but
still magnificent defeat of Hitler. Khrushchev was resurrected as Moscow Party boss in the thirties, nailing up
posters on a busy street, young and vigorous in a jaunty
workman's cap, receiving an Order of Lenin with a radiant, boyish grin on his face just about the time when
the previous generation of leaders was about to get it in

the neck in NKVD cellars. Then, after paying homage to
Khrushchev's de-Stalinization campaign, the film cut to
footage of him haranguing a crowd of uncomprehending
peasants about corn. Brezhnev was also presented as a
good guy for a while, before he turned bad. No explanation was offered of how so much good and evil could
coexist so peacefully under one Communist roof.

The film was riveting. It was also infuriating. It would
be comforting to conclude that the filmmakers were simply being cautious, that it was too soon to tell more of
the truth. Indeed, Itzkoff's post-screening comments implied as much, addressing several related issues more
candidly than the film had. And when we later asked
him point-blank whether he was really as evenhanded
as he seemed to be, he answered with an enigmatic
smile and an ambiguous reference to the way the prolific
Marx could be read to justify almost anything.

But what amazed us at this early point in our stay was
the way the audience used such occasions as experi-
ments in civic dialogue. "What's going on in Armenia?"
Itzkoff was asked. Though the then-very-recent disorders in Armenia had nothing to do with the topic at
hand, Itzkoff answered with complete frankness and, we
suspect, no small satisfaction in showing how well informed he was.

While we were watching Soviet films, Soviets were
lining up to get their first look at a wide range of Western
films: *One Flew Over the Cuckoo's Nest, Amadeus, A
Chorus Line, Short Circuit, Crocodile Dundee, Purple
Rose of Cairo.* (Even sophisticated Russian film buffs
knew nothing of Woody Allen.) Early in March, Jane
attended a special meeting of an informal film discussion society, most of whose members were faculty or
graduate students at the university. This was a special
occasion: the previous week there had been an unprecedented festival of American films shown in Moscow.
The twenty or thirty members who attended were ob-

viously knowledgeable about foreign films and tossed around the names of European, particularly Italian, directors and actors. But American films were terra incognita.

Of the more than thirty films shown during the week, most members had managed to see four or five. The American organizers had taken pains to present a broad time span and a broad range of genres, putting particular emphasis on films in which Americans criticize their own society. None of the films had been shown publicly in the Soviet Union before. *The Dead* was universally admired but seen as "English rather than American." *Hoosiers* was called "a patriotic film in the best sense," and reminded at least one speaker of the popular Soviet trend of "village prose" in the 1970s. The audience was particularly grateful for the opportunity to see American films of the 1950s and 1960s, which had been a blank in their film education; several expressed unexpected delight in *Singing in the Rain*. They were suitably horrified by *The Killing Fields*, but at least one of them felt the film would have been more interesting if it had more explicitly raised the question "How could this happen?"

The discussion at the meeting struck Jane as more formal than she would have expected. A chair called on various members of the group in turn, and there was little give-and-take but rather a series of set speeches, impressively articulate, which sounded as if they had been thought out in advance. Jane had the feeling they were as involved in learning the art of free discussion, something that had never been a part of their education, as they were with the films.

PESSIMISTS

AND OPTIMISTS

I t became more and more apparent to us that something very significant was happening. But exactly what? Clearly, some people felt free to speak out with breathtaking boldness, but others did not. Obviously there were still limits. Where did they begin and end? And how did one fit together the new openness in intellectual life with the utterly unchanged or perhaps even deteriorating conditions of everyday life? Even if *glasnost* was real and growing, how long could it go on if *perestroika* did not take hold?

As always, we checked with friends, both close and not so close, to see what sense they were making of the events we observed. Some thought what was going on was exactly what was needed. Others thought change had barely begun. Some thought the reforms had a good chance to succeed. Others saw virtually no hope.

Seryozha had worked for years as a journalist on

second-rank national newspapers. His assignments had taken him around the country, especially into plants and factories of all kinds. Ultimately he tired of the grind and abandoned daily deadlines to become what he always wanted to be, a fiction writer. A warm-hearted, bushy-haired teddy bear of a man, he had joined the Party in the fifties in hopes that Khrushchev's reforms would work out. When those hopes faded in the late sixties, he tried to use his status as a Party journalist to help individuals. Given his background, we assumed he would take heart from Gorbachev's renewed effort at reform. And at first he did. In January 1986, he had been guardedly optimistic; in the summer of 1987, a bit less so. By the fall of 1987, he was getting depressed. When we saw him in January 1988, he had just about abandoned hope.

We were puzzled. His gloom deepened in direct proportion to reform's progress. The farther Gorbachev seemed willing to go, the more Seryozha feared he wouldn't get there. When we put the paradox to him, Seryozha denied that the reforms had progressed very far. On the contrary, he detected signs of a retreat. Most ominous was the defeat and humiliation of Boris Yeltsin, the outspoken former Moscow Party chief who had lost his job the previous fall. Yeltsin stood for more radical reform than Gorbachev favored, and at a faster pace. The specific behavior that brought on his fall—criticizing the leadership and especially Yegor Ligachev at a Central Committee meeting just prior to the celebrations marking the seventieth anniversary of the Revolution—lent some credence to Kremlin-circulated stories that he was mentally unstable. Bill himself had detected a slightly hysterical note in Yeltsin's speeches. But Seryozha had no doubt that what Yeltsin objected to was worth getting agitated about.

Early in February, several of our friends independently told us of a *samizdat* text of Yeltsin's speech. It hit hard at the privileges of the Party elite, asking, "How long can we keep feeding at this trough while the man in the street stands in line for lousy sausages?" It also asked to "spare us from the petty tutelage of Raisa Maksimovna [Gorbachev]." A French newspaper had published the text, but other Western correspondents in Moscow held back; they smelled a forgery designed to discredit Yeltsin, who later disavowed the French version. Yet it was precisely those lines that convinced our friends the speech was real.

Rumor had it that on his dismissal from office Yeltsin was taken directly to a hospital with heart trouble. Seryozha told us about an older woman, an idealistic Communist and a great Yeltsin fan, who learned which hospital and went there with flowers. "Who said he is here?" a nurse asked suspiciously. "Who are you, anyway?" The woman took fright and left with her flowers. Later in the spring we saw graffiti in elevators proclaiming "Free Yeltsin!" Even the kids in the apartment house courtyards got the message. "Have you seen them playing 'Yeltsin'?" Seryozha asked. "One kid is Yeltsin. The others, led by 'Gorbachev,' run him down and 'destroy' him."

Seryozha had other evidence of retreat. He compared a recent meeting between Gorbachev and writers and editors with a similar session two years earlier. Then, Gorbachev had asked the press to provide the "opposition" otherwise lacking in a one-party state. This time, he demanded they "consolidate" their forces to provide a united front of press and Party. According to Seryozha, the retreat began at the January 1987 Central Committee plenum, which had been delayed several times by conservative opposition. Either the opposition, led by Ligachev, would ultimately take over, he said, or Gorbachev would be compelled to lead the retreat himself.

Where did Seryozha get his information? Like most of

his compatriots, from reading and decoding the news-papers. Doubtless he also heard rumors, sometimes from well-informed sources, but he was not close enough to the Kremlin to know for sure. He was an unreliable guide to who was up and who down at the top. His pessimism was based on other evidence; the economy, he insisted, was the key. Its deterioration had prompted the reforms in the first place; now it would seal their fate.

The trouble could be seen in the stores. Ten years ago, there were five or ten kinds of cheese, now just one or two. If that was the case in Moscow, imagine how much worse things must be in the provinces! Econo-mists and factory directors openly admitted on TV that the reforms weren't working. As of January 1, 1988, most firms were supposed to be supplying one another ac-cording to contracts. But the ministries were still dictat-ing. The troubles of the much-heralded cooperatives were another bad sign. Young people who had re-sponded to the call to engage in "individual labor activ-ity" were getting discouraged.

These results were built into the system itself, Ser-yozha said. Take the famous "Arkhangel'sk *muzhik*." The press and television had carried stories about a hard-working farmer who managed to turn a far northern island into a prosperous cattle farm. His success was a triumph of Gorbachev's new principles. But the nearby state farm whose land he rented closed him down. Why? Because they felt threatened by his ability to produce more than they could with thirty bureaucrats and a whole state farm full of peasants. Despite the opposition of local Party authorities, central television showed a laudatory documentary about the Arkhangel'sk *muzhik*, and *Izvestiya* chimed in with no fewer than three articles. But the situation on the ground had not im-proved. A classic example, said Seryozha, of how there could be *glasnost* without *perestroika*.

Another example: Gorbachev swore he would end the long-standing practice of mobilizing city people to bring in the harvest, a practice that disrupted industrial and other urban activities without helping peasants as much as more machines and better rural organization would. Yet Seryozha knew for a fact that every single functionary in a particular ministry had spent a week in the fields in the summer of 1987. There was simply no alternative, no other "technology" for harvesting carrots and potatoes.

How could Gorbachev claim things were getting better when they were palpably worse? Unfortunately, there was a way. The latest statistics cited gains that could only be phony. They did so because three years into the Gorbachev era it was too late to blame Leonid Brezhnev. It was time to show results even if they had to fudge and fib to do so. If Gorbachev came to believe in his own statistics, he would be one of the few who did. Others could already see the handwriting on the wall and hedged their behavior accordingly. Seryozha mentioned friends who avoided him because he had relatives in America. His friends were champions of change and knew that seeing him was not very risky, but they were afraid to take the chance.

The trouble was the system itself. Seryozha recalled Andrey Tarkovsky's science-fiction film *Solarius,* whose star is the mysterious living, breathing "atmosphere" around some nameless planet, an eerie force field with a life of its own which swallows travelers who venture into it. The Soviet system behaved the same way. Shortages begat shortages. In the face of political as well as economic scarcity—the former being a way to describe a situation in which everyone worked for and hence depended on the state—people made the necessary accommodations, compromises that doomed the effort at reform.

Anya and Pavel were engineers, good liberal people whom we had seen on all our trips over the years. Even in the darkest days of stagnation they welcomed us to their home, shared with us candidly their sense of the times, even introduced us to colleagues brave enough to break bread with Americans. Yet now that Brezhnev was gone, they hesitated before inviting us. The "special section" at Pavel's plant, a euphemism for the KGB presence in every major Soviet institution, had called him in for a chat. Did Pavel have anything he wanted to tell them? In a long, strained "conversation," they pointedly mentioned that he and Anya had been in contact with old friends who had emigrated to America.

Pavel returned home in shock. He and Anya were torn, afraid—and ashamed of being afraid. They were determined to live as before but were fearful of the price. Finally, through friends, they invited us to dinner. They were not optimistic. Rank-and-file workers at the plant were sick of revelations in the press about the Stalinist past. There were many who thought that Lenin had begun what Stalin continued, or that the Revolution had gone wrong from the start. But Anya and Pavel never heard them say so in public. The Afanasyev institute lecture and the seminar Bill had attended were very rare exceptions.

What did they think of the newly instituted elections in the workplace and the prospect of multicandidate elections to political office? We expected them to dismiss both with a sneer, but they spoke warmly of their duty as citizens to use even the most limited opportunity to improve things. Their native idealism, which had sustained them for so long, was not entirely crushed after all. Their children, young professionals in their late twenties, did the sneering for them. "Come on, Mamochka," said Anya's daughter, "you should know better. What good will voting do? None at all."

Optimists were harder to find, less likely to insist they

were right, and less convincing when they did. We were relieved to find a few believers. But not, thank God, true believers. We are hardly the first to notice that there is something in the Russian soul, and in the Marxist-Leninist creed as well, that craves certainty. The real reformers, as opposed to the careerists and opportunists who merely mouth new platitudes in the old way, were refreshingly tentative and self-critical.

We met the daughter and son-in-law of a longtime refusenik. After a bitter struggle, the old man had gotten permission to leave. But the daughter's family was trapped: in order to take her older daughter by a previous marriage with them, her ex-husband's permission was needed, and he refused. They might have been bitter, but they were surprisingly upbeat. Under *perestroika* their lives and fortunes had improved. She had found work in her profession, and he had taken advantage of the new law on individual labor activity to develop his craft independent of pressures and restrictions. He too was full of stories about contradictions in the reforms. But the trend toward democratization on all continents convinced him that sooner or later the USSR too would become more democratic.

We also met three men, front-line fighters for reform, whose nonstop activism radiated optimism. Their hopes could be dismissed as self-deception. Or you could write off their optimism as a reflection of the power they enjoyed. Still, their example gave us hope.

The first was Gorbachev's science adviser, Yevgeny Velikhov, a big, balding, heavyset man, physically powerful, with a quick, darting mind. About fifty-five, he looks older and acts younger. During the Chernobyl disaster, he directed efforts to smother the reactor fire and decontaminate the site, winning Gorbachev's respect in the process. He struck Bill, who met him only on semiofficial occasions, as a "yes man" of a new and different kind. The traditional Soviet yes man said yes to his boss and hardly ever to anyone else—certainly not to Americans.

In Bill's admittedly limited exposure to him, Velikhov never said no. Equally striking was the way he got others to say yes. When Martin Sherwin flew into Moscow to rescue his spacebridges, Soviet television people had delivered their verdict: there was no way they could mount all these programs. Bill could understand their decision and even sympathize with it, but they had committed themselves and then, after Sherwin made his arrangements, backed out, denying that they had ever agreed.

One of Velikhov's young assistants suggested putting the heat on Gostelradio by leaking the story to *Literaturnaya gazeta*. The fact that two Americans were in the room when the suggestion was made was testimony to *glasnost*. Western Sovietologists argue about whether Soviet officials send each other covert messages through the Soviet press. Here was Bill sitting in on just such a strategy session. But Velikhov rejected the aide's suggestion. Public pressure, he said, got people mad, and when they were mad, you never knew how they would react. He preferred the straightforward approach. With that, he picked up the phone and called the key man at Gostelradio. Velikhov got his way. He seemed to be fighting and winning battles in a war that may yet be lost, but not for his lack of trying.

Fyodor Burlatsky maintains a frantic pace as a columnist for *Literaturnaya gazeta*, author of several books, including studies of Machiavelli and Mao Tse-tung, and plays on the Cuban missile crisis and the politics of *perestroika*, frequent commentator on TV, chair of the philosophy department at the Central Committee's Social Science Academy, and head of the new Soviet Human Rights Commission. He is close enough to Gorbachev to have traveled with him to several U.S.-Soviet summits and to Yugoslavia. Bill first met Burlatsky at Columbia

University several years ago. In October 1986 they spent several days together at a Harvard University conference on the Cuban crisis. At the time of the crisis, in 1962, Burlatsky was a speechwriter for Khrushchev; before that, he worked for a Central Committee department then headed by Andropov. He also led a Khrushchev "brain trust" that included Arbatov and Georgy Shakhnazarov, who recently became personal assistant to Gorbachev for Eastern European affairs.

Burlatsky's conversion under Khrushchev is typical of many current reformers. He is closer to the reins of power than most reform-minded intellectuals but more willing to speak out and risk his neck than one might expect, especially since he found out in the late 1960s how risky it is. He and a co-author published a ringing defense of two avant-garde theaters in *Pravda*. Either Brezhnev read the piece himself and took offense or his gray eminence Mikhail Suslov did. *Pravda* fired both men. Burlatsky landed on his feet at the Social Science Academy. His co-author was kicked out of the Party.

While we were in Moscow, Burlatsky published the first serious profile of Khrushchev, a long, candid article that praised the former unperson's contribution while recognizing his faults, as well as several other pathbreaking, pro-reform pieces. Back in Cambridge in 1986, he had seemed unsure how far Gorbachev could or would go. By the spring of 1988, he had either repressed or overcome such doubts.

Burlatsky is quick and mercurial, short and chunky, warm and outgoing, always on the move. Getting through to him on the phone at work is not impossible, but it is very gratifying when it happens. Burlatsky is rarely at his Academy office; either that or he doesn't take phone calls. He has a helpful secretary at *Litgazeta*, but her help usually consists of telling you that he is on another line. When the shock of learning that there is more than one telephone line per person wears off, you're back to square one.

Burlatsky paid Bill the high honor of giving him his home phone number—a practice official Soviets never used to engage in . The joy of being able to reach him at home at 9:00 A.M. quickly wore off when we realized that the phone rang almost as much there as it did at the office, and it was his wife who had to do most of the answering. She was always good-tempered, but Bill hated to impose on her. When we were later invited to dinner, we witnessed firsthand the everyday burden of being a reformer: poor Burlatsky could barely get through a sentence or a mouthful without a ring. *Perestroika* will really have succeeded when it boosts technological innovation to the point where telephone answering machines, now virtually unknown, become available.

Sergo Mikoyan is less highly placed than either Velikhov or Burlatsky, but in some ways he is even better connected. His job is editor of *Latin America,* an academic journal published by the Academy of Sciences' Latin American Institute. Each time Bill dropped by his office, he found Mikoyan besieged by writers, editors, printers, and delegations from Latin American countries. Mikoyan's connections, as well as a great many of his current concerns, are linked to his father, the late Anastas Mikoyan, the wily Armenian Bolshevik leader whose career began under Lenin, prospered under Stalin, flowered even more under Khrushchev, and didn't end until Brezhnev dumped him. At about fifty-five, with a slim build and boyish face, Mikoyan, like Burlatsky, is a man of the 1950s and 1960s. He is proud that his father was at Khrushchev's right hand in the anti-Stalin campaign of 1956 and that he tried to restrain Khrushchev from some of his greatest blunders. What about his long and loyal service to Stalin? As a trained historian and skillful writer, Sergo Mikoyan has been in the forefront of the campaign to scrutinize the Stalinist past. He has written a mordant insider's profile of Stalin's sadistic police chief, Lavrenty Beria. He has been

pushing for complete publication of his father's memoirs, which started coming out in the 1970s in bowdler-
ized, abbreviated form. He also gives lectures, at which
the question of his father's complicity in Stalin's crimes
always comes up.

Mikoyan has no good answer. That is one of the most
impressive things about him. He tries to explain some
of the contributing factors, such as fear and ambition,
but he offers no excuse, no justification. The only thing
he can say in mitigation is that at least his father tried to
make amends by supporting Khrushchev's reforms, the
very reforms that other former Stalin henchmen struggled to limit or defeat. Together with other children and
grandchildren of Stalin-era leaders whom we met, Mikoyan constitutes what we came to think of as a kind of
"aristocracy" in the good sense of the word. Once associated with almost limitless power, they have a healthy
respect for the damage it can do, plus an impressive
refinement that must reflect the elite educations they
received.

Mikoyan has been a driving force in breaking down
barriers of secrecy in foreign affairs. At Harvard, along
with Burlatsky and Shakhnazarov, he managed to put on
the record more inside information about Soviet behavior in the Cuban missile crisis than had been hinted at,
let alone released, in the twenty-six years since it happened.

Bill asked Mikoyan how he felt about the prospects
for change to which he was devoting so much effort,
quoting to him the argument that the changes hardly
penetrated beyond the newspapers. Usually the soul of
gentle politeness, he got angry. It was a "grave mistake"
to think the changes affected only what appeared in the
newspapers. They were beginning to affect the way people viewed authority itself. But still, he added with a
wistful smile, there was a long way to go.

MEET THE PRESS

In previous years, conversations with friends would have been almost our only way of double-checking our impressions. But this time we had something else to go on—the Soviet press itself.

A cynical Soviet diplomat once described journalism —his own country's as well as ours—as "the second oldest profession." Suddenly, the Soviet press was the cutting edge of change. We hardly looked at a Western paper the whole time we were in Moscow. We grew so addicted to Soviet newspapers that it took a real effort to put them down and get out into the city. In this, we were only imitating our Soviet friends and neighbors. Before departing for Moscow we had heard on the academic exchange grapevine that it would make sense for us to subscribe early on to the most popular Soviet publications. This could be done quickly and easily at the nearest post office; but in the month it took for the papers and magazines to start arriving in our mailbox, we had to make do with newsstands. The first day, having been warned to buy our papers early, we dropped by our neighborhood stand at nine thirty in the morning, only to find that the only paper still available at that hour was *Pravda,* and it too was almost sold out. Such hot items as *Socialist Industry, Rural Life, Construction Gazette,* and *Soviet Russia* were long gone. The next day we were back at eight o'clock: same result. We asked friends how they managed. "Be out there at six thirty," they said. So we were—only to find a long line of readers waiting in the pre-dawn, twenty-degree-below-zero darkness.

One day while waiting in line, Jane noticed that desirable papers discreetly appeared from under the counter —even the distinctive red-bordered *Ogonyok.* Greasing the palm of the elderly man who worked at the kiosk was clearly the answer. We offered him American cigarettes from the dollar store. "I don't smoke, thank you," he replied. A jar of coffee? Ah, yes. After that he occasionally produced "something interesting" from under the counter. But what really produced results were copies of *Amerika,* the glossy Russian-language magazine which the United States Information Agency has been producing for years in an exchange agreement with *Soviet Life.* Though legally distributed in the USSR, it never seems to be available at kiosks. The U.S. Embassy gives copies away, and we always picked up some to pass out to friends, even the most sophisticated of whom used to receive it eagerly. This year, our friends were no longer interested; they were too busy reading their own press, but the kiosk man, evidently an avid reader, was delighted to get it.

Moscow Spring had many faces and features—economic, political, social, cultural—which were reflected in the media mirror. But what helped most to make sense of our first impressions was working out the complex connection between past, present, and future. The present that reformers find so in need of change is rooted in the past. History explains both what needs to be done and why it is so difficult to do it. More than anything else, Gorbachev seems to want to energize the Soviet economic system. For many of his liberal supporters, the most important lesson of the past is the need to build safeguards against tyranny, to devise guarantees against a reversion to the Stalinist past. But the same history that teaches this lesson militates against learning and acting on it—or so said some of the most interesting writers we read in Moscow.

It is only now that the Soviets are beginning to find out exactly what happened under Stalin. Khrushchev and the writers of his era told part of the story. Gorbachev added to it in his November 2, 1987, address. But one of the most important facts remained hidden until the spring of 1988—the staggering, numbing numbers of people killed during collectivization, starved to death by Stalin's man-made famine of the early thirties, liquidated in the Great Purge, sacrificed unnecessarily as a result of the dictator's incompetent military leadership during World War II. Until this spring, only the purge itself was recognized as an atrocity. And it, according to Gorbachev, destroyed "thousands." Later estimates would reach numbers—as many as fifteen million killed during collectivization—that even Western demographers consider exaggerated.

Ogonyok's several million readers were treated in January 1988 to a two-part account of how Stalin's favorite charlatan, Trofim Lysenko, trashed Soviet biology by destroying its most distinguished geneticists. The fact that the author, Valery Soifer, was a refusenik biologist who had been waiting nine years for permission to emigrate made *Ogonyok*'s decision to publish the story even more daring. The magazine also told the full story of Sergey Korolyov, who suffered imprisonment under Stalin before going on to direct Khrushchev's successful effort to put the first man in space.

The kind of straight talk Bill had heard at Afanasyev's institute about how and why Stalinism happened was not yet published in the press. The issue of whether Stalin himself was responsible or whether the trail led back to Lenin and beyond was posed in a somewhat roundabout way, but not so indirectly that the guardians of orthodoxy failed to detect it. Those who posed the question were not historians—Mikhail Shatrov, for example, is a playwright, one of several important writers who have moved in where professional historians fear to tread.

Bill spent some time with Shatrov, a short, stocky man of fifty-eight, with a thick shock of white hair and a classic 1930s biography. The son of an engineer and Party member, Shatrov suffered Stalinism, as the Russian saying goes, "on his own skin." In 1937 his father was taken away, never to return. His mother was arrested in 1949, and he himself was denied access to higher education on the grounds that his parents were "enemies of the people." He was reluctantly admitted to the Moscow Mining Institute when he finished at the top of his high school class. He wrote his first play in 1955, a year before his father was posthumously rehabilitated and his mother returned from the camps. Inspired by Khrushchev's 1956 secret speech and instructed by long talks with surviving old Bolsheviks, he began to write the documentary political plays for which he is now famous. Every one of them was banned.

Shatrov's first docudrama, *The Brest Peace*, was written in 1962. First published in June, 1987, it finally reached the stage not long before we arrived in Moscow. When we saw it, we were stunned, not by its boldness but by the fact that so tame a play had struck fear in the censors' hearts. The play treats the Bolsheviks' agonizing decision in early 1918 to pull out of World War I by signing the punitive Treaty of Brest-Litovsk with Germany. Trotsky and Bukharin, among other historical personages, appear on stage for the first time since Stalin had them murdered. The constructivist staging by Georgian director Robert Strura starkly evoked the revolutionary spirit of the time. What bothered us about the drama was that it lacked just that. The actual outcome was, of course, never in doubt. Moreover, the quarrel between the two sides was inherently unequal. The long-standing Party line on the Brest peace is that it was necessary to compromise the cause of world revolution in order to preserve Soviet power at home. Even Western historians would agree with their Soviet counterparts that Lenin, who at first stood alone for the peace, was tactically right, and Bukharin, who held out for turning the world war into a revolutionary crusade, was wrong. Bold as he was to make Bukharin a sympathetic figure (unlike Trotsky, who appeared looking like Dracula in a diabolic cape to the sound of ominous organ music), Shatrov was not about to give him the better arguments. Whatever pathos was supposed to attach to the retreat from "first principles" was lost on those who, like us, were never fans of world revolution in the first place.

Still, the image of Lenin standing alone against his closest revolutionary comrades was striking. Even more unusual, especially for two young women sitting in front of us, were scenes where the leader was embraced and comforted by an elegantly dressed and coiffed comrade named Inessa Armand. "Who was she?" the two whispered to each other in puzzlement. The official culture, which had fed them since childhood the canonized image of Lenin's wife Nadezhda Krupskaya, had of course never mentioned the woman who, according to the tsarist police and most Western historians, was Lenin's mistress.

Even *The Brest Peace* brought out the wolves, in the

form of an attack on Shatrov in *Pravda*. But their gorge
rose much higher in reaction to his latest play, *Further,
Further, Further,* published in *Znamya* in January,
1988. Shatrov leaves no doubt in his public appearances
and writing that he considers himself a true Leninist.
But like any work of art, his play is more ambiguous than
his politics. *Further, Further, Further* begins in October
1917 with the Bolsheviks debating whether or when to
seize power. But its historical characters range freely
across the decades, debating among themselves
whether first Lenin's and then Stalin's decision to take
the Revolution "ever further" account for the disasters
that later befell it, including the sad state at which it
arrived toward the end of the 1980s.

This time, *all* the characters get good arguments. Stalin is shown to be a sadistic, bloody tyrant, especially in
a devastating scene in which he drives one of his oldest
and closest colleagues, Sergo Ordzhonikidze, to suicide.
But the same Stalin gets to argue persuasively that Lenin's New Economic Policy had outlived its usefulness
by the end of the twenties and had to be superseded by
sterner stuff. Bukharin, whom Shatrov obviously pre-
fers, is not nearly as convincing on the issue. Lenin himself is shown agonizing in retrospect—not about
whether his party should have seized power in the first
place, but about making it possible for Stalin to take
control. Other characters, ranging from the Marxist theo-
retician Plekhanov to the liberal politician Miliukov to
the White general Denikin, all charge that the fundamental error from which all else followed was the decision to take power in October 1917.

All this was much too much for conservatives. Their
response took the form of a *Pravda* piece by three historians whom no one we knew had ever heard of. How
dare Shatrov, they demanded, portray Lenin as weak
and self-doubting when everyone knew the great man
had been ever strong and resolute? What good did it do

to have Lenin, who had been dead for sixty-four years, grieve at the state of socialism after Brezhnev? Shatrov's portrait of Stalin was one-sided, they charged; it lacked precisely the sort of balanced perspective that Gorbachev had insisted on in his November 2 speech. The play's implication that the Great October Socialist Revolution was "accidental," rather than fated by historical laws as laid down by Marx, was an outrage. So was the way Shatrov put the Bolsheviks on trial while calling on their class enemies as accusers and witnesses. The historians' attack was a classic example of a tactic used against other writers in the long years before *glasnost*. It identified the author's view with the words of his characters, turned the artist's open-ended exploration into political dogma and then beat it over the head for heresy.

Dimitry Volkogonov, a longtime specialist on political indoctrination for the Soviet military who became one of the top-ranking officers in the Ministry of Defense and is now director of the Institute on Military History, has been writing the first more or less objective Soviet biography of Stalin. Judging from the excerpts that have appeared in *Literaturnaya gazeta,* it will be a mixed bag. He is willing to say that Stalin committed crimes, not just "mistakes," but insists that the resulting social order still deserves the sacred name of socialism. His theory that power corrupted Stalin and that his deep personal insecurity transformed itself into rage against others is not new; Western biographers have been over this ground before. And, although he is willing to admit that Stalin's rise was "not accidental," he is not about to offer a full explanation. The disaster of the 1930s needn't have happened if only Leninist democracy had been developed, he insists, as if the case hadn't been made over and over in the West that Leninism's fatal flaw was its lack of democratic guarantees against the abuse of power.

Ogonyok offered an equally limited image of Stalin in excerpts from Anastas Mikoyan's memoirs as edited by his son Sergo. These, however, confirmed a crucial fact about an event that triggered the 1930s purges: Stalin indeed received far fewer votes than Leningrad Party boss Sergey Kirov in the election of Central Committee members at the Seventeenth Party Congress in 1934. The delegates were expressing their deep reservations about their leader; most of them didn't live to see the next congress five years later. Kirov himself loyally reported the embarrassing result to Stalin, and got a bullet in the back from an assassin several months later as his reward.

Mikoyan's fellow henchmen were the subject of other profiles published early in 1988, several of them by Arkady Vaksberg, a veteran journalist and jurist who, we were told by admiring readers, in contrast to certain other born-again Gorbachevites, had never sold out but been as honest as it was possible to be and still get published. The first Vaksberg piece we read was a full-page profile of Andrey Vyshinsky, the Menshevik-turned-Bolshevik who prosecuted the major show trials of the late 1930s. According to Vaksberg, the past Vyshinsky needed to live down combined with vaulting ambition and dread fear to turn what had been a good mind into an automaton. Vyshinsky was not a creator of Stalinism, Vaksberg points out, but the archetypal implementor of his master's system. (Vaksberg, too, shies away from asking where that system came from, but he insists, in a stirring peroration, that it is the source of much current legal malfeasance.)

Daniil Granin is the author of widely read novels about the lives of scientists. Back in the 1970s, he and others set out to memorialize the heroic defenders of wartime Leningrad by interviewing survivors for a book on the 900-day blockade. But like Vaksberg, Granin ended up contemplating a system that somehow turned individuals, even the most powerful of political men, into cogs in the Stalinist machine. As he recounted in *Znamya*'s February 1988 issue, one of the survivors he wanted to interview was Aleksey Kosygin, who had been the Soviet premier ever since joining with Brezhnev and others to overthrow Khrushchev. Only with difficulty and after long delays was the interview arranged. Granin had been warned not to expect revelations from the notoriously taciturn Kosygin, but he was stunned to encounter not a man, but a machine. Mild and gentle as Granin's questions were, Kosygin avoided answering them: "He held his tongue. It was as if he didn't trust himself. To hear him tell it, no one connected with the blockade was guilty of anything; there had been no conflicts, no blunders; millions of Leningraders had died, and not only at the hands of the Nazis, but everything was beyond reproach." Someone suggested to Granin that this was Kosygin's way of keeping out of trouble at a time when the cult of Brezhnev's non-personality was nearing its peak. But the question Granin really raised was whether the man of stone he interviewed hadn't been created long ago by the system first put into place by the man of steel, Joseph Stalin.

Andrey Gromyko, Soviet head of state during the early Gorbachev years, was cut from the same cloth as Kosygin. Renowned for his reticence and self-control, especially when working for bosses like Stalin and Khrushchev, Gromyko took the uncharacteristic step of providing his own profile in a two-volume memoir published early in 1988. The book reveals that its author is actually a snob who relishes dropping names of politicians, businessmen, and other celebrities who were his friends, as well as some, like Boris Pasternak, who no doubt were not. It also shows that working high up in Stalin's apparatus, being exposed to the dictator himself on a daily basis, was the key formative experience of Gromyko's political life, an experience to which he de-

votes more nostalgic pages than to any other in his long
career. He is, of course, entirely uncritical.

At the opposite end of the spectrum from profiles of
individual Soviet leaders were articles about the imper-
sonal forces that account for Russia's seeming aversion
to democracy. So grim and relentless were some of
these, so convincing in their depiction of the deep-
seated structural obstacles to democratization, that it
was hard to see how their authors could end up the
champions of democracy that they in fact were. We tried
to meet some of them so as to unravel the contradiction.
They were either too busy to see us or too careful, given
the controversy caused by their writings and the sensitive post held by at least one of them.

Philosopher Igor Klyamkin, we were told by friends,
taught for many years at a low-status night school and
was now on the staff of the Institute on the Economy of
the World Socialist System, which harbors some of the
fiercest fighters for reform. The Klyamkin piece that had
intellectual circles buzzing when we arrived appeared
in *Novy mir*. Its title, "Which Road Leads to the
Church?" was taken from the last lines of Abuladze's
Repentance. The "Church," for Klyamkin, is a modern,
liberal, democratic Russia. The fear that haunts his article is the same one that depressed so many of our
friends: that the road the Soviet Union is on, and that
Russia has been on for centuries, leads not toward but
away from that goal.

The essay mounts the most withering criticism in an
acceptable manner. Klyamkin's question—where Russia
is heading and why, and whether the direction is worthy
or not—has been debated by Russians for centuries. In
the nineteenth century, the warring camps were "Westernizers," who wanted their country to adopt Western
ways, whether liberal or socialist was another matter,
and "Slavophiles," who thought Russia should build on
its own unique traditions. In the sense that Marxism was

originally a Western European doctrine, the Bolsheviks were Westernizers of an extreme left-wing sort. As such, they have been accused by latter-day Slavophiles like Solzhenitsyn of forcing an utterly unnatural and hence ruinous foreign system on the Russian body politic. What makes Klyamkin's article politically acceptable is that he seems to defend the Bolsheviks against precisely this charge. Their revolution was not unnatural, he contends; it was foreordained by nearly all that went before. The October Revolution was not an accident, not a minority coup d'état that might as easily not have happened; it was the logical culmination of all of Russian history.

In the great debate on Stalinism, it is the Stalinists who have argued that forced collectivization, all-out industrialization, political terror, and the rest were necessary, whereas the anti-Stalinists insist there were viable alternatives, like the communism with a human face championed by Lenin in his late articles and then by Bukharin after Lenin's death. Klyamkin agrees with Soviet conservatives that the forces offering an alternative to Stalinism were weak and undependable because they cut against the grain of Russian history. Even on the potentially explosive issue of guilt and responsibility for Stalinist atrocities, Klyamkin offers comfort to the Stalinists: "Until we've finally freed ourselves of the question 'Why?' we'll keep dissolving without a trace in the question 'Who's to blame?' "

But Klyamkin is not justifying Stalinism by rooting it in Russian history; he is indicting Russian political culture by charging that it led directly to Stalinism. On the one hand, his historical survey makes it clear why *perestroika* and *glasnost* are so important: they mark a break with almost everything that has gone before, not only since 1917 but for a millennium. But why should Gorbachev succeed where all the others have failed? Klyamkin tries to end on an optimistic note by pointing

to the existence of a new social base for political change
—"highly skilled workers, those representing the most
advanced productive forces, scientific-technical and humanistic intelligentsia." But the happy ending seems
tacked on—as in so many Soviet movies—not so much
perhaps to please the authorities as to give hope to Klyamkin himself.

Hope needs a better grounding than that, especially
when the most brilliant writer we read on political-eco-
nomic issues catalogued even more obstacles to change,
although he, like Klyamkin, was working tirelessly for
the very reforms his own analysis suggested could never
be effected. Gavriil Popov, longtime dean of the economics faculty at Moscow State University, has recently
taken over the editorship of *Questions of Economics*,
the leading Soviet journal in his field. Even more important, he has been called upon by the Central Committee
to work on the most sensitive issues of economic reform.
He writes frequently for *Moscow News* and other popular publications.

Oddly enough, Popov's most striking contribution
came in what amounted to extended reviews of two novels. Aleksander Bek's *New Assignment*, which was accepted by *Novy mir* in 1964 but published for the first
time in *Znamya* in late 1986, is the story of a high-level
Stalinist bureaucrat, the kind who served his master so
faithfully and well he survived Stalin only to come to
grief later for thinking the system had changed when it
had not. Daniil Granin's *Zubr*, Russian for a breed of
buffalo now nearly extinct, tells the story of Soviet ge-
neticist Timofeyev-Resovsky, who chose in 1938 to remain in Nazi Germany, where he had been doing
research for thirteen years, rather than return and risk
the fate of his fellow geneticists under Stalin. Both characters were based on real individuals, and Popov took
both novels as mirrors in which the strength and resil-
ience of the Stalinist administrative command system
are revealed.

Bill was struck by the resemblance between Bek's hero Onisimov and Khrushchev. Both were hyperactive yet reserved, personally modest but eventually corrupted by power, dedicated and disciplined yet capable of erratic, seemingly irrational behavior. Bill had attributed many of Khrushchev's traits to his personality. Popov showed that they could be traced back to the conditions under which men like him had to function.

Even Stalin was such a creature, bound to play by the rules he had invented, with no choice once the massive bloodletting began but to fear those who feared him. Stalin was also an obstacle to the system's perfection; he was too arbitrary, too changeable, too powerful. What the system needed was regularity and predictability. And these neither Stalin nor Khrushchev was able to provide. The system Stalin established, Popov insisted, found its ideal in Leonid Brezhnev, a leader who left the bureaucrats alone to do their job, who didn't terrorize them as Stalin had or rock the boat incessantly as Khrushchev had. In Popov's reading of Bek's novel, Onisimov misunderstands the meaning of Stalin's death. Thinking a new day has dawned, a day he does not necessarily like but is determined to adapt to, he tries to tell the truth and is fired for his trouble. Khrushchev, Popov wrote, was similarly misguided in his belief that he could dismantle the system Stalin designed.

Popov's reading of Granin's *Zubr* stressed the unspoken deal Stalin made with the country's scientists. In return for forsaking politics, they were allowed to pursue science even, in many cases, while incarcerated in the *sharashkas* made famous in Solzhenitsyn's *First Circle*. The scientists accepted the deal for love of science, assuming the nation's long-term interest transcended and would outlive the Stalinist system. In the end, however, Soviet science paid the price in terrible backwardness in many areas, while the system outlived whatever usefulness it ever had.

The moral of Bek's and Granin's novels, wrote Popov,

is that what the country needs most of all is *citizens*—not functionaries who excel at taking orders or intellectuals who allow themselves to be segregated from political life, but citizens who insist on sounding the alarm when things go wrong and help to set things right, who take the measure of their country's past in order to plan for its future.

As we have noted, the role of citizen is a new and strange one for Soviets. One of our friends attributed his countrymen's "slave mentality" to not only political subordination but economic scarcity as well. With too little of everything to go around and the state controlling access to all of it, people were used to begging for favors and being grateful for any bestowed. We witnessed the transformation of subjects into citizens, but it did not come easily.

Early in March 1988, *Ogonyok* published a symposium in which scholars from various institutes pressed the boundaries of permissible debate to the limit. The announced subject was how to make the reforms irreversible, how to devise guarantees against a reversion to tyrannical rule. The discussion included for the first time in public the sort of criticism of Stalin's foreign policy that Bill had heard at the seminar he attended, but on the subject of guarantees, it was underdeveloped. One panelist spoke of "psychological guarantees," apparently hoping that the "new thinking" would itself constitute a barrier against the old behavior. Another believed the "scientific-technical revolution" would prevent a reversion to the past. A third contended, more convincingly, that a freer and more open economy could provide the material basis for political activity not entirely dominated by the state.

Americans feel most comfortable with constitutional guarantees. Russians, who have never lived under a constitutional order, are more likely to trust a "commitment to justice." Even liberal Soviets occasionally surprised us by proclaiming, "*We* are the best guarantee against tyranny"—as if having in mind a high-minded band of intellectuals not so very different from the revolutionaries who brought Russia the Bolshevik Revolution in the first place.

Apart from the kind of guarantees needed, there was the tactical issue of how to obtain them. Gorbachev had in effect given his answer at a lengthy meeting with ideological and cultural leaders held just before we arrived in Moscow. In contrast to Khrushchev, who reveled in confrontational tactics, Gorbachev was trying to preserve the widest possible united front for as long as he could, implicating conservative rivals in reforms about which they had grave doubts and thus depriving them of any excuse to move against him until he was ready to move against them. His more radical supporters, among them our liberal Soviet friends, worried that he was deceiving himself. In their view, the struggle he wanted to avoid was already raging; the only question was how to fight it. They wanted him to exclude his enemies from the process, but this approach struck us as dangerously wrong.

We found Gorbachev's admission that the reforms have opponents immensely refreshing in a way. For decades the Party line was that Soviet society was monolithically in service of Communist ideals. Now we were told that interests, not ideals, make the Soviet world go round, and were warned by people with various axes to grind to beware of almost every possible interest one could think of—from entrenched bureaucrats to self-righteous intellectuals to the untutored, anarchic, potentially explosive masses. Almost everyone had his or her own notion of how to dissect the body politic, of who was for or against which brand of change. Yet the phrase "enemies of *perestroika*" came too easily to the lips of intellectuals whose forebears had suffered from abuse of the term "enemy of the people." Russians, it has always seemed to us, too quickly identify "opponent" with "enemy." The parliamentary tradition of "my respected opponent" and an understanding of the importance of open debate are not strong elements in the Russian tradition.

The most systematic, coherent statement of the liberal view was found in a two-part article in *Novy mir* by a specialist on aesthetics, currently the vice-director of the Scientific Research Institute on Film. Andrey Nuikin's essay "Ideals or Interests?" analyzed a series of newspaper and magazine articles that had expressed alarm about the social results of economic reform. One fear was that in their effort to boost economic efficiency, the reforms would increase inequality to levels far higher than were consistent with socialist ideals. Another was that the socialist commitment to fraternity and community would suffer from the focus on material incentives. Nuikin rejected these claims, arguing that inequality was already rampant; it was hidden from view because it rewarded the wrong people, like bribe-taking bureaucrats and black marketeers. Now was the time to reward the right people—those with enterprise, energy, and imagination whose hard work benefited not just themselves but society.

We parted company with Nuikin when he insisted that the expression of the socialist ideals of fraternity and community only masked the selfish interests of bureaucrats and black marketeers who, as the prime beneficiaries of "stagnation," were the leading opponents of reform. His contention that a similar unholy alliance had supported Stalin when he liquidated the market-oriented New Economic Policy and launched his genocidal war against the peasantry in 1929 was fascinating. But we resisted reducing virtually every professed ideal to naked self-interest. As social analyst, Nuikin didn't allow for sincere if misguided disinterest or for the way the system—as described by Popov, or compared by our

pessimistic friend Seryozha to Tarkovsky's living, om-
nivorous "atmosphere"—forced everyone to do its bidding. As political tactician, Nuikin seemed bent on
turning everyone who disagreed with him into an
enemy. But if every bureaucrat in the USSR is an
enemy, reform will have precious few friends. It will
find even fewer if reformers fail to reach out and touch
what may be a "silent majority" of skeptics, people who
sincerely believe in the ideals that Nuikin reduces to
interests. They may be deluded, but they sincerely believe *perestroika* will undermine socialism. Socialism,
as they understand it, seems to amount to social envy,
the insistence that "my neighbor not live better than I
do," even if the prospect of doing so prompts him to
produce more for us both. This attitude is deeply self-
defeating. But the way to cope with it is not to condemn
it as a cover for self-interest but to try to understand its
roots and remedy it.

The silent majority may or may not be a majority—
only the KGB is really counting, and they aren't saying
—and it is not really silent. The letters columns of papers and magazines are filled with remarkably outspoken criticism of both *perestroika* and *glasnost.* Terrible
ironies abound. Not only do poor and oppressed people
defend the very political and economic arrangements
that ensnare them, but some of Stalin's surviving victims
have become his most eloquent defenders—"vulgar Stalinists," some of our friends called them, to distinguish
them from the more highly placed elitist variety. It is
one thing for a high-living official to wax nostalgic about
an era that raised him to the heights. It is another when
a widow cries out that the escalating attacks on Stalin
demean those who believed in him, who went to their
deaths in World War II crying "For Stalin! For the
Motherland!"

How can a cry like that be answered? We pondered
over it when told by innumerable taxi drivers that most

of the reforms didn't amount to a damn. Most thought *glasnost* was a good thing, that telling the truth about the past was long overdue. Some said efforts to democratize the workplace had given them a voice on the job. But nearly all denied that their basic lot had improved. And many dismissed the excitement that had us in thrall as "just another campaign," another attempt by the bosses to pull the wool over the people's eyes.

Our first reaction was shock and dismay. If the intended beneficiaries of the reforms didn't respect them, how could they succeed? On the other hand, their resistance to changes that could better their lives was yet another result of their long victimization. To ask them to be patient after all they had lived through, to demand sacrifices of people who had already sacrificed so much, to expect them to hail reforms that might be reversed tomorrow with dire results for the reformers, was too much. But what alternative was there? To let fail what even our pessimistic friends agreed was the last best chance for change?

The reformers need to find a way to praise those who gave up so much in Stalin's name, to explain that their achievements were in spite of, not because of him. The gap between the pro-reform intellectuals and the people is deep and dangerous. It can only be bridged by recognizing the social pathology that has infected both, the fatalism and passivity bred by lifelong dependence on an all-powerful state. Even the dreaded bureaucrats are only human beings trapped by forces they cannot control. If only they could see themselves as fellow victims of the system rather than as its guardians against change!

Our friends laughed at our ideas. We didn't know what they were up against, they said. We didn't know the Russian people. We didn't know the typical Soviet bureaucrat. How many hard-core conservatives had we encountered? The only language they understood was strength. This argument, too, appalled us, for it reeked of the intolerance of Soviet political life. Conservatives were supposed to be everywhere. But where were they exactly?

Just about the time we were asking that question, in the middle of March, the conservative voice was heard in such a way as to change the very life we were leading by threatening to put an end to Moscow Spring.

THE
INTERREGNUM

On March 13, while Gorbachev was visiting Yugoslavia, a nearly full-page open letter entitled "Why I Can't Waive Principles" appeared in *Sovetskaya rossiya*. It was signed by Nina Andreyeva, a chemistry teacher at the Leningrad Polytechnical Institute, and turned out to be a barely disguised broadside against *perestroika, glasnost,* and virtually every other aspect of Gorbachev's reforms. Some of our friends admitted afterward that when they saw it they feared all was lost. It seemed impossible that it could have been published in an organ of the Communist Party Central Committee without authorization from the very highest levels. It must therefore be a signal: either Gorbachev had been forced to acquiesce in the death of his own reforms, or he was on the way out. In either case, Moscow Spring was over.

In pre-*glasnost* days, such signals really were signals.

Now, however, they might not be. Even liberal Russians were uncomfortable with not knowing for sure. But until *Pravda* spoke out against Andreyeva on April 5, the press was silent, and no one knew. Because we didn't read *Sovetskaya rossiya* regularly, we at first missed the importance of the manifesto, and not all of our friends wanted to talk about it. If indeed *glasnost* was ending, it was no longer safe to lament its fate to foreigners.

To be sure, many Russians never read the Andreyeva article. We later made a point of asking around, and quite a few people—although not those in intellectual circles—had never heard of Andreyeva or the *Pravda* rebuttal. Nor did all those who read it react with panic or despair. Some fought back even before *Pravda* indicated it was safe to do so.

Before plunging into what we saw and heard and didn't see and hear during the three weeks that followed, we should report on certain pre-Andreyeva encounters with conservatives. There weren't many of them. Our circle of acquaintances grew as we were passed from friend to friend, but none of them were particularly friendly with people they regarded as the enemy. The few conservatives we got close to were people we sought out on our own. Still, our exposure to the "other side" was sufficient that, when we finally read Nina Andreyeva, we knew where she was coming from.

There was Nikolay, a young engineer we had encountered unexpectedly. His hobby was American politics. He was also related to one of Stalin's bloodiest henchmen and had been quite close to him during his childhood. We didn't let on that we knew Nikolay's family history, even though we assumed he assumed we knew, but we signaled our interest by stressing how objective we tried to be when evaluating even the most dreadful episodes in Soviet history. He asked his own seemingly innocent questions to test our capacity to empathize

with those the world regarded as evildoers of the lowest
sort, and eventually we got to hear a bit about the old
man—not much, but enough to realize that Nikolay's
loyalty to him was as touching as it was chilling.

When we saw Nikolay again after the Andreyeva article appeared, he said he agreed with every word of it.
His politics were conservative, but in a far more complex way than one might expect. For example, Nikolay
agreed that the American practice of providing early access to counsel—unlike Soviet law, which does not per-
mit recourse to a defense lawyer until the preliminary
investigation of a defendant is concluded—would make
for fairer trials, even though there were some people
who could never be treated fairly under current circumstances. He thought *glasnost* was such a good thing that
not only reformers but conservatives too should be allowed to take advantage of it. He was as caustic in his
criticism of Brezhnev-era corruption and mismanagement as any liberal we knew.

Most of the conservatives we encountered in the
weeks before the Andreyeva interregnum appeared in
the press. There was the conservative campaign against
Shatrov. Other liberal voices—*Ogonyok* and *Moscow
News*, writers like Aleksander Bek and Daniil Granin,
the historian Yury Afanasyev—had come under withering fire in *Molodaya gvardiya* and its conservative al-
lies.

Writers for the conservative newspapers and magazines did not dare criticize Gorbachev and his program
directly. Instead, they took out their anger on his most
liberal supporters. Nonetheless, they were not only allowed to wage ideological war, but were encouraged by
honors and awards to their editors. It was clear that
someone in the Politburo was giving them the kind of
protection that Gorbachev ally and Politburo member
Aleksander Yakovlev reportedly provided for *Ogonyok*,
Novy mir, and other liberal journals. All signs pointed

to Yegor Ligachev, Gorbachev's number two man, as the instigator, and the Andreyeva incident would release a torrent of "inside stories" about his efforts to undermine his chief. But even before then, his speeches had combined with rumors to convey the impression of deep differences between him and the Soviet leader. Gorbachev pushed de-Stalinization, democratization, and movement toward market socialism. Ligachev seemed to resist all three. Of course, the two denied any tension between them, and not everyone in Moscow agreed that Ligachev was out to do in Gorbachev. A handful thought he was playing "tough cop" to Gorbachev's "nice cop" in a calculated division of labor. But most believed that if Ligachev could speak his real mind, he would sound even less like Gorbachev and more like the most outspoken reactionary of them all, Yury Bondarev.

Bondarev is the writer and literary politician who in 1987 compared the onset of *glasnost* to Hitler's invasion of the USSR in 1941; the only hope was a new "Stalingrad," that is, the eventual and in all likelihood bloody routing of the reformist foe. Shortly before the Andreyeva letter appeared, Bondarev expanded on this view in a speech at the Union of Soviet Writers. *Perestroika* was the "new radicalism," and *glasnost* and *demokratizatsiya* had ushered in a wild, hedonist night. Quoting some misguided youthful manifesto, Bondarev took its endorsement of group sex as the essence of the new freedom. All the old values—truth, patriotism, family, authority—were going under.

Whatever underground political vibrations were encouraging conservatives on the eve of March 13 reached liberal ears as well. In the last issue before the Andreyeva letter, *Ogonyok* editor Korotich published an unusual warning in his own name about often unsigned letters that denounced anti-Stalinist writers and editors to "higher organs," a euphemism for the Party Central Committee or the KGB. By what right, these letters de-

manded to know, did *Ogonyok* criticize the past or the
present? "By the right of democracy," Korotich declared.

Andreyeva, too, mentioned Gorbachev only to praise
him; she insisted his struggle was hers. But she accused
his supporters of near-treason and his policies of under-
mining the authority of the Politburo, the Party, even
the nation itself. As a woman and a teacher, she wept for
Mother Russia and despaired over the corruption of Russian youth. The fact that her arguments weren't entirely
consistent seemed a sign of conservative confidence and
strength. It wasn't important to make a perfect case; it
was important to show the flag so as to inspire the silent
majority and the not-so-silent minority as well.

"I decided to write this letter after lengthy delibera-
tion," the letter begins. Andreyeva claimed to be
pleased by her students' new *perestroika*-engendered
political activism. Strolling together along the snow-
covered paths at Peter the Great's magnificent mini-
Versailles by the Baltic Sea, "we argue. We do argue!
The young souls are eager to investigate all the complex-
ities and to define their path into the future. I look at
my loquacious young interlocutors and I think to myself how important it is to help them find the truth."

She was not pleased, however, with the way they discussed issues raised on Voice of America, the BBC, and
other Western broadcasts, or by "those of our compatriots who are not firm in their conceptions of the essence of socialism." Andreyeva named these issues first
in fairly neutral fashion: "A multiparty system, freedom
of religious propaganda, emigration, the right to wide
discussion of sexual problems in the press, the need to
decentralize the leadership of culture, abolition of compulsory military service." But her real outrage is visible
when she quotes her wards' "verbiage about 'terrorism,'
'the people's political servility,' 'our spiritual slavery,'
'universal fear,' 'domination by boors in power.' "

She was especially put out by their reaction to a Colonel of the Army Reserve and Hero of the Soviet Union who gave a talk in a student dormitory. Given all the media discussion of Stalinist repressions, the students were bound to press him for examples he had encountered. Out of caution if not conviction, he replied "that he had never come across any repressions." Some students were disappointed by this reply. That proved to Andreyeva that "the subject of repressions has been blown out of all proportion in some young people's minds and overwhelms any objective interpretation of the past." What other reaction could be expected, she asked, from students indoctrinated with "revelations about 'the counterrevolution in the USSR in the late twenties and early thirties,' or about Stalin's 'guilt' for the rise of fascism and Hitler in Germany?"

Andreyeva added her own potshots at Shatrov, charging him with "deviating substantially from accepted principles of Socialist Realism." She proclaimed her lasting interest in "the questions that directly influenced young people's ideological and political education, their moral health, and their social optimism." "Take for example," she wrote, "the question of I. V. Stalin's position in our country's history."

For example? The Stalin question was the essence of it all. She condemned "the obsession with critical attacks . . . linked with his name," the travesty on "an epoch linked with unprecedented feats by a whole generation of Soviet people."

She was quick to deny any personal connection with "Stalin, his retinue, his associates, or his extollers," painting herself as an ordinary person whose relatives had even suffered under Stalin. She "shared all Soviet people's anger and indignation over the mass repressions which took place in the thirties and forties and for which the Party-state leadership is to blame." But she had taken careful note of nostalgia for the past. Those best suited to judge the past were not "persons distant both from those stormy times and from the people who had to live and work in those times," who were "an inspiring example for us today."

Even Stalin himself, she implied, could be a source of inspiration, citing as her authority Winston Churchill, of all people, who had allegedly praised the Soviet leader's "exceptional energy, erudition, and inflexible will-power." Andreyeva praised the "personal modesty verging on asceticism" that was the norm in Stalin's time, when "we prepared young people not for the niceties of consuming wealth accumulated by their parents but for Labor and Defense, without smashing young people's spiritual world with masterpieces imported from 'the other side' or home-grown imitations of 'mass culture.' "

She blamed Jews and other ethnic and social groups for "anti-Stalinist" excesses. And she condemned the "spiritual heirs" of historical figures like Trotsky, who were widely known to be Jewish, while recalling that Marx and Engels "once described entire nations at a certain stage of their history as 'counterrevolutionary.' "

She ended her letter with an appeal to both Communist conservatives and Russophile nationalists. She distinguished two enemy camps, which she labeled "neo-liberal intellectual socialists" and "traditionalists" trying to "return to the social forms of pre-socialist Russia." But she was much harder on the former, charging them with not only glorifying something so unsocialist as the "intrinsic value of the individual," but "writing off the slightest expressions of Great Russian national pride as manifestations of great-power chauvinism."

Who was Nina Andreyeva, and how had she come to publish her piece in *Sovestskaya rossiya?* When the smoke cleared, that is to say after the April 5 *Pravda* rebuttal, everyone we knew was asking that question. There really is such a person. Fyodor Burlatsky con-

firmed that in an interview with a French journalist,
adding that Andreyeva's husband had been expelled
from the Party for sending anonymous letters of denun-
ciation, and that she herself was known in Leningrad for
denouncing local leaders to the press. Several Western
journalists reached her on the phone in April but
elicited no comment on the furor she had raised. After
we left the USSR in early June, several reporters actually interviewed her. According to a Yugoslav correspondent, she insisted that she was the sole author of
her famous missive, claimed that she had received more
than a thousand letters in response, of which 85 percent
were favorable, and even revealed that she had written
a new letter to the Party conference scheduled for late
June. She had "not had any unpleasant experiences with
the Soviet authorities over her stands so far."

None of our Soviet friends believed that Andreyeva
acted alone. Giulietto Chiesa, the well-connected Moscow correspondent of the Italian Communist Party
newspaper, *L'Unità,* reported in May that he had obtained a copy of an earlier version of Andreyeva's letter,
dated July 9, 1987. It had been sent to several central
newspapers in September of that year and rejected by
all of them. According to Chiesa, the letter was "ex-
humed, transformed, and rewritten" by *Sovetskaya rossiya* editors. His comparison of the two versions
revealed that only about five pages of the original text
were retained; "the rest disappeared entirely or was re-
vamped, softened, and made more 'acceptable.'" Explicitly anti-Semitic passages were among those toned
down. The attack on *Further, Further, Further* was
added to coincide with the anti-Shatrov campaign.

A rumor swept Moscow in April: Ligachev was said to
have called a meeting of newspaper editors (not including those of the leading liberal papers and magazines) at
which he held the Andreyeva manifesto aloft and endorsed it. Chiesa quotes Andreyeva herself—at a public

meeting at the KGB higher school in Leningrad at the
end of March—as confirming that she had sent the letter
to Ligachev. (If the KGB does indeed have a higher
school in Leningrad, since when does it hold open
meetings?) Two facts that need no confirmation are that
Gorbachev was in Yugoslavia when the Andreyeva letter appeared, and his chief ideologist, Aleksander
Yakovlev, was in Mongolia. Our friends insisted these
absences were of key significance. "If Gorbachev or
Yakovlev were in town, *Sovetskaya rossiya* would have
had to clear the article with them. With them gone, the
editors could pretend that they thought the piece was
permissible under the rubric of 'socialist pluralism.'"

Why in fact was the piece *not* permissible under the
rubric of "socialist pluralism"? If all *glasnost* means is
that everyone now says the opposite of what they used
to say four years ago, it is *not* real. We could imagine a
high-minded reply that the kind of reactionary stuff Andreyeva was peddling was beyond the pale. But *Molodaya gvardiya* and other conservative periodicals were
already publishing equally objectionable material and
would continue to do so. Why did *Pravda* eventually
come down so hard on Andreyeva and *Sovetskaya rossiya*? The answer involves not so much the letter itself
but the uses to which it was put.

Perhaps the whole thing was a trial balloon, an effort
to see how much support was out there. If so, Party and
state officials opposed to the Gorbachev line immediately sprang into action. The letter was reprinted across
the country in provincial and local papers. The armed
forces' political education network was said to have in-
corporated it into its program. The news agency TASS
pressed the piece on its subscribers. According to *Moscow News,* a Byelorussian youth newspaper received a
TASS message that "many newspapers would like to reprint the publication in compliance with their readers'
requests, and that if we wanted to do the same we could

consult Party authorities." When the editor called the Byelorussian Central Committee for advice, he was told to make his own decision. He decided not to reprint it.

The Soviet Union is not rich in copying machines, but enough were found to produce a small avalanche of copies of the Andreyeva letter. "Did Party and Komsomol committees call meetings to condemn those committed to restoring the old order?" asked a Leningrad journalist in a mid-April edition of *Komsomolskaya pravda.* "No, just the opposite—conferences were arranged in support of N. Andreyeva's article." Similar sessions were arranged in other institutions. The Moscow Physico-technical Institute is an elite agency that does classified work for the Ministry of Defense. Back in February its vice-rector attacked leading reformers in a long, nasty letter to *Ogonyok.* Perhaps at his instigation, the Andreyeva piece was photocopied at the institute, recommended for study, and discussed at a special seminar sponsored by the institute Party cell. A friend of ours who worked in a factory reported that certain older workers who had been moping around since *perestroika* began suddenly cheered up on March 13 and began crowing to pro-reform co-workers that they had "told you so" all along.

The reformers were frightened. A friend described her elderly mother-in-law's "post-Andreyeva panic." "This is the end of *perestroika,*" she cried. She called all her friends and found them equally distraught. A Leningrad journalist reported that his paper received letters criticizing Andreyeva and didn't dare publish them. Anatoly Strelyany, author of hard-hitting anti-Stalinist pieces, thought to himself, "Isn't it time to make some dry toast?" Under Stalin, people had taken dry toast with them to prison. On March 13, he recalled afterward in *Moscow News,* "I lingered a little longer over the slices of bread, but didn't put them in the oven."

When he learned that army newspapers had started re-printing Andreyeva, "I put the slices in the oven."

It so happened that we saw several of Andreyeva's prime targets between March 13 and April 5. Martin Sherwin and his Tufts students were invited to the *Ogonyok* and *Litgazeta* editorial offices for lengthy brief-ings, and we went with them. Bill met with USA Insti-tute economist Nikolay Shmelyov and playwright Shatrov in the course of his Khrushchev research. Be-sides being a brilliant social scientist and short-story writer, Shmelyov had been married to Khrushchev's granddaughter while the old man was still alive. Khrushchev had not yet appeared in a Shatrov play, but Shatrov appeared more capable than any of the histori-ans Bill had met of thinking his way into Khrushchev's head.

Only once in the course of all these meetings and conversations did the Andreyeva letter come up. Burlat-sky mentioned it in passing in his *Litgazeta* briefing. The *Ogonyok* and *Litgazeta* editors seemed anything but embattled. On the contrary, they radiated confi-dence and assurance. The only odd thing was that they spent so much time with the American students, more than two hours at each place, which we chalked up to the Soviet weakness for delegations. Later an editor told us that *Ogonyok* had thought long and hard about how best to answer Andreyeva and had opted for a "steady as you go" response (which reassured many of the maga-zine's faithful readers), trying to make the point that this time, as contrasted with the Khrushchev era, the reform-ers would not change course in reaction to every con-flicting signal at the top.

Looking back, it strikes us that all the attention lav-ished on the Tufts delegation at both periodicals was indeed their way of coping with the Andreyeva threat. Editors waxed so eloquent in praise of *glasnost* that it seemed almost like propaganda. We suspect they were defending themselves by cultivating Americans, just as *Ogonyok* had developed professional ties with magazines like *U.S. News & World Report*. When reformist Soviet media come under threat at home they can cite the Western reaction: "What will Western public opinion think if we go under?"

Ogonyok editor Korotich has become one of the most controversial figures in the USSR. Like many other heroes of *perestroika*, he has a checkered past. Once associated with dissident Ukrainian writers, he later became impeccably establishmentarian. His book about his experience in America bore the kind of title that was required in the Brezhnev years: *Face of Hatred*. Many people, including some of Korotich's current admirers, have not forgotten. One of the brightest young reformers we met all spring mentioned Korotich's past, not to detract from his present achievements but to argue that they were all the more significant given his history. If a man with Korotich's establishment connections was now in the forefront, that meant reform had a broader base than we knew.

At *Litgazeta* the editors were pleased to report that their paper's circulation had recently risen by 500,000 to reach a total of four million. Burlatsky talked to the Tufts group about how best to institutionalize *glasnost*. A paper like *Litgazeta*, which was officially an organ of the Writers' Union and had actually been a creature of the state, should become a cooperative. The theoretical next step would be to establish private publishers and publishing houses. But that, said Burlatsky, with an ambiguous smile, would be beyond the boundaries of socialism. And indeed, within weeks the dissident *samizdat* journal *Glasnost* had its premises wrecked by the KGB for crossing just that boundary.

Nikolay Shmelyov had published a stunning piece of economic analysis in *Novy mir* the previous summer. At a time when Gorbachev was only flirting with the idea of encouraging market mechanisms, Shmelyov called upon him to go all the way, even to countenance the unemployment that would necessarily accompany truly radical economic reforms. The very mention of unemployment, something that had been declared ended for all time under socialism, brought an outcry. Gorbachev felt compelled to respond to an apparently prearranged question shouted out by a reporter. No, he didn't agree that unemployment was desirable, but yes, he agreed with Shemlyov's overall analysis of Soviet economic problems and their causes.

Now Shmelyov answered his critics in an equally controversial *Novy mir* piece arguing that the economic changes on which the whole reform process depended needed emergency shots in the arm. More than anything else, the reformers needed to put goods in the stores. One way was to import such goods from capitalist countries as a stopgap measure. They could be paid for by selling off some gold reserves or even by cutting the military budget.

Bill managed to catch up with Shmelyov just before this latest piece appeared. Their meeting in his USA Institute office was hurried, but Bill got a clear impression of a man who seemed quintessentially Soviet in everything but his willingness to challenge the basic tenets of the Soviet system. He was pleasant enough but so sure of himself as to seem arrogant. He seemed unfazed by the Andreyeva manifesto. At the end of their conversation Bill asked how he felt about the current situation. Shmelyov characterized his views as "restrained optimism." "*Very* restrained," he emphasized, but optimism nonetheless because there was simply no alternative to radical reform.

Several weeks after the *Pravda* response, at an important conference of historians and writers, Mikhail Shatrov chastised his colleagues as well as himself for their Andreyeva-imposed silence. "How would this conference have gone," he asked, "if it had been held seven days after the infamous article in *Sovetskaya rossiya?*" Hardly a single newspaper had dared to criticize Andreyeva. Only one artistic union, the cinematographers, had immediately protested; the others remained silent. Where had the historians been until April 5? Or the writers? "Why are we so afraid to think for ourselves? That we waited for authorization from above is a gigantic reproach to us all. . . . The fate of each of us is at stake, and yet we once again require permission to act." If *perestroika* fails in the end, he concluded, "Andreyeva and her ilk won't be to blame. We'll be the guilty ones, we who today pledge allegiance to *perestroika* but yesterday were silent."

Bill had called Shatrov several times before they met. The playwright never refused to see him, but put off naming a date. With a storm raging about his head, was he hesitant to take the risk, however small, of hobnobbing with an American Sovietologist? In the end, he was not, for a reason he mentioned at a literary/political evening he invited Bill to attend on March 30: "Fear deprives us of our humanity. If we don't fight against the lie in our own lives, then we will always be afraid."

Shatrov suggested that Bill meet him outside the House of Unions, where he was to speak. He was waiting with other friends when Bill arrived, then ushered them all past the crowd and up the stairs to a backstage anteroom where he made last-minute preparations. When the evening began, Bill had a reserved seat in the first row in front of the speaker. The setting couldn't have been more suited to meditations on the burden and ironies of history. For it was in that same attractive, white-columned October Hall with its blue walls and friezes that the 1936 show trial of Old Bolsheviks Zinoviev and Kamenev took place. Shatrov himself made reference to the fact during his presentation, as if to exorcise the ghosts of history.

Bill stood and cheered with the rest of the audience at
Shatrov's final words: "These reforms are our last
chance. And not just ours. Back in the twenties, people
didn't know what lay ahead. We can't use that excuse.
The welfare of future generations depends on us. We
must succeed!"

WHO'S AFRAID OF

NINA ANDREYEVA?

T he fact that many Russians reacted to the Andreyeva affair with fear and caution was a de-
pressing reminder of how far the reforms had to go. That
others were not intimidated was a sign of progress, of
many people's determination to press on despite the
risks.

Looking back, we see signs of tension we did not pick
up at the time. The political meetings we attended during this period were more restrained than previously.
Least changed were cultural and literary evenings. If
the press was largely silent during the interregnum, the
writers, poets, and critics were not. It was during these
three weeks that the literary evenings Jane attended at-
tained the intensity of the talk Bill had heard back in
February at the Historical Archives Institute. Participants took upon themselves the traditional role of Russian literature in the struggle for democracy and justice.

Some of our friends seemed absolutely unaffected. For others the affair deepened an already profound pessimism about the prospects for change. Still others seemed just plain scared.

We had first met Volodya and Valya Ivanov fifteen years ago in the United States. A physicist, he was here on a scholarly mission. Valya was with him, a rarity in those days when family members usually stayed home to guarantee the traveler's return. We spent a lot of time with the Ivanovs that year despite a certain amount of political tension. It was not that we argued about politics; on the contrary, they carefully steered clear of the subject, and we learned to follow suit. We sensed they were reform-minded—Valya dropped thinly veiled hints that Leonid Brezhnev was not her ideal—but in those times we felt certain things were better left unsaid. We kept up the friendship after they returned to Moscow, dropping in to see them on all our trips. In January 1986, less than a year into the Gorbachev era, we saw the first signs of change. They themselves tentatively broached the political issues we had learned to avoid, indicating that they welcomed Gorbachev's reforms. A year and a half later, in the summer of 1987, we found them transformed. Only now, they said, could they tell us what had been on their minds all those years, how unhappy they had been about things they could only hint at when talking with us.

This breakthrough lifted our friendship with the Ivanovs to a new plateau. Our next meeting was a week after the Andreyeva letter in March 1988. We didn't think of it that way at the time, but our evening at their home was a kind of litmus test. None of our friends had been more circumspect than the Ivanovs during the decade of stagnation. If anyone could have been expected to regress now, it was they. Instead, the evening proceeded absolutely normally; after years of avoiding controversy, and then the confessions of the summer before,

we could now act like ordinary people, talking politics
when we pleased, ignoring it when we wished. That
evening we discussed rumors of a struggle in the Politburo. The Ivanovs assumed that if the wrong men won,
the reforms would be reversed. But that didn't affect
their own behavior. Like most Russians we knew, they
were fatalists, convinced that, despite their importance
in the scientific establishment, they had no power to
affect their country's future. But unless and until the
worst happened, they were determined to act as if it
would not.

Seryozha, the pessimist, was gloomier than usual during the interregnum. Previously, his somber prognosis
had had an economic underpinning. This time, it was
political. The biggest obstacle to reform, Seryozha now
insisted, was arbitrary political power. The highest authorities in the land had passed a law decentralizing
economic management. But government planners and
Party *apparatchiki* felt free to ignore the decree. Economic reform depended on the supremacy of the law,
but that in turn required punishment for those who dis-
obeyed it. Neither the police nor the courts could be
counted on, since both were under the Party's thumb.
The key was to get Party officials to obey the rules the
Party itself made. But that could only be done by some
outside force stronger than the Party—which by definition was impossible in a one-party system. Ergo, a multiparty political system was needed.

Bill objected, as he usually did in conversations with
Seryozha, that prospects were not so hopeless. Theoretically, intraparty democracy could provide some of the
benefits to be obtained from multiparty competition. If
factions were allowed to operate freely, as they had until
Lenin's 1921 ban, and if the debate were decided by
voting, not violence, then the outcome Seryozha wanted
might still be obtained. He shrugged. There was no way
even Gorbachev was going to reverse Lenin. After all,

Lenin was the only leg he and the Party had to stand on
once they had jettisoned Stalin, Brezhnev, et al.

"If you don't believe me," Seryozha said, "go ask
Dimitry and Linda." Dimitry is an artist; his wife, a retired engineer. Both have tragic histories. His father, a
high-ranking official in the 1930s, was exterminated in
the Great Purge. She is actually British by birth. Her
parents came to the USSR in the 1920s to help build
socialism. When the dream soured a few years later,
they returned to England, but Linda, full of adolescent
rebellion, refused to go. "It was the worst mistake I ever
made," she had told us on an earlier visit. In the 1940s
she paid for it with arrest and exile, later with limited
job opportunities and no chance to visit her native land.
A half-century later, she was still paying. But instead of
being bitter, she was relentlessly analytical in elegant if
old-fashioned English. As an engineer, she knew what
was wrong from the inside: it took sixteen Soviet workers on the Fiat-supplied assembly line in Togliatti to do
the work of four men in Rome. Radical economic reforms could not work in the absence of prices that reflected real costs, but a thoroughgoing price reform,
including higher food costs, would produce political
chaos.

Linda and Dimitry had a run-down dacha in the country several hours by train from Moscow. They described
a dying village that resembled the place Andrey Amalrik
depicted in *Involuntary Journey to Siberia*. The few
peasants who hadn't fled to the cities were usually
drunk. At the drop of a rumor that vodka was on sale in
a neighboring town, they would set off on tractors that
were supposed to be working the fields, often taking up
to two or three hours to find out the town next door was
dry as well. Nearby was an old wood-working mill that
had been revived as a cooperative. So hard and well did
the participants work that they made up to 2,000 rubles
a month, more than all but the most highly paid officials

in Moscow. The cooperative was fully legal; it was precisely the sort of operation the new law on cooperatives was designed to encourage. But that carried no weight with local authorities. They were damned if they were going to tolerate "exploitation" (of whom or what was unclear) on that scale. They closed the place down. The mill attracted another set of entrepreneurs. A group of young scientists commuted in from their research station for two days each week, which netted them 400 rubles a month, or twice what they earned doing science. So far, the local authorities had deigned to let the new group continue.

Besides the deepening gloom of old friends, there was the nervousness of new ones. Even before arriving in Moscow we had been fans of *Moscow News*. As long as *Moscow News* kept the faith, others would defend it too. Bill had dropped by the offices, hoping to find out what kind of men fought this good fight. He got the brush-off. It was his fault for not calling first, he reasoned, so he was pleased when an editor responded to several phone calls by inviting him in for a chat. The editor was pleasant but reluctant. When Bill asked why *MN* had not published much if anything on Khrushchev, the answer was that the time wasn't right. Anything written on Gorbachev's predecessor would inevitably be taken as an indirect comment on the current situation. A few weeks after *Pravda*'s anti-Andreyeva attack, *Moscow News* published two full pages on Khrushchev.

The time wasn't right either, apparently, for getting to know one of the brightest and most engaging men we met. Andrey was a chemist. His hobby was economics and politics, and he knew well the senior social scientists preparing key reform legislation. The mutual friend who introduced us warned that Andrey was depressed these days. But the stocky, muscular young man who joined us for lunch at a fashionable new cooperative restaurant was a marvelous combination of warmth, energy, and wit. It turned out he was a baseball fan, a regular reader of *Sports Illustrated* and completely *au courant* on batting averages. If ever a Russian and an American found a common language in a hurry, it was Bill and Andrey in the course of gauging the Red Sox' chances of parlaying young talent into an American League pennant. After that, there seemed to be no stopping them. According to Gorbachev, *perestroika* consisted of two phases—planning and implementation. In fact, said Andrey, there were three: analyzing the mess, deciding what needed to be done, and then figuring out how to do it. The third stage was the hardest, he added, and it had hardly begun. Besides, the top leaders themselves were deeply divided. We wanted to press him to be more specific, to say exactly who was for and against what. But we were afraid of scaring him off. Something did, for we never saw him again. He must have had some special reason for wanting to meet us in the first place. Bill was sure it was his eagerness to compare notes with an American Sovietologist. Jane, who has learned the lengths to which sports addicts will go for a fix, thought it was baseball.

Ilya Matveevich Ignatov was as different from Andrey as could be imagined, a shy, retiring, absentminded professor deep into middle age. We had encountered him before on semiofficial business, but he had always kept his distance. He was a true intellectual, a man of learning and curiosity with a passion for the Russian past. In former years, he had signaled his dissent in subtle ways, a raised eyebrow, a barely audible sigh. This year, emboldened by *glasnost,* he was determined to go public, yet unsure exactly when or where. When Bill first encountered him in February, he blurted out his delight that Bill was working on a book on Khrushchev, then quickly looked around at his colleagues as if afraid he had overstepped himself. Later, in a quiet corner, he whispered that he intended to take us to the theater and concerts to show us the Moscow he loved.

Nearly two months passed without a further word from him, which was not surprising in the case of a man who, as the Russians say, is not entirely "of this world." Nor was it surprising that when he finally did call us, it was just when he shouldn't have. Not only did he invite us in late March to a posh restaurant where he himself had never been, but in what must have been a superhuman effort for a shy, retiring man, he did battle at the door to insist the restaurant honor the reservation he had made on the phone.

For a while, he talked more boldly than ever before about the "monsters" who had ruled culture under Stalin and after. But somewhere in the middle of the evening, something clicked shut and he lapsed into apolitical clichés about the importance of human contact and mutual understanding. As we parted, he talked once more of going to concerts and the theater. We never heard from him again.

Did Ilya encounter official "unpleasantness" because of our evening together? We heard of no such incidents throughout the spring except for one involving a couple we met at the home of an American correspondent several days before we dined with Ilya. He was a sociologist with Jewish activist friends, she a historian specializing in increasingly restive non-Russian nationalities. Nothing they said that evening at dinner was a state secret. But just to be seen at a newsman's home was risky. We heard later that the police had begun following them the next day. We doubt very much that Ilya received such treatment, however. More likely, he just thought better of his own boldness, such as it was.

In the past we had found that the less Russians had to lose, the more modest their stations in life, the more willing they were to be seen with us. That was not so during Moscow Spring—*except* during the Andreyeva chill. Of all Bill's sources on Khrushchev, one of the most engaging was Dima, a former photographer who now worked as an illustrator. Dima had been recom-

mended to Bill by two much more highly placed former
Khrushchev aides. He couldn't have been more relaxed
about receiving him, and he was obviously flattered by
the attention. A man of a million contacts, he prided
himself on his knowledgeability. Bill found his Khrushchev stories revealing and enjoyed listening to him talking on the phone, which rang every other minute. The
Russian language is full of wonderfully expressive di-
minutives, which Dima further embellished with old-
fashioned politeness. "Dear, dear Anyushechka," he
would coo into the phone. But Dima was puzzled by the
attention. Why had Bill been sent to him? He confessed
to having mulled over the question at length before arriving at an answer: the referral fit the time perfectly,
right after the Andreyeva letter when more highly
placed people were reluctant to spend much time with
an American Sovietologist but willing to pass him along
to someone on the fringe.

Bill encountered real fear on just one occasion. He
had been invited back for a second time to Velikhov's
course on the history of the arms race. This time, with
Martin Sherwin and his Tufts students present, the class
featured a screening of *Dr. Strangelove*. One of the Soviet students wanted to know why the film's tone was so
anti-Soviet. Either he had missed something in the
translation (which was bravely ad-libbed by Sherwin's
assistant), or he was out to show what a good ideological
watchdog he was. Another Soviet student correctly insisted that the film was much more anti-American, although not so much so as some recent Soviet films like
TASS Is Authorized to Announce. . . One of the American students asked whether such a bitingly anti-military
film could now be made in the USSR. Not yet, Velikhov
answered. The first question, Bill thought, was whether
such a film could even be *shown* in the Soviet Union.
Private screenings were one thing; doubtless *Dr.
Strangelove* had been shown many times that way, but
it had never been released for a mass audience.

As the class was breaking up, a student who had asked Bill a series of seemingly ordinary questions proposed that they take a stroll outside. While they walked beside the thirty-three-story skyscraper with its high-Stalinist towers, he confessed he was deeply religious and hence torn by the path that was inexorably taking him toward a career in science, perhaps even in the defense sector, where the best jobs were. Rigid with fright, he declined to give his name or even his academic specialty and insisted on speaking with his back to the building, lest unseen observers read his lips through binoculars.

Shortly after the Andreyeva article appeared, Bill attended a talk at the Academy of Sciences' Institute of Economics on "Was There an Alternative to Collectivization?" For years the question could never be publicly asked in the USSR. Now it seemed every intellectual in town volunteered an opinion. The all-out, forced-draft industrialization had long been justified as necessary for "socialism," and for the successful defense against Hitler. But wouldn't industrialization have proceeded more efficiently in cooperation with the peasantry rather than in the teeth of peasant opposition? Twenty-five years before, Bill had written a paper on this question in his first year at graduate school. He couldn't wait to hear some of the USSR's leading economic minds address the issue.

He is still waiting. The speaker at the Institute of Economics turned out to be a junior scholar. His talk was virtually unprecedented by Soviet standards, according to a young man sitting next to Bill in the lecture hall. It concluded there *had* been an alternative, namely, the use of economic means such as higher taxes and voluntary forms of agricultural cooperation to obtain the raw materials and other resources needed to industrialize the country. But the overall quality of the lecture, and especially of the questions that followed, was nowhere near what Bill had expected. If some of the USSR's leading economic minds were in the hall, they weren't heard

from. Among those who did hold forth were two elderly
Stalinist hacks. "Without collectivization," one asked,
"would we today have all that we have?" "What exactly
do we have today?" whispered the man sitting next to
Bill, and then answered his own question under his
breath: "A disaster, that's what we have."

"Without collectivization," intoned the other commentator, "we would be deeply in debt, like Mexico,
Brazil, Singapore, and Finland." At the mention of Singapore and especially Finland, whose economic
successes put the USSR to shame, the original speaker
bent over to stifle a fit of laughter. He did not, however,
otherwise reply.

The day after the Economics Institute talk, we attended one on "Osip Mandelstam and the World of the
October Revolution" at the Historical Archives Institute. This time the lecture was first-rate; it made clear
that the great poet had not been against the Revolution
from the beginning, but that the Revolution had turned
him against itself. The questions from the audience
were noticeably milder than they had been in February.
One question, however, struck us. "Where is Yury Ni-
kolayevich?" a note inquired, referring to Afanasyev
who usually sat just behind the speaker but this day was
nowhere in sight. "He's home with the grippe," the
young student-chairman answered. The audience
laughed at its own uneasiness. Back in February, when
the lecturer spoke of the need to take risks, someone
had joked, "When the reforms are reversed, Yury Niko-
layevich will be the first to go."

A third meeting revolved around a path-breaking film
called *The Cold Summer of 1953.* The film's action took
place a few months after Stalin's death in a somnolent
northern village where two political prisoners were living out their endless exile. A short time before, criminals had been released under the so-called Beria
amnesty by Stalin's surviving police chief, in the expec-

tation that they would create such havoc that his MVD troops would be needed to quell the disorders, thus increasing his power. In the film, criminals from a nearby camp sweep into the village with guns blazing, massacring the police, robbing and raping the villagers, meeting resistance only from the two "politicals," one of whom, a former army intelligence officer, is still paying for the "crime" of being captured by the Germans, though he escaped within twenty-four hours.

When the smoke clears, just about everyone is dead except the former officer, who almost single-handedly wipes out the criminals. The film ends with his return to Moscow in 1957. He visits the widow of his slain companion, who renounced her husband at the time of his arrest in 1939. She and his son still find it hard to believe that he was innocent. The newly freed officer goes out alone into a city bustling with preparations for the anniversary of the Revolution. Another wanderer with a similar worn suitcase approaches; wordlessly they recognize each other, light up from the same match, and go their separate ways.

Our friends in the audience were enthralled by the film. They loved the notion of a political prisoner as hero, and they ate up the American-style shoot-out. We thought the real drama began as the film ended—the drama of the exile's readjustment to "freedom," a theme never before touched on in Soviet film. What was unusual about the evening was that Bill got the chance to say this and a lot more to several hundred Soviets who had been invited by a film discussion club under the sponsorship of the district Party committee.

We had been told that Sergo Mikoyan would lead the discussion. When he turned out to have another speaking engagement, his replacement was Valentin Berezhkov, a septuagenarian with an unlined face and thick white hair who had been Stalin's wartime interpreter in meetings with the Americans and British and now edited the USA Institute's monthly journal, *SShA* ("USA").* Like Mikoyan, he had been recruited by a group of young Americanists to whom either Party authorities or perhaps the club had subcontracted the job of booking the films and their discussants. Just three days before, Bill had spent an afternoon with Berezhkov, who regaled him with wonderful stories about the talks between Hitler and Molotov in November 1940 for which he had been the Soviet interpreter.

When, without warning, the young moderator summoned him on stage for an off-the-cuff, open-ended discussion in Russian, Bill suddenly felt sympathy with conservatives who insisted *glasnost* was going too far. But there was no way to escape. Bill took his seat next to Berezhkov. The first question was to Bill: "How do Americans perceive and comprehend Stalinism?" "With horror," he answered. "Like you, we are aghast at the extent of the terror and violence. We try to understand it. But the full extent of it is beyond comprehending. We have some ideas about how to explain it. We think some of them would interest you. That's one reason why we're glad that you finally have the opportunity to read what we write, to hear our point of view. But what is even more satisfying to us is that you yourselves are finally free to confront your own past. After all, this is your country, and you should write your own history. We're confident that when you do so, you will have a lot to teach us."

Bill was pleasantly surprised by the words that came to his tongue. He badly wanted to strike just the right note for the occasion, to speak politely but candidly. The discussion, however, entered trickier territory. Did Bill think Stalinism was inevitable in the Soviet system?

---

* Berezhkov achieved a different sort of notoriety in the West a few years ago as the father of a young man who reportedly did not want to return to the USSR with his family.

(The question wasn't asked so directly, but that's what it amounted to.) Bill had answered this often enough in his Amherst class on Soviet politics. With a gulp, he gave the same answer here. Nothing was inevitable. If Stalin had been hit by a truck and killed in 1925, history would have turned out differently. But the ideas and institutions Lenin left in place made the rise of someone like Stalin possible, even probable. Lenin saw the danger just before he died; he tried to remove Stalin as general secretary and to erect other obstacles to dictatorial rule. But the basic flaw in the Soviet system was that Lenin himself, a mortal and by then ailing man, was the primary obstacle—so that when he was gone the road to Stalinism was wide open.

Having gone this far, Bill resolved to go the rest of the way. The lesson of Stalin's rise, he said, as well as of the lesser tyrannies of Khrushchev and Brezhnev, was that the USSR needed institutional guarantees against dictatorship. The reformers ought to consider repealing the ban on factions that Lenin himself pushed through the Party's Tenth Congress in 1921. They ought also to take a leaf from the American book on separation of powers, the device built into our Constitution specifically to limit governmental power.

From his position on stage, Bill couldn't tell how the audience was reacting. Those around Jane were obviously rooting for him. But Berezhkov was not. He felt compelled to rebut, vigorously but not venomously, as if recognizing that an exchange of this kind was now par for *glasnost*—even a mere ten days after Nina Andreyeva. Little did either he or Bill realize that within a month calls for the USSR to devise institutional guarantees on the American model would be an almost daily feature of the Soviet press.

In mid-March, Jane was invited to an evening in honor of Joseph Brodsky. The return of Brodsky's poetry to his native land was a story she followed with particular interest. She had long been an admirer of his work; in graduate school, she had written a seminar paper on it. Then Brodsky came to western Massachusetts as Five-College Professor of Poetry in 1975, and in the 1980s he had taught there each spring semester. Jane had attended many of his seminars on Russian poetry, and Bill had had many arguments with him about Soviet foreign policy and the American response to it.

In May 1987, after a historic meeting between emigré writers and Soviet literary figures in Washington, Brodsky had confided with a twinkle that *Novy mir* wanted to publish some of his poems. At the time, it seemed an impossible dream: no living emigré had yet been published in the Soviet Union. Six months later, there were Brodsky's poems in *Novy mir*'s December issue, along with a carefully worded footnote in tiny print: "After this number of the journal with the poems of Joseph Brodsky, a Russian poet now living in New York, had been set in type, news came that he had been awarded the Nobel Prize in Literature." A second selection of Brodsky poems appeared in the March 1988 issue of the Leningrad journal *Neva,* with another footnote: "In connection with this publication, J. Brodsky requested the journal to convey 'his sincere regards to the readers of *Neva* and to the city which I love.' " In a complimentary afterword, an old friend of Brodsky's, the Leningrad poet Aleksander Kushner, praised his "combination of poetic power with wonderful refinement and remarkable virtuosity."

And so, that evening in mid-March, Jane found her way to the house of culture of the Zuev factory, not far from the Byelorussia railway station, and met her friend among the mass of people on the sidewalk, hoping somehow to acquire tickets. Once inside the hall, she looked with curiosity at the audience. The majority seemed to be of Brodsky's generation, in their late for-

ties, or ten to fifteen years younger. They were an interesting crowd, well but not showily dressed, a blend of
the Soviet yuppie and the literary and technological intelligentsia—all of which probably said more about the
way tickets were distributed than about Brodsky's read-
ership.

The evening's first speaker was Fazil Iskander, who
writes in Russian but sets most of his work in his native
Abkhazia, a small, ancient land on the shore of the Black
Sea. *Sandro of Chegem,* his magnum opus, was published during the 1970s with some of its anti-Stalinist
chapters removed. These had been published abroad;
now they were coming out in the USSR. He spoke about
his first encounter with Brodsky's poetry, confessing
that he had found the early poems "strange, they didn't
move me, they were rather bookish and not economi-
cal." But later, on reading "A School Anthology," Iskander knew "this was a really major poet." He concluded
by announcing confidently that "in the near future, all
or almost all of his poems will be published in his
homeland."

The program was organized and moderated by Yevgeny Rein, another Leningrad poet and old friend of
Brodsky's. In 1979, he was in political difficulty for par-
ticipating in *Metropol,* the unofficial literary almanac
which resulted in Vasily Aksyonov's emigration. Now
he was giving his own readings, publishing poems in
Litgazeta, and preparing to spend a semester at Yale.
Evidently out of an excess of good will, he had included
far too many people in the program. Jane's favorite candidate for elimination was a middle-aged actress who
read Brodsky's poems at great length in a stilted, overemotional style. We had heard Brodsky himself, many
times, reading his verse in his incantatory yet under-
stated way; it was hard even to recognize them in this
rendition.

Toward the end of the evening, a slight, graying man

wearing glasses and a sweater walked on the stage with a guitar and an impish smile and began to sing some of Brodsky's poems in the style known in Russia as "author's song." Somehow, it worked; Alek Mirzoyan had chosen only Brodsky's early poems, and his accompaniment brought out the insouciance and irony in them.

But the most interesting part of the evening was the give-and-take between Rein and the audience. Notes flooded the stage, asking for the most basic information about Brodsky: How many books had he published, and what were their titles? Did he have a family? When and why had he left the Soviet Union? What was he doing now? Would he come back to visit the USSR, and when? Was it true that Nabokov praised his poetry just before he died? Rein responded with candor, often with warm humor. Question: "What does he live on?" Rein: "He pays in dollars."

Rein described in frank detail the scandalous 1964 frame-up and trial in Leningrad that resulted in Brodsky's eighteen-month exile to a collective farm in the far north. When he added that Savelyeva, the presiding judge, had later been demoted to notary for her unprofessional conduct during the trial, the audience cheered.

Brodsky was currently teaching in America at "the branch of the University of Chicago in Ann Arbor," Rein informed the audience. Jane could not let this inaccuracy pass; during the intermission she slipped him a note correcting his error and included a copy of the latest issue of *Amerika*, whose cover story on women's colleges featured photos of Mount Holyoke College, where Brodsky is currently Mellon Professor. Rein thanked her profusely for the information, and she was amused to watch him as he sat on the stage during the slower moments of the second half of the program leafing through *Amerika* along with Iskander, both of them showing considerable interest in this "American propaganda."

Another high point of the evening was the appearance of Tatyana Tolstaya. Her personal style was as striking as her prose style. Slightly chubby, wearing a fashionable white dress that set off her black hair, she commanded attention. She had recently returned from her first trip to the States with a delegaton that also included such establishment figures as Viktor Karpov, first secretary of the Writers' Union. This in itself was a tribute to the new attitude in the cultural establishment. Despite her talent, probably in fact *because* of it, Tolstaya had not yet been accepted into the Writers' Union. She is only very distantly related to Leo Tolstoy, but her grandfather was the Soviet writer Aleksey Tolstoy.

While in New York, Tolstaya had met Brodsky in his Greenwich Village apartment, which she described in loving detail. Mikhail Baryshnikov had arrived for the evening, bringing a bundle of logs for the fire. Brodsky is not poor, she explained; it was just a cold evening, and a fire was very pleasant. After she finished, there was a note from the audience: Why hadn't she described the poet himself? Her plausible answer: She met him only that one time, and since everyone is different on different occasions and in different company, she thought it unfair to characterize him on the basis of one meeting.

Others who paid tribute to Brodsky included the young critic and short-story writer Viktor Yerofeyev and the actor Lev Prigunov, another of Brodsky's Leningrad friends. What was missing, and what the audience most wanted, was the voice of the poet himself. They had to be satisfied with a few minutes of his Nobel acceptance speech in a low-quality recording, obviously taped off Voice of America. They wanted much more, but even this was a big surprise—a clandestine recording from VOA played openly at a public gathering.

Another note inquired about a planned evening in the same hall in honor of Aleksander Galich, the poet-bard who had been forced into emigration in the 1970s for his biting satirical songs about Soviet life. The speaker explained with a proud smile, "They're trying to prohibit our evening, but we're going to hold it anyway." "*Who* is trying to prohibit it?" someone in the crowd called out. "The KGB," replied the speaker, boldly uttering that still-taboo word from the stage. The audience roundly applauded his courage. In retrospect, we realized that this gathering took place only three days after Andreyeva's manifesto, a factor that must have weighed on the minds of both participants and audience. By May, Galich evenings were going on unimpeded—but that was May, and this was still March 16.

The Brodsky and Andreyeva stories merged in a bizarre manner three days later when an unsavory piece by one P. Gorelov appeared in *Komsomolskaya pravda,* the organ of the Young Communist League. Gorelov, who signed himself "research associate at the Gorky Institute of World Literature," is known as a hatchet man for Feliks Kuznetsov, the conservative director of the institute. ("They couldn't even find someone with an advanced degree who would do the job," muttered one of our friends, as much in praise of those who wouldn't as in contempt for Gorelov who would.) Gorelov's piece recalled some of the worst literary slanders of the Brezhnev years. Not all Nobel laureates, he reminded his readers, were of equal caliber; Brodsky was worse than most. Some former recipients "weren't even mentioned in the *Literary Encyclopedia.* I. [sic] Agnon (the 1966 laureate) and A.[sic] Singer (1978) even though they are found there, don't, in general, say anything to the Soviet reader." Of course they don't, since S. Y. Agnon, an Israeli who writes in Hebrew, and I. B. Singer, who writes in Yiddish, have never been translated in the Soviet Union. The anti-Semitism of the references was crude and obvious, and the appearance of the article just six days after Andreyeva's was not at all accidental, our friends assured us. Gorelov intentionally misread two Brodsky poems, trying to paint him as a rootless "cosmopolitan" (a code word for Jew). Quoting carefully selected lines out of context, Gorelov implied the disdain of the "emigré Jew" for the glorious Russian motherland. Gorelov's title, "I Have Nothing to Say," is, in Brodsky, the pessimistic cry of the exile, torn from his native readers, not knowing for whom he now writes in a foreign land.

> I have nothing to say to the Greek or the Varangian.
> Since I don't know which earth I'll lie in.

Gorelov tried to make it seem a confession of artistic sterility.

Gorelov's piece was supplemented by brief items of reportage under the heading "Our correspondents provide additional information." The Paris correspondent quoted a French writer who explained the "amazingly vague understanding" of contemporary Soviet literature in France as follows: "In France, publishing is a commercial business. They publish those writers who sell, and those are the ones who are cleverly advertised." The implication, of course, was that Soviet publishing was *not* commercial but magnanimously published authors who *don't* sell only because they and the publishers are novices at the suspicious Western game of advertising.

Komsomolskaya pravda's New York correspondent had chosen to visit a Russian-language class at Lehman College taught by Professor Robert Whittaker. Of the three students in the class, he reported, two knew that Brodsky had been awarded the Nobel Prize, the third was hearing his name for the first time. None of them, however, had ever read his poems in either Russian or English.

After we returned, Jane called Professor Whittaker,

who remembered the incident well. The class, he explained, had been a second-year Russian class, a level at
which few students are prepared to tackle Russian
poetry of the complexity of Brodsky's. Three students is
not a large scientific sampling, but given the cultural
level of the average American college sophomore, Whittaker's class actually did pretty well. The catch, of
course, was that the Soviet reader, knowing that Russian
university students are on the average quite well-informed about contemporary American and European literature, not to mention their own contemporary poets,
would assume that the American students' ignorance at-
tested to Brodsky's general reputation.

Several days later, as Jane sat in the imposing lecture
hall of the Lenin Library waiting for another literary
lecture to begin, she overheard three women in the row
behind her gossiping about Gorelov's piece. One had
read it, the others had not yet gotten hold of the text.
Jane introduced herself and offered to let them have a
look at the article, which she happened to have in her
briefcase. It turned out that they worked at Gorelov's
institute, though they had never heard of him and were
indignant that his signature had seemed to imply institute support for his views. They were glad to see the
piece, but after they had read it they seemed hesitant
about continuing the conversation. The Andreyeva and
Gorelov articles were clearly having a chilling effect.

Among those who were not chilled were Tolstaya and
Viktor Yerofeyev, whose joint letter of protest to Gorelov
appeared in the letters column of the always gutsy
Ogonyok. Komsomolskaya pravda itself refused to print
it.

Late in March, Yelena Chukovskaya, granddaughter
of Kornei Chukovsky, invited Jane to an evening in
honor of Aleksander Tvardovsky, the late poet and editor of *Novy mir* during its best and most liberal days in

the 1960s. Tvardovsky was the first to publish Solzhenitsyn and much else that was fresh and truthful in Soviet
literature. He managed to hold out against the rising tide
of Brezhnev dogmatism till 1970, when the journal was
taken away from him. His death from cancer a few
months later is widely blamed on that defeat.

This evening was held in the Nekrasov public library
just off Gorky Street. An overflow crowd listened
through loudspeakers in an adjoining room. It turned
into a tribute to "the sixties" and the journal that symbolized the era, as much as to the editor himself. The
mood, however, was not nostalgic but militant. Fazil Iskander said, "You don't know the critical articles that
didn't get through the censors," and lamented the "general falling-off of morality" in the intervening twenty
years. "We wouldn't be in the dramatic situation in
which we find ourselves now," he continued, "if *Novy
mir* had been allowed to continue as it was in its glory
days." Such is the Russian intellectual's traditional faith
in the moral power of literature!

Anna Berzer, a grandmotherly lady in thick glasses
who would look at home in any New York editorial office, was the head of *Novy mir*'s prose section under
Tvardovsky. She recalled how one of the magazine's opponents, after the invasion of Czechoslovakia, declared
that her office, not Prague, was where the tanks should
have been sent. She also revealed that the army brass,
miffed at a story by I. Grekova (a pseudonym for one of
the sixties' few women authors who taught mathematics
at a military institute), ordered that all army base libraries cancel their subscriptions.

Many of the speakers compared the role of Tvardovsky's *Novy mir* to Nikolay Nekrasov's *Contemporary,*
the crusading liberal journal of the 1860s that published
Turgenev, Tolstoy, and Dostoevski. The editors and
writers tried to re-evoke and summarize Tvardovsky's
civic achievement as a model for a new generation

which had barely been born when he died. That
younger generation was present, and they were in-
tensely interested, but they had not all gotten the hang
of *glasnost*. A note came forward with the indignant demand, "Tell us the names of the eleven bastards who
signed the letter denouncing Tvardovsky!" and signed
"A group of students." "You can read it in a footnote to
my recent article in *Ogonyok*," snapped Natalya Ilina,
author of the exposé of corruption among Writers' Union
officials, with the wry amusement of a professor catching
out a student who had not done his reading assignment.
"And by the way, why didn't you sign your own note?"

The evening's most dramatic moment was provided
by Dimitry Yurasov, who, at the age of nineteen, had
become the youngest hero of *glasnost*. At the tender age
of thirteen, Yurasov was struck by the fact that the lives
of so many Old Bolsheviks had ended abruptly in the
same fateful year of 1937. He began to investigate their
biographies, first as a hobby, then through access to
closed archives when he got himself a low-level job as a
page at the Museum of the Revolution, and then in the
archives of the procurator, where he wangled a similar
job. During slow moments at work he pored through the
dossiers of purge victims, using his nearly photographic
memory to compile a card file now rumored to contain
100,000 names. Eventually he was caught, but quietly
let go since publicity about the case would cause more
harm to his superiors than to him. He found a protector
in Yury Afanasyev, who arranged for him to be registered as a part-time student at his institute. Yurasov
worked during the day as a laborer, loading trucks.

Jane had heard stories of this legendary young man,
but she had no suspicion it was he when she noticed a
tall, broad-shouldered, rather American-looking youth
being ushered in through a back entrance to the speaker's platform. Yurasov's was the most daring contribution to the evening in its explicit concentration on

Solzhenitsyn. Solzhenitsyn's name was still almost taboo, but it was hard to evoke Tvardovsky's accomplishments without mentioning his most important literary discovery. Yurasov recounted how Tvardovsky had nominated Solzhenitsyn for the Lenin Prize in 1964, in honor of *One Day in the Life of Ivan Denisovich*, only to be told that "Solzhenitsyn collaborated with the fascists during the war." Not one to give up easily, Tvardovsky addressed himself to the KGB, asking for confirmation of that charge. In return, he was sent a copy of Solzhenitsyn's official rehabilitation document exonerating the writer which Yurasov proceeded to read aloud, to resounding applause.

But Jane sensed a touch of ambiguity about Tvardovsky himself, muted because of the celebratory nature of the occasion and the presence of his two daughters. Tvardovsky's family had been peasants, and the family was exiled to Siberia in the murderous anti-kulak campaign of the early 1930s. Already a rising literary star living in Moscow, Tvardovsky was visited one day by his father and younger brother, both on the verge of starvation, who had managed to escape from exile and come to him for help. Without even offering them food or a night's lodging, Tvardovsky sent them back with a few empty words about his "confidence that the state would take care of them." Tvardovsky's brother told the story in his memoirs, just published in the March issue of *Yunost*, and everyone was talking about it.

The evening had one other luminary, though she sat in the audience and didn't say a word: the eighty-one-year-old Lydia Chukovskaya, the daughter of the writer Jane was researching. Inspired by her father's principles, and somewhat protected by his fame and wealth, Chukovskaya had been one of the most outspoken defenders of persecuted writers and dissidents in the late sixties, for which she was expelled from the Writers' Union in 1974, after her father's death. Chukovskaya's

monumental memoir of Anna Akhmatova has been published in many languages.* Now, finally, there are plans
to publish at least the first volume in the USSR. Chukovskaya returned to public view in May 1987, when she
spoke at another packed event—a memorial evening in
honor of Boris Pasternak—and received a standing ova-
tion. *Sofia Petrovna*, her short novel of the purges, written in 1939 and hidden for many years, was finally
published in the February 1988 issue of *Neva*.† She has
become the literary heroine of Moscow, admired for
never compromising, never emigrating, and finally
achieving vindication. Chukovskaya's presence at any
event was enough to distract attention from the event's
honoree, but she felt compelled to pay tribute to Tvardovsky.

Every year Kornei Chukovsky's family, friends, and
admirers gather to honor his memory on April 1, the
anniversary of his birth. Stopping at the market for the
customary flowers, Jane made her way to Peredelkino
on the electric suburban train. Another flower-bearing
Chukovsky admirer spotted her on the platform; they
introduced themselves and together slogged through
the snow in the Peredelkino cemetery, trying to find the
grave, not far from Pasternak's.

A small group of family and friends circled the flower-
bedecked grave as a feisty and vigorous Chukovskaya
spoke of her father's two best-known books, *From Two
to Five* and *Alive as Life*. Both had been immensely
popular, but how many of his readers, she asked, realized what militant and political books they really were.
Whether exploring children's creativity or defending
the Russian language from Soviet bureaucratese, Chukovsky was really talking about the preservation of truth.

---

* Though not in English. The American publisher is waiting for the completion of Volume 3 to publish the work in its entirety.
† It was published in the 1960s in the West under the incorrect title *Abandoned House*. A revised and corrected translation was published in 1988 by
Northwestern University Press.

Chukovskaya's own rehabilitation was cause for celebration. Though she had been offered readmission to
the Writers' Union, she had proudly refused it on the
grounds that they had no authority to expel her in the
first place or to reinstate her now. At the Chukovsky
dacha, the dining room was filled to overflowing with
the largest crowd in many years. Chukovskaya opened
the after-dinner festivities by reading an unpublished
letter of her father's to . . . She paused dramatically, her
eyes twinkling behind their thick glasses, ". . . Iosif Vis-
sarionovich Stalin." A hushed gasp came from the
crowd.

The letter, she explained, had been written in 1938,
in defense of her late husband, the theoretical physicist
Matvey Bronstein. The Leningrad laboratory in which
Bronstein worked was particularly hard-hit by the
purges—the fact that so many of its scientists were Jewish was surely not irrelevant—but Bronstein's case
seemed based only on the fact that he was the unfortunate namesake of one Lev Davidovich Bronstein (no relation), better known as Trotsky. By the time Chukovsky
found an opportunity to have his letter personally
passed to Stalin's secretary—there was no other way to
transmit such documents—Bronstein had been many
months in his unmarked grave, an NKVD bullet in his
head, but Chukovsky and his family had no way of
knowing.

Yelena Chukovskaya read excerpts from her grandfather's diary, a 4,000-page document which spans the
decades from 1902 to his death in 1969. For many years,
she and Chukovsky's literary secretary, Klara Lozov-
skaya, had been working to prepare the manuscript for
publication. It is a treasure trove for students of Russian
literature and culture. Chukovsky knew everyone who
was anyone in Russian culture during his life span—he
was the recipient of the last letter written by Leo Tolstoy before his death, and he lived to give refuge to the
persecuted Solzhenitsyn in the Peredelkino dacha. Sol-

zhenitsyn's was only one of the "forbidden" names in the diary that had prevented its publication. Now the family had a contract, and a publisher was rushing it into print.

The mood at the April 1 gathering, like that at the earlier Tvardovsky and Brodsky evenings, was one of defiant celebration. These representatives of the literary intelligentsia were not going to let themselves be intimidated by the likes of Nina Andreyeva.

PRAVDA

TO THE RESCUE

I n the old pre-*perestroika* days, one of the few things worth reading in the daily Soviet press was speeches and other pronouncements by the top Party leader. Even if what he had to say was dull and uninteresting, it affected people's lives. Gorbachev pronouncements were always worth reading, but toward the end of March they took on a striking new tone. Whereas previously he had called for unity and a "consolidation of forces," now suddenly he seemed to be striking out at unnamed foes who threatened to scuttle his reforms.

"We are learning to live under conditions of expanding democracy and *glasnost*," he told Italian Communist Party leader Alessandro Natta. "But from time to time this causes some people to think that socialism itself will collapse." These "internal opponents of *perestroika* in effect close ranks with our foreign foes." The equating of domestic doubters with foreign foes was pretty strong stuff. The phrase "some people" has often been used by Soviet leaders to refer to other Soviet leaders they did not want—not yet, anyway—to name. Why did Gorbachev suddenly seem embattled?

Suddenly, on April 5, the fog lifted. *Pravda*'s full-page blockbuster, "Principles of *Perestroika:* Revolutionary Thinking and Action," made several things clear. There had indeed been a political crisis. It was linked to the Andreyeva article. It was now over. For the time being at least, the reformers had won.

We and our friends breathed a great sigh of relief. How sweet it was to have *Pravda* on our side for a change! Not only that, the piece despite its deadly title had been written by someone with a brain. Yet even as we read and rejoiced, we had doubts of our own—about the arguments made and the way *Pravda* made them, most of all about the way it smashed opposition that this time happened to come from reactionaries but next time might come from reformers.

The best part of the piece was its anti-Stalinism. Like Gorbachev's November 2, 1987, speech, the article mentioned Stalin's "indisputable contribution" as well as his "flagrant political errors." Then it took a giant step in the right direction: "Sometimes it is said that Stalin did not know about the acts of lawlessness. He not only knew, he organized and directed them. That is now a proven fact. And Stalin's guilt, along with that of his close entourage, before the Party and people, for massive repressions and lawlessness is enormous and unforgivable." Just the day before, a taxi driver had insisted to us that Stalin did not know, that all the criticism of Stalin insulted those who built and defended socialism in the thirties and forties.

Another satisfying thing about the *Pravda* piece was that it had at last found the right words. It condemned "attempts to play on the dearest thing a person has—the meaning of the life he leads":

If Stalin was guilty of crimes, it is asked, then how are we to evaluate our past achievements? What value are we to place on the work, the heroism of people who brought the land of socialism its historic victories? Are we not denying these too in condemning Stalin and rejecting his methods?

No, we are not denying them, we are praising them. Honest workers, soldiers on the field of battle, all Soviet people who proved their patriotism and their devotion to the motherland and to socialism through their work were doing—did do!—their duty. It was their work, their selflessness, their heroism that lifted our country to unprecedented heights. Only an immoral person would cast doubt on the people's work and achievements. Today we are more aware than ever of how hard it was to do one's real duty at that time, a time that was hard in every respect.

It would be wrong now to write these people off as advocates of Stalin's lawlessness. Wrong because we realize, because we are obliged to realize, how much greater the results of their labors would have been for the whole country, for each of us, if their creative energies and material efforts had not been hindered.

We quote at such length because these words really did stir us. So did those that begged people who were nostalgic for the past to understand that radical reforms were "the only way we could hold on to what has been gained by the labor and heroism of the preceding generations."

Pravda lambasted Andreyeva's smear tactics. "Those who scream about alleged 'internal threats' to socialism, who join certain political extremists and look everywhere for internal enemies, 'counterrevolutionary nations,' and so on, are not patriots. Patriots are those who fearlessly act in the country's interests and for the people's benefit."

And yet the same piece that lifted our spirits reminded us how far reform still had to go. The conservatives were so strong it took the most important paper in the country to turn the tide against them. As usual, *Pravda* arrogated to itself the right to speak for all Soviet citizens. "*We* have changed over the past three years. *We* have raised our heads and straightened up, *we* look facts honestly in the face, *we* speak aloud and openly of painful things, and together *we* are seeking to resolve problems that have built up over decades" (emphasis added). Nothing wrong with the sentiments expressed. But if everyone was of one mind, what was the rest of the article about anyway? The truth, as the Andreyeva affair itself showed, was that there were deep differences. Why shouldn't conservatives be free to express their views?

Under Gorbachev, the limits on factional politicking were loosening. Virtually all our friends welcomed that change. But they were also glad to see *Pravda* crack down on *Sovetskaya rossiya. Pravda* insisted that "Communist writers and editors have a sense of responsibility." In the past, our friends dreaded precisely those words. Now they feared that if the Party did not impose such responsibility, the reactionaries would win. Either they would constitute a majority, or they would play on mass doubts about democracy. Ironically, reactionaries feared the same scenario in reverse, with reformers coming out on top. What both sides had in common was the traditional Russian conviction that democracy can be understood and operated only by a minority.

What was heartening was that *Pravda* itself was not as central as it used to be, because the Soviet press was no longer monolithic. It still required Party sanction before even the boldest reformers would speak out against Andreyeva, but once *Pravda* spoke, it was quickly overtaken by those who had been radicalized by their own impotence. Aghast at how easily they had been cowed, they were determined not to let it happen again. A few days before, they had feared all might be lost. Now they were determined to give voice to what they had been holding back. If the worst happened, the truth would still be on the record.

Pravda's April 5 broadside triggered an explosion of civic activity. The media overflowed with unprecedented articles, television and radio programs. Each morning's paper brought a new revelation about Stalinism, each evening's newscast a fresh proposal for reform. The pace of political and literary evenings picked up. We ourselves were in constant demand to speak, to lecture, to be interviewed, to appear on television. Friends from February whose ardor had seemed to cool during late March reemerged; new acquaintances overwhelmed us with warmth. It felt to us at the time, and our Soviet friends agreed, as if all hell had broken loose. We use that term not because the experience was unpleasant—on the contrary, it was exhilarating—but because it must have seemed to conservatives that the very ground beneath their feet was shaking.

Yet every now and again we were reminded that this was still the USSR, a country where reformers were more numerous in Moscow and Leningrad than in the provinces, where bureaucrats did not necessarily share intellectuals' animus against bureaucracy, where democrats oscillated between feeling constrained by the limits on democracy and dreading what would happen if those limits were removed, where what they feared most was the people whose interests they were trying to advance, where at least some of the ordinary people we met seemed a lot closer to the intellectuals than either realized, but where even we worried, when confronted by speech and action of breathtaking boldness, that radical supporters of Gorbachev were going too far too fast.

April 5 was a Tuesday. By this time we were experienced newspaper hunter-gatherers; we knew *Pravda* was available until at least 8:00 A.M. at our neighborhood kiosk. But not on April 5. The bus downtown resembled the ads that used to depict "almost everyone" reading the Philadelphia *Bulletin*. Everyone's *Pravda* was open to page 2, with the attack on Andreyeva topped by a banner headline. The kiosks downtown were stripped clean. It wasn't till the next day that we managed to cadge a used copy.

Bill had made an appointment on April 5 with a senior historian with a reputation as an intelligent, responsible conservative. Actually, compared to some establishment historians, he was almost liberal, but compared with our liberal friends, he was distinctly right-wing. Bill's purpose was to widen the ideological range of his acquaintances. In the same spirit, he leaped at the chance to attend a lecture that same afternoon by another historian on Stalin's role in World War II. The senior historian described new projects he was working on—a demographic accounting of Stalin's victims and a study of how the idea of *perestroika* germinated during the Brezhnev era. Less impressive was his defensiveness when asked why journalists and writers were publishing more and better history than many historians themselves: "These days, everybody thinks he is a historian. They think they know what they're talking about, but they don't." On the central issue of the day, how to evaluate Stalin overall, he waffled. "To some extent," he said, "Stalin may be said to have deformed socialism, to have prevented it from living up to its potential."

The afternoon's lecture was even more puzzling. Bill had expected, if not a defense of Stalin, then an exercise in praising with faint damns. What he heard was an all-out demolition job. But while the speaker's heart was in the right place, his talk was primitive. It consisted of a series of assertions without much argumentation or evidence to back them up. Bill concluded that he had encountered for the first time a new breed of human being —the anti-Stalinist hack. Had the lecturer read *Pravda* that day? Had he revised his talk to take account of it? He made a sneering reference to Nina Andreyeva.

Surely he wouldn't have dared do that the day before. And what about his senior colleague? Had he read and underlined his *Pravda?* Or was waffling simply part of his intellectual makeup?

The next few days posed more puzzles. Fyodor Burlatsky had several times mentioned inviting us to dinner at his home, but each time something had come up. Burlatsky's life was so frantic that such postponements required no special explanation. Yet was it sheer coincidence that we ended up having a wonderful evening with the Burlatskys shortly after April 5?

Burlatsky bubbled over with speculation about what lay behind the Andreyeva affair and with his own plans to answer her in *Litgazeta.* He came up with a wonderful theory of *homo politicus Sovieticus* that may owe something to his Andreyeva-inspired fears. The trouble with Soviet politics, he said, is that there is only one power game in town, only one political hierarchy to climb. The greatest fear of Soviet political man is that he will fall or be pushed off the Party/state ladder that leads to the top. In America, he knew, power and influence reside in many places, in executive suites, foundation board rooms, university presidencies, etc. In the Soviet Union, all these are part of, or rather subordinate to, the same power structure. The upcoming Party conference was likely to consider a proposal to limit Party and state officials to a fixed term in office. The whole issue would be less traumatic if there were more independent social organizations in which people with leadership ability could find satisfying work. "People? Leadership abilities? Satisfying work?" Jane asked teasingly. Wasn't Burlatsky also talking about men whose manhood was threatened, for whom power and self-image were one? He was man enough to take the idea under consideration.

Sergo Mikoyan had also been less visible during the interregnum. For part of the time, he was in the United

States. Yet he too called shortly after April 5 to invite us to lunch. Like Burlatsky, he was buoyant and full of speculation, convinced the Andreyeva article had been a group project and that it signaled a major anti-Gorbachev effort. Nor was it the only such attempt. The ethnic turmoil in Armenia and Azerbaijan, which conservatives attributed to Gorbachev's reforms, had deep local roots, Mikoyan said, but anti-reform forces in Moscow were also involved. Every time the tension died down, a tendentious story or editorial in a central newspaper "just happened" to stir it up again.

Something as un-Soviet as sheer giddiness seemed the order of the day after April 5. The gathering of former Belousov underlings all agog with *glasnost* at the Academy of Sciences occurred on the morning of April 6. That same afternoon we had a long chat at a suburban sanatorium with a distinguished scientist taking a much needed rest cure. He was incurably optimistic. Everybody knew there was no alternative to reform, he said, even its opponents. What about the possibility of a military coup, if not tomorrow, then down the road a bit? No way. Although the military as a whole had force on its side, individual generals were too scared of the Party and police to conspire. He even found a silver lining in the Armenian protests in Nagorno-Karabakh. The ethnic fratricide graphically illustrated the dangers of a fanatic nationalism; extremist Russian nationalists needed that reminder. So did patriotic Russians who were revolted by Pamyat's anti-Semitism but complacent about the possibility that it would ever get out of hand.

In some ways the press reaction was even more stunning. Pieces that struck us and our friends as unprecedented appeared not only in periodicals like *Moscow News*, *Ogonyok*, and *Litgazeta*, but in *Pravda* and *Izvestiya*, which we had followed out of a sense of duty, and even in *Sotsialisticheskaya industriya* ("Socialist Industry"), which we had completely ignored.

On April 7, Gavriil Popov called reformers to arms in *Sovetskaya kultura,* the biweekly that overtook *Litgazeta* by the end of our stay as the most radical paper other than *Moscow News.* The piece didn't mention Nina Andreyeva by name but refuted several of her arguments. Popov warned that the decisive battle was not over but had just begun. The June Party conference could be decisive. All would be lost if reformers "ignore the laws of struggle." Opponents of *perestroika* could be beaten if they were deprived of mass support. They were "dangerous only if they succeed in poisoning part of the working class against *perestroika.* If they can do that, then they can crush the reformers and grab the levers of power."

What was remarkable about the piece was its cold, brutal realism. Just a few weeks before, Gorbachev had been preaching unity and consolidation of all forces, including the conservatives. His own change of tone, along with *Pravda*'s, allowed his most radical supporters to go public with the kind of harsh anti-conservative sentiment that we had been hearing from our liberal friends all along. Seryozha, for example, had been saying economic reform required political change. The most trenchant public case yet made for this point of view appeared in *Sotsialisticheskaya industriya* on April 12, once again from the pen of the prolific Popov. His argument was revolutionary: The Party could never maintain the country's superpower status unless it relinquished its own arbitrary rule. The time to begin was now, during election of Party conference delegates. Party officials should constitute no more than one-third of the delegates. The remaining two-thirds should be chosen in competitive elections.

Popov was highly respected as a leading economist. Even so, the fact that he told the Party how to restructure itself was extraordinary. But the habit of giving unsolicited political advice to the Politburo was spreading to even less likely people. Aleksander Gelman is a playwright and movie scenarist. On April 9, *Sovetskaya kultura* published his keynote speech to an open Party meeting of the Cinematographers' Union. At Gelman's suggestion the meeting had voted to advise the Party conference to publish all its speeches without cuts, to hold all Central Committee plenums openly from now on, to limit Party officials to one term of office of eight to ten years, and to require them to justify their worthiness to the public. Too many former leaders had been suddenly revealed, once they were safely out of office, to be unworthy. Even Gorbachev's fate was already being prepared. "Just you wait," one of Gelman's readers had written him, "your Gorbachev will yet be thrown out for '*glasnost* without limits.'" "You see," Gelman continued, "he has the formula all ready."

Gelman didn't invent his proposals; some had been circulating for years. A month or so later they were standard in all the major newspapers. But not on April 9. The friends who pointed out Gelman's speech alerted us to other important features. The text included a long paragraph criticizing Nina Andreyeva. An introductory note to the speech said that Gelman had delivered it on March 23. He had had the courage to speak out before permission was given. But the text was not published until after April 5.

Yury Feofanov's piece in *Izvestiya* on April 18, "The Truckloader Ivan Demura in Nina Andreyeva's Scheme of Things," told how a simple young worker had been caught up in Stalin's terror, arrested for no good reason, tortured, and killed. "There is a rumor going around," wrote Feofanov, "not in the press, but among the people, that Stalin destroyed the bosses, that he decapitated his own 'boyars' with his own hands, and that he was right to do so because all the evil came from the boyars, not the Tsar. . . . If Ivan Demura was an enemy of the people, then *who on earth were the people?*"

But were the people themselves reading Feofanov? More so than one might think. Several days before, we had asked a taxi driver whether people's opinions of Stalin had changed as a result of all the revelations. "They sure have," he said. "That's why you don't see so many pictures of Stalin on dashboards anymore." During the Brezhnev years, Stalin's portrait had indeed appeared in innumerable truck and bus windows. We, like other Westerners, had been dismayed, even after being told the portraits were a protest against Brezhnev-era corruption and stagnation. "We didn't know how many Stalin killed," remarked our taxi driver. "It's only recently that we learned Stalin cared only for himself, and that he killed to increase his power." How many? we asked, thinking of Yevtushenko's famous report of a 1960s Siberian campfire conversation in which students ventured estimates of Stalin's victims ranging up into the hundreds. "Ten million before World War II alone," he answered.

One taxi driver hardly outweighs hundreds of pro-Stalin letters to the editor. Still, it was a sign that the anti-Stalinist message was getting through. Another revelation that made a big impact on the mass reader was Stalin's slaughter of Soviet military officers. Next to shots of the crumbling Cathedral of the Saviour in *More Light,* the film's most devastating image was a long list of army officers executed by Stalin, their dates of death listed in an even row, all murdered by their commander-in-chief in 1937. At an Army Day music-school concert to which Phoebe and Jane were invited by a Russian girl who lived on our block, a middle-level officer who had brought along a group of young soldiers offered a greeting. After hailing the unique Soviet unity between soldiers and civilians, he reminded the audience of times gone by. "Of five marshals, three were liquidated. Of four army commanders, three were executed." And on and on. That these somber statistics would be inflicted on children at a holiday concert was as encouraging as it was startling.

When *Pravda* itself did the talking about Stalinist butchery, we and everyone else listened. Like other major papers in Russia, *Pravda* is tacked up page by page on glass-enclosed bulletin boards around town. In pre-*perestroika* days, hardly anyone was seen reading it. Now, with copies hard to come by at newsstands, small crowds gather to read particularly sensational pieces. We noticed just such a throng on April 29, jockeying for position as they read. The object of this scrutiny was a full-page exposé entitled " 'Conspiracy' in the Red Army," which quoted from secret-police archives as well as the testimony of torturers who were arrested when murdered military officers were rehabilitated in the 1950s. According to this testimony, the sadistic, gnomelike NKVD chief, Nikolay Yezhov, had chosen people with doubtful pasts as his main investigators, precisely because they would go to any lengths to obey his orders. The piece revealed that when some of the accused appealed to Stalin, trying desperately to get word to him that incomprehensible injustice was being done in his name, the "Great Leader and Teacher and Friend to the Armed Forces," as he liked to be known, dismissed their pleas with "some cynical phrases" and sent them to their deaths.

"Some cynical phrases"—clearly the notes scribbled in the margins by Stalin and his cronies were curses. *Pravda* was still a little squeamish. But Arkady Vaksberg was not. The stunning thing about his piece in *Litgazeta* on the fate of Meyerhold and Babel was that he described in sickening detail just how the great theater director and the master short-story writer were beaten and tortured.

The list of path-breaking pieces went on. It included Space Institute director Roald Sagdeev's devastating dissection of Soviet scientific backwardness, warning

that only in full openness to the outside world can a cure
be found, and literary critic Yury Burtin's call to move
the rubber-stamp soviets toward the status of real legis-
latures by allowing multiple candidates to be nominated
without Party control. Yury Levada, a sociologist, and
Viktor Sheynis, an economist, found an original way to
give voice to their own deepest doubts in their conversation with "Skeptic," who worried, among other things,
that a revolution from above could never produce real
democracy from below.

Foreign policy had been mostly off limits until Foreign Minister Eduard Shevardnadze signaled in several
speeches that public criticism was needed and welcome. It began to appear in professional journals with
small circulations. But these efforts paled in comparison
to a long mid-May piece in *Litgazeta* that turned the
standard interpretation of Soviet foreign policy upside
down. Bill had never heard of its author, Vyacheslav
Dashichev, who, we later learned, was a specialist on
modern German history.

Dashichev mocked the fact that "you will not find a
single mention of the slightest mistake or error in books
and articles about our foreign policy. No matter what
was done, everything is depicted as infallible. Is it possible seriously to believe that, while we were commit-
ting major mistakes in internal development, we
managed to avoid them in the international arena in all
those seventy years? This simply cannot be." The long-
standing Party line pictured the USSR as standing almost alone against the dread capitalist encirclement. According to Dashichev, "the hegemonist, great-power
ambitions of Stalinism . . . repeatedly jeopardized political equilibrium between states, especially those of East
and West." The Western response, to join forces against
what was perceived as the Soviet threat, could and
should have been predicted. Instead, "on the one hand
we heightened the level of military danger by advancing

on the West's positions, and on the other we mounted a broad campaign in defense of peace. . . . It is no accident that a joke current in the fifties said: 'There will be such a struggle for peace that everything will be razed to the ground.' "

Dashichev went so far as to accuse "the Brezhnev leadership," whose leading foreign policy specialist, Andrey Gromyko, was still the President of the USSR, of "miscalculations and incompetence." But he did not go so far as to include Lenin in the roster of Soviet sinners. Much more than historical truth is at stake here. As long as Lenin's halo remains intact, so does the legitimacy of the Party itself.

That's why a long article in *Novy mir*'s May issue was the most astounding piece of all. Vasily Selyunin is a largely self-trained economist, we were told, who had acted as gadfly to economic reform since 1985. In 1987 he and another economist, Grigory Khanin, charged in *Novy mir* that the very statistics on which both the economy and efforts to reform it were based were fatally flawed. His latest foray challenged the sacred authority of Lenin. The roots of Stalinism were to be found, Selyunin contended, in the early history of Bolshevism, in the harsh regime of "War Communism," including forced agricultural labor and use of terror against "class enemies." The article went on to argue that such forced labor, which had some precedent under the Tsars, had never been as economically efficient as free labor.

Although we read Selyunin with great excitement, an embarrassing question kept nagging at us. The problem of just how far reformers *should* go is even more painful than how far they *could* go. When did they risk more by giving ammunition to reactionaries than they gained by telling the truth? What about an unbelievable television program we watched one evening in the middle of May?

Called "Public Opinion," the program had two parts. The first revolved around three panels of "experts," on economics, politics, and ideology. Each consisted of people ranging from district Party officials to teachers, students, and workers. The task of each panel was to argue that its area was the key to *perestroika*, the place to focus reformers' energies. At the end of the first hour and a half of the roughly three-hour program, viewers were invited to phone or telegraph their reactions. People watching in Leningrad, where the show originated, were invited to come down to the studio to voice their opinions live on the street. Presiding over the affair, in a booth high above the three panels, was a harried but enthusiastic young woman who was advised by two superexperts, including sociologist Yury Levada.

The first half of the show was fairly predictable. Eager reformers on each panel made their case with genuine excitement. Party officials on each panel paid what sounded like lip service to *perestroika*. Of the three groups, the ideologists were the most spirited, the politicians the most calculating, the economists the most boring (at least to us). The calls and wires that started coming in at half-time surprised the experts. They had expected economics to win, reflecting the widespread demand that *perestroika* prove its mettle by delivering goods in the stores. Instead, politics took the lead, with ideology next.

Meanwhile, crowds were heading down to the studio, surrounding a young newsman who was bravely trying to get them to speak into the microphone one by one. The first few mumbled banalities. The next man, longhaired, bearded, with intense staring eyes, shouted that a Party official on the politics panel had fired him several years ago for no good reason. Would the official like to answer the charge on the screen? the moderator asked. Of course not, but he had no choice but to try. "Dear Ivan Ivanovich," he began in his most unctuous official manner. "I remember you well. Surely you remember the unfortunate circumstances which required

that you be released." If ever a person looked out of
place it was this powerful Party bigwig. Strong men usually trembled in his presence, yet here he was having to
justify himself on television to a long-haired noncon-
formist.

The following scene topped even this. The next per-
son-in-the-street demanded the Communist system's
monopoly of power be replaced by a multiparty system.
Immediately several homemade signs popped into view
proclaiming similar sentiments: "Down with the One-
Party System!" "Let's Have More Than One Party!" We
couldn't believe what we were seeing. The merest whiff
of such sentiment, even in private, had been risky only
a few months before. Suddenly there it was on television, for all the world to see. To be sure, it was late
evening, when the more controversial shows we had
seen were televised. But what if Nina Andreyeva were
up watching in Leningrad, with or without her impres-
sionable students? What would they think of the sight of
people milling around on the street shouting what we
had assumed until then would be treated as "anti-Soviet" slogans? Strangely, the show's moderator and her
advisers seemed unperturbed by the spectacle, as if the
USSR had a tradition of free speech and assembly dating
back more than five minutes. We felt like shouting out,
"Turn off that camera, you fool! Get those idiots off the
screen before they screw up *perestroika* for good!"

FEMINISM?

Item: Nina Andreyeva's reactionary letter railed against "discussion of sexual problems in the press."

Item: Andreyeva's role as a stalking horse for the conservatives reminded Soviets with long memories of the even more infamous Lydia Timashuk, a physician who in 1952 triggered a purge of Kremlin doctors with mostly Jewish names by accusing them of poisoning top Soviet leaders.

Item: During our March visit to *Ogonyok* the letters editor revealed a startling fact: about 90 percent of those who write to defend Stalin are women. When Jane asked for an explanation, an older *Ogonyok* staffer, only partially in jest, snapped back, "Longing for a strong man."

Item: On a recent Seattle–Leningrad spacebridge, when an American participant inquired whether sexually suggestive advertising existed in the Soviet Union,

a Leningrader leaped up and defended his homeland:
"We don't have any sex!"

Item: We realized some time ago that in Russian
"feminism" is a negative word. This spring, when she
tried to figure out why that was, Jane was told, "Feminism is bad because it means the feminization of men."

All these items raised issues that Jane in particular
had been puzzling over for some time—issues concern-
ing the role of women in Soviet society and in Moscow
Spring. From the perspective of American politics, in
which the "gender gap" has become an important reality, we expected women to be among the strongest supporters of Gorbachev's reforms, with their new concern
for the "human factor" and the interests of the consumer. We already know that the anti-alcohol campaign
was popular with women; alcohol is the major cause of
family strife, wife-beating, and divorce in the USSR. In
a televised visit to a factory in Latvia last year, Gorbachev was heard to remark, "Women are my greatest
supporters," and Jane was already working out a hypothesis on the unappreciated importance of the "women's
lobby" in Gorbachev's reforms.

On the other hand, we were increasingly puzzled by
a persistent pattern in which women were the strongest
supporters of the status quo, fighting to preserve a system that, it seemed obvious to us, oppressed them even
more harshly than their brothers. We recalled our reaction to the BBC-TV *Comrades* series last year. Its portraits of Soviet citizens left us with the strong impression
that it was the women at the low and middle levels of
society—teachers, a judge, a Party boss in a small Pacific
coast city—who provided the glue that kept this un-
workable system from falling apart altogether. Perhaps,
we were beginning to think, that was the answer: faced
with the primary task of keeping their families function-
ing and raising their children, women had a strong inter-

est in making the existing system work. No matter how
flawed, it was a system they had learned to live with,
and change was not guaranteed to bring improvements
—it might just make things worse.

Such female conservatism raised another question:
Why had no women's movement emerged from Moscow
Spring? Was it possible to speak of "women's consciousness" in the Soviet context? Was there such a thing as
Soviet feminism? We recalled some gloomy precedents.
A small group of Leningrad feminists, toward the end of
the 1970s, began publishing an underground journal
voicing feminist concerns. Almost all of them, including
Tatyana Mamonova, their most vocal spokesperson,
were promptly expelled from the country. Yet when Mamonova was invited to speak at Amherst, Jane as translator found herself caught in the middle between the
speaker and our closest emigré friend, Vika, a woman
who had taken an active role in the dissident movement
before leaving the USSR in the late 1970s. Vika has
never had any sympathy for Western feminism, which
she sees as a plaything for the pampered; in the Soviet
context, she felt, the problems facing society in general
were far more important than any particular to women.
Though a few women—notably Natalya Gorbanevskaya,
Larissa Bogoraz, and Elena Bonner—played important
roles in the dissident movement, many women close to
the movement felt their role was to provide psychological, spiritual, and material support to the men who were
its most visible leaders and who most often drew prison
sentences. Vika and Mamonova, before a packed hall of
students, publicly accused each other of being KGB
agents.

If the Soviet mind is not receptive to feminism, it is
even less receptive to open manifestations or discussions of sexuality. Strangely enough, political taboos
have fallen more rapidly than sexual ones; a Victorian
reticence about discussions of anything remotely sexual

remains the rule, a legacy of Stalinism. Homosexual
practices are still punishable by law. But even here
there are hints of change. The Leningrad spacebridge
anecdote quoted above was told to us by several different friends with a sense of satisfaction that Soviet society was now overcoming such attitudes and could laugh
at itself. But the recent flood of explicit sexuality in
Western films, videos, and rock music threatens chaos to
Nina Andreyeva and her like. Is there indeed, as that
Ogonyok staffer's flip remark seems to imply, any connection between sexual and political repression? All we
can do is offer some of the evidence we collected. Here
are two passages from the recent Soviet press:

> I'm not inclined to idealize women. But one must see
> clearly how and in what ways they differ from men. In
> the male sex we more frequently encounter bright tal-
> ents; both genius and evil are more clearly expressed.
> The peaks are the lot of men. Woman has the firm
> golden mean. Men are more varied in their inclina-
> tions and aptitudes, they are the innovators in the or-
> ganization of life. Women are more conservative and
> stable precisely because they are the transmitters of
> life. For that reason, they become major criminals far
> less often than men. Much in them is defined by the
> function of childbearing. It's bad when that is forgot-
> ten.
>
> There can be no return to the past, but I don't like
> some of the results of emancipation. Women have de-
> cided to place the entire burden of cares upon their
> own shoulders. As a result, men have nothing to
> "carry," while women bear a double load. We now
> see women pressing men in spheres where they
> shouldn't. There are many weak, effeminate men and
> aggressive women.

The authors of these two quotations sound like dyed-in-

the-wool male chauvinists. Actually, the first is acade-
mician Tatyana Zaslavskaya, head of the Soviet Socio-
logical Association and one of Gorbachev's most
influential advisers on economic reform and social policy, and the second, the talented young writer Tatyana
Tolstaya. What are we to make of these two statements?

Nowhere in conversations, public statements, or rare
discussions in the press did we find objections to
"macho" attitudes in men, but rather the reverse—an
appeal for "more masculinity." Soviet women often express longing for a strong man in their private as well as
their public lives. Far from complaining that they and
society are dominated by men, we were often told by
both men and women that most families are in fact dominated by women, because the men are unwilling or unable to take a stronger role. A popular proverb goes,
"Man is the head of the family, but woman is the neck;
whichever way the neck turns, so turns the head." One
tentative hypothesis is that the stifling bureaucratic hierarchy of Soviet society has indeed emasculated men,
who have to kowtow constantly to their superiors in the
workplace. From their wives, they expect (and get) a
great deal of emotional support, almost to the point of
mothering.

The women's consciousness that is very tentatively
beginning to evolve in the Soviet Union will take different forms from that in the West because of a very different historical background. The "woman question" was
always an element of Russian nineteenth-century radical ideological baggage—so much so that by the end of
the century Chekhov was satirizing "bluestockings" like
Uncle Vanya's mother. The October Revolution ostensibly solved everything by giving women full legal and
economic rights, equal pay for equal work, and equal
access to professional education. The Soviet Union
today presents the odd spectacle of a society that has
overcome many of the educational and professional ste-

reotypes still common in the West while maintaining what seem to us antediluvian sex-role stereotypes.

Women make up more than half of the chemistry students at Moscow University; many Russian women are engineers, and "math anxiety" does not seem to be a problem among women students at any level. Yet within society and the family, traditional sex roles remain far stronger and less challenged than in the West. Though men often help with grocery shopping (necessity requires it), we never saw a Russian man cook more than a snack or boast of his culinary skills. The kitchen remains women's domain—indeed, for many Soviet women, their only area of autonomy. They seem to find this a powerful role, and they don't welcome offers of help from guests. The kind of gallant yet down-putting gestures American men have learned to forgo in the last dozen years are all too common in Soviet society, and women don't seem to notice or object. Recent Soviet films are rife with insensitive male behavior that women forgive again and again. The bureaucrat in *Forgotten Melody for Flute*, for example, seduces his visiting nurse after persuading her to stay and do the dishes. She readily agrees because, she says, "it's not man's work."

The husbands in the families we know best, all of them members of the literary or scientific intelligentsia, are the most sensitive and gentle of men. Equality seems to reign in these homes, with the husband respecting the wife and her profession and taking a large role in childrearing. But it is difficult to know how widespread such families are—we were often told they were found almost exclusively among the intelligentsia. And these are not the patterns and attitudes one sees in films and on TV or hears in many unembarrassed public statements.

At a question-and-answer session with rural schoolteachers in Odessa, Jane was told that the shortage of male teachers in Soviet schools is a big problem, because "they are more intelligent and have stronger character." This comment, from a self-assured middle-aged woman teacher, evoked approving nods from a roomful of her largely female colleagues.

We had expected that Raisa Gorbachev would be widely admired, as she is in the West. Instead, we found most Soviets do not like her. Our friends criticized her shrill, not very cultured Russian and the clichéd expressions to which, as a teacher of Marxism-Leninism—a subject regarded as a joke at most universities—she often has recourse. Working-class women, we were repeatedly told, despise her for "not knowing her place." Some resent the fact that she draws a sizable salary for her position on the board of the new quasi-independent Soviet Cultural Fund. Few if any see her new prominence as a step forward for Soviet women in general.

While Western women are still struggling for full access to the workplace, particularly in the professions, many Russian women are struggling for the opportunity to put more of their time into motherhood. An article in the International Women's Day issue of *Sobesednik*, the weekly magazine supplement to the youth-oriented *Komsomolskaya pravda*, articulated this point of view: "Motherhood is also a creative profession. And the sooner we realize that a talented mother and wife is just as significant a member of society as a good professional, then the more possibilities there will be for women to realize themselves either in the family or at work." A selection of readers' letters accompanying the article emphasized the theme of family happiness in childbearing, along with the problems posed by current conditions: "It's boring and lonely for our husbands at home. A husband with many children won't cheat on his wife. But for a man to support such a family without exhausting himself, his salary should be raised by a factor of two." The author goes on to propose a computer matchmaking system (never hinting that such things already exist in the West) as a solution to the large number of single "and unhappy" women. "The most terrible thing in life is loneliness. It seems to me that the greatest harm is done to society by a single woman and a lazy man."

Such articles and the letters they inspire reveal a new wave of concern about the importance of the traditonal family. Many of the younger families we met had two children rather than the one which was long the urban norm; on the other hand, due to the alarmingly high divorce rate, the two children often had different fathers. We knew several couples who had consciously decided to make their children's upbringing their first priority, at the expense of the wife's, or even the husband's, career. They had arranged their work schedules so that one of them was always at home with the children, keeping them as long as possible from the state-run day-care centers where both viruses and intellectual regimentation are rife. The traditional babysitting grandmother is fast fading from the scene; the grandmothers of today's preschoolers are themselves still working, many at rewarding professional jobs. Many young parents look with hope to the parent coop day-care centers now being organized under the new economic reforms.

Despite Gorbachev's much-touted anti-alcohol campaign, alcoholism still remains the major threat to the family. Though drinking among women is serious enough that the USSR has a significant birth-defect problem from fetal alcohol syndrome, male alcohol abuse is so taken for granted that the *Sobesednik* article begins: "Good husbands don't come ready made—you have to create them. Nature works on the principle of 'but . . .': talented and intelligent—but drinks. Or—he doesn't drink, and he's talented, but greedy. . . . A woman must understand what she can accept, and what she cannot make her peace with."

There are some tentative stirrings—an article here and there in *Literaturnaya gazeta* or *Moscow News* raising women's issues—but feminist theory and feminist scholarship, as they are known in Western intellectual circles, are unknown. Whenever Jane began to explain the simplest premises of feminist scholarship, merely raising the question "Does the gender of the reader make any difference in the reading of a work of literature?" or "Might the gender of the historian affect the questions asked of history and the questions assumed to be most important in social science?" she would always get a positive, thoughtful response: "I never thought about that. That's interesting." Not only our close friends but some of Bill's political contacts were astonished when Jane asked why the infamous Andreyeva letter appeared over a woman's signature when the vast majority of political leaders and political commentators in the country are male. The question had never occurred to them.

Women are only beginning to see sexual discrimination in certain kinds of consumer goods shortages. In the spring of 1988, *Moscow News* featured a full-page article by a pregnant journalist complaining about the impoverished state of Soviet maternal health care, including the reusable syringes used to draw blood samples right underneath a poster warning of the spread of AIDS. The situation was no better in a maternity shop where she sought to buy a female undergarment that was "first mentioned openly in the Soviet press" only recently. She asked for an "85S in cotton and fastening up the front." She was told: "No, we haven't got that size. They come in very rarely. We have size 105B and I advise you to take it while it's available. You'll sew in the straps and the rubber band at the back. Besides, it'll shrink anyhow after laundering." Moscow's first-ever beauty-contest (at least in living memory) was not a development Western feminists are likely to applaud.

Nevertheless, *Moscow News,* which put a photo of the winner on its front page, reported that "the contestants all complained about the bad conditions: one makeup room for 36 girls, no hot water, no place to get decent food." In a much starker vein, the press has debated possible causes of a rash of self-immolations by young, Westernized women in Uzbekistan.

Sex-role stereotyping extends to holidays; Soviet Army day on February 23 was clearly a male holiday. Little girls congratulated little boys in school (as future soldiers), women in offices ceremonially congratulated the men. But International Women's Day, two weeks later on March 8, was the occasion for a long weekend, during which the university library was closed for two days, the Lenin Library for one. As commemorated in the USSR, the holiday was a combination of Mother's Day and Valentine's Day with a celebration of spring and fertility thrown in. Celebrations began the previous Saturday evening, with a televised gala in the Bolshoi Theater. Mikhail Gorbachev and most of the Politburo occupied center stage, but, for once, he never said a word. The keynote speech was given by Valentina Tereshkova, who since her pioneering space flight has served as the Soviet Union's leading "official woman." She was followed by a popular middle-aged film star, whose speech was a model of old-fashioned chivalry: "woman as wife, mother, inspiration." The audience, evidently composed of women Party activists, loved every word of it.

Tributes to Soviet women occupied newspaper headlines for three days. On the holiday itself, *Pravda* proclaimed in big red letters above the masthead: "Happy Holiday, Glorious Daughters of the Motherland!" The front page featured portraits of a woman eye doctor and a milkmaid who had won both the Order of Hero of Socialist Labor and the State Prize. The two front-page portraits in *Izvestiya,* which now has the reputation of being livelier than *Pravda,* were of an ancient Russian country woman in her Sunday best and kerchief, posing in front of a laden tea table with samovar and china, and a young doctor or nurse, her eyes sparkling above her gauze mask, proudly holding aloft a chubby, squalling newborn girl.

The Communist Party leadership may suddenly have discovered the importance of women's issues; Ronald Reagan certainly made a big hit in Moscow with his praise of Russia's hard-working, self-sacrificing women. Moreover, in down-pedaling defense spending while tackling a bloated bureaucracy, Gorbachev is taking on two overwhelming male constituencies, though one could argue that behind each pampered bureaucrat or general there stands a wife accustomed to the privileges her husband's position has brought. The Women's Day celebration was aimed at not only young working mothers but traditionalist older women like Nina Andreyeva who are frightened that loosening political and cultural controls will undermine the very foundations of Soviet society.

On the eve of the holiday, *Izvestiya* featured a long interview with sociologist Tatyana Zaslavskaya. She first attracted attention in the West in 1983 as the author of the unpublished "Novosibirsk Memorandum," which made the case for far-reaching economic and social reform based on recognition of the "human factor." Attached to the Siberian branch of the Academy of Sciences, Zaslavskaya long resisted the temptation to move to Moscow. Only in the spring of 1988 did she agree to become the Moscow-based head of the Soviet Union's first institute for polling public opinion, a science she is the first to admit is in a primitive state.

Yet Zaslavskaya's professional concerns were raised only at the end of the interview. The beginning of the full-page piece and the large photo that accompanied it reflected traditional sex-role stereotypes. Other photos we had seen of Zaslavskaya showed a businesslike woman with her gray hair in a short, no-nonsense cut. In the *Izvestiya* photo, she is wearing a softly draped dress and a big smile, her hair freshly coiffed in a fluffy, feminine style. But the real stunner is the pose—she is proffering a samovar! Her typewriter and eyeglasses are barely visible on a table in the background, but it is as hostess that *Izvestiya* chose to portray her.

The interviewers began by raising the issue of sexual inequality in positions of power and influence—a question unlikely to have been broached in print even a year earlier. Zaslavskaya denied any personal discrimination but went on to say that "the majority of women don't have the ambition to rise to the highest levels in their careers." As explanation, she is not afraid to point to the barrier that Soviet family life poses: "If a woman wants both family and career, then in our conditions she is placed in an extremely difficult position."

On the subject of *perestroika*, she suggested that "first and foremost the life of women will be lightened by a richer marketplace." But the example she used struck us as odd. Food shortages, she noted in passing, were obvious. She complained instead about hair dye—not only its poor quality, but its irregular availability: one month only henna, the next black, the next bright blond. We had noticed how many Russian women dye their hair—the quality of the dyes makes it hard *not* to notice—but we still wondered why Zaslavskaya chose this particular item on which to base her case.

The two best-known contemporary women writers, Tolstaya and Grekova, have both taken pains to deny that they are "women writers." In an interview last year, Tolstaya responded in this vein:

Q. Why is it that Russian literature, which is rich in women poets, can boast of only a few women prose writers?
A. I don't know why. But so-called "feminine prose" is abundant. It has a variety of hallmarks: confusion of

daily routine with Life, sugariness and "beauty" smacking of a fancy-goods store. One feature is particularly notable—the authors' mercantile psychology. As often as not, an author of this kind gives himself away in small things. For example . . . "a green Zhiguli" or "a red Mercedes" instead of simply "a car"; a "Finnish leather coat" instead of a "black coat."

This is not surprising from Tolstaya, whose prose conveys the poverty of lives whose vision of the world is limited to such details. But, always full of surprises, she continued:

> "Femine prose" is mostly written by men. But, on the other hand, there are also women eager to write "men's prose." I find this deplorable, for a woman painting a moustache on her face is disagreeable.

She concluded with the remark about "effeminate men and aggresssive women" cited earlier.

The USSR has several talented women film directors. Premature death cut short the promising careers of Larissa Shepitko and Dinara Asanova, and Kira Muratova's films *Brief Meetings* and *Lengthy Partings* lay on the shelf for years until they were released in 1987. These, and Muratova's newest film *A Change of Fortune,* chose women as their central characters, but they are mercilessly critical of their heroines in ways only a female viewpoint allows. Muratova's films are idiosyncratic; though they are acclaimed by film critics, Jane found herself watching them in nearly empty theaters, surrounded by puzzled moviegoers.

In 1988 sexual taboos began to fall, at least a little. Several articles in the press, including a wide-circulation magazine for youth, *Smena,* and a popular Soviet film magazine, complained about the prohibitions on erotic scenes in the Soviet cinema. *Soviet Screen* even interviewed three of those in the department responsible for editing and dubbing foreign films bought for the Soviet market. One of the bureaucrats insisted that prudish or political cuts were no longer being made, promising that Coppola's *The Conversation*, Milos Forman's *Amadeus*, and Fellini's *Ginger and Fred* would all reach the Soviet viewer in the coming season "without a meter cut."

We noticed a more forthright attitude toward sexuality in recent Soviet films, and somewhat greater frankness in its depiction. Respected film director Mikhail Schweitzer managed to bring to the screen a version of Leo Tolstoy's sexually obsessed classic, *Kreutzer Sonata. The Observer,* a production of the Estonian film studio which premiered in late May, broke new ground with a sensitively photographed, yet totally explicit, scene of male and female nudity in a traditional Russian bathhouse. Roman Viktiuk, one of the most active and experimental of Soviet stage directors, was rehearsing a production of Tsvetayeva's *Phaedra* at the Taganka theater, with the marvelously talented Alla Demidova playing the lead. The play's subject matter, though based on Greek myth, is not likely to make a Soviet cultural bureaucrat's heart leap up—incestuous passion and homosexuality in a single package. At one rehearsal, Viktiuk worked on a suggestive scene between Demidova and a young man playing the role of death. Demidova had no trouble with either Tsvetayeva's lines, some of the most frankly erotic ever written in Russian by a poet of either gender, or with the appropriate movements. But the young man couldn't get the hang of it—time and again the director demonstrated how he needed to loosen his hips, but he just couldn't. "Soviet education!" the director muttered under his breath.

We don't think Nina Andreyeva would have liked the production.

SOME ENCHANTED

EVENINGS,

SOME NOT

The sense we got of Russians taking heart, beginning to believe, gathering their courage, was almost palpable after April 5. It was not only what they were doing, but that they constantly asked us to do it with them. Bill's previous public appearances had all been arranged by people we regarded as committed reformers. Now, to his surprise, he was asked to give a public talk on American views of Soviet history and politics at two history institutes that he regarded, if not as bastions of conservatism, then at least as outposts of the uncommitted. Jane had been getting more involved with people she met at the first Brodsky evening, who were planning a second. Even before April 5, they had asked her to help get a tape of Brodsky reading his poetry. Shortly after April 5, they asked her to speak at the evening herself, before what turned out to be an audience of more than a thousand people.

By the time we left Moscow we were both fending off almost daily invitations to speak or be interviewed. Jane's Brodsky performance brought a plea to do an encore at yet another evening in the poet's honor. When she declined on the grounds that we would be in Leningrad, the persistent organizer offered to pay her round-trip fare if she would come back for just the evening. The same woman, whose job was to organize cultural or political evenings for one of the professional unions, wanted us both to discuss American views of *perestroika*, if possible with a couple of Soviets to give balance to the evening, by ourselves if we preferred. When the date slipped past the Reagan-Gorbachev meeting, she added the summit and American views thereof to our agenda. When it turned out we couldn't appear after all, due to pre-departure pressures, she made us swear on a stack of *Pravdas* that we would appear in her hall on our very next trip.

All this activity was as heady as it was instructive. *Perestroika* itself might or might not be lifting off into orbit, but we certainly were. And yet, just as there had been a "Yes, but" in the dead of winter, so there was even at the height of Moscow Spring. Virtually every one of the evenings, lectures, and meetings we attended had a "down side," an aspect or epilogue that gave cause for concern about the future of reform.

On Friday, April 15, we headed for the Hammer and Sickle factory's Palace of Culture for a four-hour celebration of Joseph Brodsky, who had been twice exiled in his native land, once to the far north from Leningrad as a "social parasite," and later to the West. The evening had not been publicized in the press, yet a block from the entrance we encountered a small horde of people trying to get tickets. It was hard to believe a poet who had only recently been published in the USSR for the first time in two decades had that many fans. Most of them didn't even know what he looked like. Fortunately, Jane had brought along a copy of Brodsky's English prose collection, *Less Than One,* which has a portrait on the back cover. Later in the evening, when a note came forward lamenting that "we young people don't even have an image of the poet's face," she slipped the book to the evening's master of ceremonies, who held it up for all to see.

The evening began at seven o'clock and lasted nearly five hours with only one brief intermission, but the audience was absorbed and attentive throughout. The host, Yakov Gordin, a Leningrad writer and historian, was an old friend of Brodsky's. He and other friends reminisced about the poet, reading his poems to them and some of theirs to him. An intense, charismatic actor named Mikhail Kozakov, who is one of the country's stars, declaimed several long poems from memory. Afterward he told us that he had an agreement to record them for *Melodiya,* the official state record company. Viktor Yerofeyev, the young critic and prose writer who had answered Gorelev's *Komsomolskaya pravda* attack on Brodsky in *Ogonyok,* offered a nuanced appreciation of Brodsky's work. Two bards, one of them Alek Mirzoyan, whom Jane had admired at the first Brodsky evening, sang Brodsky poems to guitar accompaniment.

The highlight of the evening was the reading of a piece of Kafkaesque prose we never expected to hear spoken aloud in the USSR, certainly not before a thousand people at the Hammer and Sickle house of culture. A brave woman named Frida Vigdorova had attended Brodsky's 1964 trial and compiled a transcript, which was published in the West in the 1960s. Why didn't Brodsky work for a living, the judge wanted to know. "I did work. I wrote poetry," Brodsky replied. Who had included him among the ranks of poets? Where had he studied? the judge demanded. "I thought it came from . . . God" was the reply.

The transcript still appalls. And was still political dynamite, we would have thought. But the only concession the evening's organizers made to its explosiveness was that they had it read by a high school teacher, a brave young man whose politically induced nervousness was masked by the uneasiness any nonperformer would have felt on reading a lengthy text on such an occasion. The audience was hushed. Only later, when it was time to answer written questions, did their horrified curiosity pour forth. "How could this have happened?" "How could it not have?" one of the speakers replied. "This is a lesson in citizenship for the younger generation." "It should be published," someone else added. Shortly after our return to Amherst, one of our friends wrote with the news that indeed it had been, in a mass-circulation magazine.

Jane had been asked to speak about Brodsky as a teacher of literature in America. Introduced as an American professor of Russian literature, she was greeted by prolonged applause—not a tribute to her talk since she had yet to utter a word, but rather to the Moscow Spring that allowed her to appear on stage. We learned later that the people who authorized her appearance were chagrined to discover what they had done. Hammer and Sickle authorities had rubber-stamped a program for the evening that included "D. [for Dzhayn] Taubman, philologist"; they had no reason to suspect she was an American. Jane's subject seemed like an anticlimax, but her remarks turned out to be unique. The other tributes inevitably had an elegiac quality about them; they recalled encounters that had occurred more than two decades ago. Jane described a man she had seen only months before, guiding students through not only Russian poetry but that of modern Europe and imperial Rome, insisting that they memorize long passages in English as well as Russian in the belief that the music in their heads would uplift their own writing, launching boldly into a course on Mandelstam and Tsvetayeva in which he never did get to Tsvetayeva.

When she was finished, the audience brought her back to center stage several times with rhythmic clapping. They wanted an encore, but what was she to perform? Someone shouted a request that she read a Brodsky poem composed in English or in the poet's own translation, but she had none with her and none memorized either. One note, passed forward from the audience, commented in touchingly broken English, "Thanks to Judge Savelyeva, that she made Brodsky to work—and *where!*"

Shortly before midnight the evening came to an end. As the audience began to file out, the sound of Brodsky's voice resounded over the loudspeaker reading his Nobel Prize lecture, this time loud and clear. A few people continued on their way home. Most stood listening in the half-darkened hall. Our own reverie was interrupted by several people from the audience who approached as we were leaving. One was an older woman with a pair of mittens she wanted us to take to Brodsky. "It must be cold there, too," she said. The other was an unkempt young man who said he had experienced life after death and wanted to talk about it on the way to the metro.

Not long after this inspiring evening, a scientist friend of one of its organizers spent another trying to convince us that it had been less inspiring than we thought. We had been invited to Oleg's apartment for an evening of poetry and song. But he was determined to deflate what he considered our overestimation of the event his friends had arranged. It did not signify, he insisted, that the reforms were for real. What the regime was really after was *peredyshka,* or breathing space, at a time when economic stagnation and military weakness made it vulnerable to the U.S. Star Wars program. Most of the reforms were simply for show, like Gorbachev's taking Raisa with him to Washington. There was nothing of "real significance."

What would constitute "really significant" change, we

asked. "Allowing other political parties to operate," he said. Oleg had other arguments. Those articles in the press that had made such an impact on us had been authorized, if not ordered, from above. They could evaporate overnight if five or ten of the leading reformist editors were ousted. When was the last time we saw Gorbachev himself criticized by name in the papers or on television? Oleg's real fear was not so much that Gorbachev would reverse himself under conservative pressure, or even that he would be ousted, but that he would be followed by a period of out-and-out fascism. Gorbachev's immediate successors would not want that; neither would they seek to return to Brezhnevism or Stalinism. But they would try to continue *perestroika* without *glasnost*, and that effort would fail as all half-measure reforms had failed before. So stagnation would return, to be attacked next time by an alliance of Stalinists and extreme Russian nationalists using anti-Semitism to blame the mess on the Jews, force and violence to try to change it, and a renewal of the cold war, or, *in extremis*, even a hot war, to justify the return to full-blown totalitarianism at home. Oleg said his fears were shared by many of his friends. Sometimes it seemed they talked of nothing else. But had we seen any such fears expressed in the media? Of course not. That, too, was off limits under the *glasnost* that we found so impressive.

But if everything he said was true, why was it worth organizing an event like the Brodsky evening in the first place? "Because it was the right thing to do," he replied.

The right thing for another group of artists and aestheticians, who called themselves the "Circle Artistic Association," was to organize a multimedia artistic happening built around *Assa*, one of the season's most talked-about movies. The film, whose sound track features the most popular rock musicians, was scheduled to open in midwinter at one of the largest downtown first-run theaters. The Udarnik's cavernous lobby was to contain an exhibit of avant-garde art, *Assa* posters and T-shirts would be sold, and the film would be preceded by a rock concert and an avant-garde fashion show. But this all got to be too much for the theater management, which panicked and cancelled the event.

The organizers would not take no for an answer. They found yet another industrial house of culture, this time belonging to the electric light factory, that was willing to take them in. Its high-Stalinist, pseudo-classical architecture provided a fine foil for the event. We were lucky enough to get tickets to the final performance on a Sunday in mid-April, and we invited some of our Soviet friends. As we waited outside to be admitted, they pointed out some of Moscow's "hottest" cultural luminaries: the woman director of Bulgakov's *Heart of a Dog*, one of the top editors of *Ogonyok*. The poet Yevtushenko, who had hosted all four Taubmans at his dacha several days before, showed up in a red and black buffalo-plaid wool jacket and cap à la L. L. Bean and elegant alligator cowboy boots. When he returned Alex's friendly greeting, "Hi, Zhenya," a teen-age friend, already in awe that we had procured tickets, was astonished at our "celebrity."

Inside we found the three floors of rooms, halls, and stairways all filled with art, much of it mocking what used to be the holiest of Soviet holies. The large lower hall was dominated by a huge construction of columns covered with reproductions of Stalin-era newspapers into which a whole forest of large nails had been hammered. On top of the columns were conical wire-mesh grids holding parts of dismembered dolls, the "souls of those victims of the years of repression," according to the pessimistic Seryozha, who was delighted we had gotten him tickets. In the "sky" over the cones hovered strange airplane-like shapes, prominently featuring a large caviar tin of the type only available to those with privileged access to special stores. Another room satirized Soviet official culture—a huge painting of Stalin waving beneficently at three blissful schoolgirls, two blown-up postcard-like portraits of pudgy Soviet all-rightniks on vacation—plus, incongruously, a larger-than-life image of pop star Alla Pugacheva in a bikini. A full room was devoted to a scene representing the "period of stagnation." A vast upside-down portrait of Brezhnev covered the floor; the walls were lined with distorting mirrors, and a square of metal, labeled in English "Iron Curtain," hung between the exhibit and the spectators.

All the political art was great fun. Though other works were less impressive, there was throughout a young, rebellious spirit exuberant at being released, much of it reminiscent of America's 1960s. For the moment, its prime subject was the years of stagnation, but where would it go next? The paradox of *glasnost* is that in freeing the artist to create as he chooses, it forces him to find something to talk about besides his former constraints.

The concert that day included an entire hour of Aquarium, the best-known and most admired popular music group in the USSR today. It consists of a flute, two violins, and a cello along with the requisite guitars, drums, and synthesizers. Its main man is the tall, pony-tailed, iconoclastic Boris Grebenshchikov, whose flair for self-promotion seems to equal his substantial musical talent. He had composed much of the score for *Assa*. We found the group's music to be inventive rather than acoustic and quite agreeable.

The next group on the bill, "Sounds of Mu" (presumably for "Music"), was absurdist and minimalist in both gestures and music. Its leader, a painfully thin man in a black zoot suit, seemed to be trying to prove that a pseudo-spastic could lead a non-band. Alex's friend told us that "Sounds of Mu" was mild compared to certain other groups, and that the audience gathered at the electric light factory had nothing on the leather-clad, purple-haired heavy *metalisty* who frequented really "in" rock concerts.

After the fashion show, in which two lines of models snaked on and off stage in black and white variations on outfits to be seen in the movie, the film itself began. Like so many Soviet films, it was a bit slow for American taste. It is set in off-season Yalta, where a Soviet gangster (we are told at the end of the film how many millions of rubles he stole from the state) is hanging out with his mistress. A group of young musicians in the hotel befriend her, and one of them falls in love with her. The struggle for the girl becomes a struggle of generations: the old and corrupt—at one point the camera lingers on a larger-than-life poster of Brezhnev, to set the historical time and theme—and the young. To underline this theme, the film is interlaced with flashbacks of the assassination of mad Tsar Paul I, condoned by his son and heir Alexander I. The film breaks new ground by legitimating youth culture and rock music. Several lines from its songs, such as "Changes—we want changes!" were featured in huge posters on the house of culture's walls. But the ending suggests that changes will not come easily. The gangster has the boy murdered before he is himself shot by his moll.

Aleksander Galich, the bard known for his bitterly satirical songs about Stalin and life under Brezhnev, was the subject of two evenings Jane attended in May. Galich was an established writer and film scenarist when he began composing his mordant song-poems. One of our favorites is the story of Klim Petrovich Kolomiitsev, "workshop foreman, holder of many orders, deputy of the town soviet," who is plucked from a drinking bout and driven off to a ritual peace rally. On the way, a speech is shoved into his hands. But it's the wrong speech, and he launches confidently into his peroration at the top of his bass voice: "Speaking as a mother and a woman, I condemn Israeli militarism. . . ." No one, however, is listening carefully, for "the phrases are never any different," and when he finishes, he's roundly applauded by "Number One."

Galich was expelled from both the Writers' Union and the Cinematographers' Union in 1971 after some of his songs had been published abroad. He moved closer to Andrey Sakharov and the dissident movement and was forced into emigration in 1974. His accidental electrocution in 1977 while plugging in a tape recorder in his Paris apartment is still regarded with suspicion by many of his friends and admirers.

Now, suddenly, the program of Galich songs that had been banned during the Andreyeva scare was playing to packed houses. The show, staged cabaret-style with minimal props and a great deal of imagination, was put on by a talented group of young actors who called themselves "The Third Direction." The production had been their graduation project the previous year at one of Moscow's theater schools, and they had finally gotten permission to perform it publicly. Titled "When I Return" it began with a spare, encyclopedia-style account of Galich's life. "Galich, Aleksander . . . Soviet prose writer and dramatist. Born in 1919 in Dnepropetrovsk. Died in 1977 . . . [long, dramatic pause] in Paris." The theme song was "Goldminer's Waltz," Galich's mordant comment on "making it" in the Brezhnev era:

> It's the say-nothings now who rule over us,
> Because, you know, silence is gold.
> Hold your tongue, you'll make number one!
> Hold your tongue, hold your tongue, hold your tongue! *

Just before intermission, the swarthy young actor who had been playing the role of Stalin or Stalinist in various

* Trans. G. S. Smith. (Aleksander Galich: *Songs and Poems* [Ardis, 1983]).

episodes came to center stage, pulled a pipe from the pocket of his military tunic, grinned sardonically at the audience, and snarled in a marked Georgian accent, "This play could be called 'When *I* Return.' " The audience, still in the euphoria of the victory over Andreyeva and company, loved it. The final sequence, as Galich boards the plane that will take him forever from his native land, was an elegy for the entire generation of creative intellectuals forced into emigration during the Brezhnev years. Many in the audience openly wept.

On May 15 Galich was posthumously reinstated in the Cinematographers' Union by many of the same people who had taken part in the unanimous vote to oust him in 1971. His reinstatement in the Writers' Union followed a few weeks later, just after we left. On May 27 there was a gala evening in his memory at the luxurious auditorium of Dom kino. When Jane and a friend arrived nearly an hour before the event was scheduled to begin, there were already no seats to be had; they managed to occupy a few square feet in an aisle.

The poet-bards had been the most genuinely popular cultural figures during the years of stagnation; their words and music helped sustain a generation by providing hints of truth in the miasma of hypocrisy and toadying that pervaded the era. The premature deaths of Galich and Vysotsky were seen by their contemporaries as symbolic. The Vysotsky anniversary just as we arrived and the Galich evening just as we were leaving provided a frame for our Moscow sojourn. Coincidentally, it was filmmaker Eldar Ryazanov who presided at both. On this occasion he publicly expressed the opinion that "most of those who emigrated in the seventies and early eighties were unjustly forced from their homeland." That would have been a bombshell in January; in late May it caused a barely perceptible tremor.

There had originally been four well-known bards. Both survivors were there on May 27 to honor Galich. Bulat Okudzhava sat quietly and unobtrusively in the

balcony, but Yuly Kim's appearance was the highlight of
the evening, and the crowd waited eagerly for him to
come on. Kim, a Korean, is less well known in the West
than his three fellow bards. His songs, now topically and
boldly political, reminded Jane of the Tom Lehrer songs
she and Bill were addicted to in Cambridge in the
1960s. Another highlight of the evening was an older
poet and former political prisoner, Boris Chichibabin,
who read a moving poem with the refrain:

> Until we . . . [Each verse naming some act of civic
> courage]
> Stalin has not died in us.

The poem was one of the few we heard or read in all
those months to tackle the really difficult question—not
of Stalin's guilt, or of the exact magnitude of his crimes,
but of a whole nation's acquiescence and shared guilt.
This question, raised by Nadezhda Mandelstam in her
brilliant memoirs *Hope Against Hope* and *Hope Abandoned,* will trouble the Russian collective conscience
for the next generation. Those memoirs, smuggled to the
West in the 1970s, began appearing in the mass-circulation magazine *Yunost* during Moscow Spring, and her
memory was honored at a literary evening in late April.

At a Peace Committee discussion-club session that
Bill attended the subject was "Freedom of Conscience."
With the millennium of the Christianization of Russia
coming up, it sounded like a propaganda circus. The
presence of Western TV crews, in town to prepare for
the Reagan-Gorbachev summit, added to the impression. But in fact the affair was more complicated than
it seemed. The organizers Bill knew really wanted a
no-holds-barred discussion. Religious believers and
nonreligious champions of religious freedom were determined to use the occasion for their own purposes.

At the entrance to the Prospekt Mira townhouse, Bill

passed a table at which a group of high school girls was collecting signatures on a Peace Committee petition. A bearded man on his way to the meeting stopped to chastise them for peddling an officially sanctioned document rather than one of their own devising. Inside, the man joined other dissident believers—those as disenchanted with the Church hierarchy as with the Communist regime—who were caucusing off to one side. The program seemed stacked against them: first there would be four ten-minute presentations by experts—a philosopher, a churchman, a historian, and a lawyer—and then a second segment devoted to questions to the same speakers. Only then would come the time set aside for short speeches, none to exceed seven minutes.

The fireworks were not long in coming, however. The archdeacon's idea of progress was to get back old churches and monasteries that the government had turned into warehouses. Dissident believers wanted Bibles for the faithful. The lawyer defended freedom of religion as enshrined in early Leninist decrees. When a man who identified himself as a "chemist and a Christian" demanded to know how such freedom could exist in a state that preached atheism, the hall rocked with applause. As the lawyer droned on, someone shouted, "Cut out the demagoguery! Your time is up." A legal scholar with a recognizably Jewish surname attacked the same Leninist legislation that his colleague had just defended. An Islamic clergyman in Western dress declared himself in favor of peace.

The dramatic climax came when a stocky, balding man in a shabby brown suit stood up to defend the rights of Ukrainian Catholics. Banned by the Soviet state, the Uniates have not been recognized by the Russian Orthodox Church either. The man said he had been harassed by the KGB, who tried to stop him from coming to Moscow for this meeting by setting up roadblocks and throwing him off trains. But a miracle had occurred; he had made it to Moscow. "We're glad you managed to get through the blockage," purred the meeting's chairman. "We're delighted you could make it to our *underground* [pause for the sarcasm to sink in] meeting."

Two last meetings Bill attended in May—one a lecture he heard, the other a talk he himself gave—revealed how much had changed since we arrived in January, and also what had not. The subject at the Historical Archives Institute was "World War II Historiography." The war had in effect become the last refuge for Stalinists. Whatever else you say about him, they insisted, Stalin won the war. The lecturer, a military historian, carefully avoided the caricature Khrushchev had popularized of Stalin planning major military offensives on an ordinary globe. He drew up a far more damning indictment. It was no news to the audience that Stalin had wiped out the cream of the Soviet officer corps on the very eve of the war. But how many suspected that the purge of Marshal Tukhachevsky and his colleagues was a sign that Stalin was already thinking in 1937 of the alliance with Hitler in 1939? Tukhachevsky had been agitating for a new anti-Nazi entente with Britain and France; he had to go. The Nazi-Soviet Pact has long been defended in the USSR as a way of postponing a German attack. "A fairy tale, pure and simple," said the speaker. Hitler attacked as soon as he possibly could. The pact did not substantially delay his assault. What it did do was prevent the kind of cooperation with Britain and France that might in fact have deterred him.

Stalin's blind insistence that Hitler would not attack in June 1941 was not new to the institute audience. But few suspected the terrible losses that followed might amount to far more than the long-established official figure of 20 million lives. That awesome figure, derived from census data, was the difference between the actual postwar population and what could have been anticipated in the absence of war. No one had really counted the casualties, said the speaker. They might amount to as many as 24 million. In view of Stalin's role in bringing on the war and then mismanaging key parts of it, the incredible, mind-numbing losses should be laid largely at his door.

While providing these revelations, the speaker shied away from other controversial topics. One questioner asked about the secret protocol attached to the Hitler-Stalin Pact that divided Eastern Europe between them. Someone else called for its publication in the USSR. "There is no such document in our archives," said the lecturer. "The issue needs study." (Later in the summer, an Estonian newspaper would confirm its existence.) How about long-standing charges that Polish officers found murdered in the Katyn Forest were dispatched not by the Gestapo, as Moscow had always contended, but by the NKVD? "I have no idea" was the reply.

About the same time, two of the Academy's history institutes invited Bill and an American colleague to give a joint lecture on American Sovietology, the first talk of this kind at either institute. This was to be a first step toward a conference on Soviet and Russian history to which Western specialists would be invited. Since it was only yesterday that many of the would-be guests had been damned in the USSR as "falsifiers of history," this too was big news. Yet, even in May, we couldn't believe that either the joint lecture or the conference would go smoothly.

Bill and his co-lecturer pulled few punches. They insisted that the Soviet Union under Stalin fit the classical totalitarian mold. Far from being the wave of the future, they said, the Bolshevik Revolution derailed Russia's evolution toward modern democracy. The audience of several hundred listened politely, but both Bill and his colleague wondered if peace would prevail during the question period. It did. One questioner implied that Soviet totalitarianism extended beyond 1953 into the post-

Stalin period. Only an older man, later described by a younger scholar as a "perfect example of a caveman," was mildly hostile.

Where were the conservatives? Two older men who fit the general description approached Bill in the corridor. They were obviously nervous, clearly not used to dealing with an American Sovietologist. One was the "caveman" just mentioned. "Don't you see," he whispered, "Stalin had no choice but to be cruel. Yes, the repressions were a bad thing, but they were inevitable under the circumstances." "May I ask you a favor?" asked the other man with a quick glance over his shoulder. "Let's imagine we're looking down on the earth from high above, so we can be absolutely objective and realistic. Don't you agree that it's in our interest that you be as weak as possible, and in yours to see us the same way? If so, why do you and other Americans favor *perestroika*? By rights, you ought to prefer stagnation for us."

The first point was a standard justification of Stalin. The second exemplified the Stalinist "two-camp" view of the world. Bill didn't accept either, yet he found himself strangely touched by the moment. Both men were the type, he supposed, who would have grave doubts about *glasnost*. Yet it had won over even them, at least for a moment. They had probably never had an opportunity to try their ideas out on an American Soviet specialist. If it had been up to them to arrange the occasion, they never would have. But once it was presented to them, they couldn't resist.

Bill explained that there were two main reasons for Americans to favor Gorbachev's reforms. One was that they aimed at improving the lives of the Soviet people, and Americans were idealistic enough to think that was a good thing. The second reason was more selfish. The notion of a superpower falling apart in the nuclear age, a prospect that was not to be excluded even by Soviet calculations, made Americans nervous. In that sense, too, Americans had a stake in the well-being of the "other side."

"In that case," responded the second man, "I have another question for you. There seems to be a big difference between the Russian and American mentality. Do you agree? How would you describe it?" Bill suggested that Americans tended to be less cynical—more naïve was a less flattering way to put it. The man looked skeptical, probably dismissing Bill's answer as a typical American attempt to pass imperialism off as idealism. But perhaps not entirely. "Well," he said with what seemed like a genuine smile, "it's been nice talking to you."

GENERATIONS

Once you've restructured yourself,
help someone else.
—Homemade button worn by Moscow
University student

N ational education in the culture of democracy will not happen overnight, or in one spring, or even perhaps in one generation. Russians are well aware that the ultimate success of *perestroika* depends not only on them but on those to whom they must inevitably hand over their society. The older generations got the USSR into the mess it is in. The younger generations must get it out. Will they be able to learn democracy in time?

Since the Revolution, the consciousness of each successive Soviet generation has been imprinted by the experiences and lessons of its youth—the revolutionary romanticism of the 1920s, the purges of the 1930s, the war, the terror of late Stalinism, the abortive reforms of Khrushchev, the stagnation of the Brezhnev era. It is not surprising, then, that each generation has responded to *perestroika* in its own fashion.

The generational difference is clearest in politics. Gorbachev is still the youngest member of the Politburo. Western observers have long predicted that sweeping changes in the Soviet Union could come only with a new generation of leadership; those changes have already exceeded their wildest expectations. The conservatives Gorbachev edged out are ten to twenty years his senior; Yegor Ligachev, at sixty-seven, is ten years older. Bureaucratic conservatives like Belousov have the most to lose if *perestroika* forces them into early— or overdue—retirement. Among women, we heard many speak of mothers and grandmothers who are Stalinist "true believers"; though they may not have any bureaucratic power to lose, they face challenges to the principles by which their whole lives have been lived.

Almost all the "heroes" of *perestroika,* the writers, editors, and scholars who are publishing the boldest and most outspoken articles, are in their fifties or early sixties. Their hopes were raised during the Khrushchev "thaw," which coincided with the bright days of their own youth. For the past twenty years, they have been "gathering stones," as one much-discussed essay put it, and this is their last opportunity to expiate their own and their society's sins.

The generation just below them, those in their forties, has been described as the "lost generation." They were coming of age just as the Brezhnev stagnation was setting in, and they had to make their careers by its rules or drop out altogether. Those who took the beaten path are now familiar villains in today's anti-bureaucrat and youth films. Others simply opted out—they either emigrated or chose the route of internal emigration through alcohol.

The next cohort, Soviet "yuppies" in their thirties, knew nothing else but stagnation, and they, we were warned several times, are the most dangerous, for they are totally cynical and preoccupied with "making it" in both the old and the new way. Yet we got to know several representatives of this generation who surprised us with their decency and courage.

Those in their twenties, so dinner-table generalization goes, are the ones who have responded fastest to the new opportunities offered by the cooperative movement; if it succeeds, this is where the new entrepreneurs will come from. Finally, there is the young generation, those now in their teens, and this is the generation about which society is most concerned. Again and again we were told that *perestroika* is a struggle for the future, and for the soul of the generation to whom that future will be entrusted.

In the spring of 1988, history exams for the high school graduating class were cancelled because it was impossible to make students mouth textbook falsehoods that had been unmasked in the press over the past year. This is symbolic of the crisis *perestroika* presents for education. The release of the draft proposal for education reform was a major event of the spring. But even more widespread than such organizational tinkering, no matter how ambitious, was the fundamental reexamination of the values Soviet education is, and ought to be, transmitting. This debate, and the proposed answers, came perilously close to the formerly taboo word "spirituality" (*dukhovnost*), which has, in the past year or two, become a commonplace in the vocabulary not only of the mass media but of Gorbachev himself.

Ludmilla Razumovskaya's play *Dear Yelena Sergeyevna* poses the problem with ruthless frankness. Suppressed for eight years, it was staged this winter by several theaters; just as we left, Eldar Ryazanov's film version opened all over town. The play's namesake, Yelena Sergeyevna, is a typical Soviet schoolteacher, a single woman in her forties, devoted to her profession and her students and genuinely convinced that she has done a good job of inculcating moral values as well as

mathematics. One spring evening, a small group of graduating students shows up on her doorstep with flowers,
champagne, and a gift of crystal goblets, ostensibly to
wish their beloved teacher a happy birthday. She re-
sponds with predictable sentimentality. It gradually
transpires that their real aim is to obtain the key to the
safe where their math exams are stored, to doctor their
papers and raise their grades. All are applying to competitive institutes, and high grades are essential. None
of them will be scientists, they assure her, so it's really
senseless that A's are demanded from them in math as
well as in the humanities. They'll never have to study
math again; who will be hurt by this tiny fraud? In the
process, of course, they reveal the bankruptcy of those
humanistic studies at which they have, at least on paper,
excelled. What is frightening about them is not that they
have failed to learn the lessons taught by their teachers
and parents, but that they have learned them too well,
rejecting the *ostensible* lessons that life has shown to be
empty platitudes.

When Yelena Sergeyevna rejects their proposal, they
turn from flattery and blandishments to threats of force,
even against their own, threatening to rape the one girl
among them if Yelena Sergeyevna refuses their request.
In the course of one terrible evening, all her certainties
are overturned, her students are revealed as moral monsters whose only code is "what's good for me is good,"
and her entire ideological arsenal proves inadequate to
cope with their cynical onslaught. In despair, she hangs
herself.

Jane saw the play at a special showing at which the
rest of the audience was ninth- and tenth-grade students
and their teachers from a special school for gifted science students attached to Moscow University. The discussion, filmed for television, that followed the play
revealed these teenagers to be as articulate as they were
good in math. Asked how close the play came to their

own experience, almost all testified to the truth of its devastating message. They indicted the sterility of the Komsomol and the universal hypocrisy surrounding its high-sounding "code of the young Communist." They gave personal testimony to the bare statistic that Komsomol membership had dropped by the millions in the past year, now that it was no longer essential for admission to higher education and cushy job placement.

Another cloud hanging over Soviet higher education is universal military service. Nearly every Soviet male at age eighteen enters the army, to return two years later, older, wiser and, many told us, brutalized by their service. More than one family spoke of their anxiety about what awaited a son in the army, even now, when the threat of Afghanistan is over. That anxiety can warp entire lives. One family we knew faced a terrible choice: should their gifted son seek admission to one of the few elite scientific institutes that offered exemption from active duty, or should he follow his own talents and inclinations, enroll in the history faculty, and face two or more years of military victimization.

The armed forces remained immune to criticism longer than almost any other sphere of Soviet society. We were told at *Ogonyok* that prior censorship is now only employed to forbid publication on grounds of "national security." But of course that definition is subject to broad application, which used to include anything even slightly critical of the military. By the time we left, even the military was no longer sacred. Articles criticized the severe hazing of new recruits. One particularly eloquent article told of a concerned father, himself a lawyer, who was so shabbily treated by the authorities when he went to complain about the mistreatment of his son that he had a heart attack and died on the spot.

One of the most popular plays in Moscow was Neil Simon's *Biloxi Blues,* acted with talent and spirit by Oleg Tabakov's theater studio. The treatment of Epstein, the Jewish intellectual misfit, brought gasps of surprise from the audience: direct reference to Soviet anti-Semitism was one of the few remaining cultural taboos. As if to underscore the message, the blues music played in the background of the American production was replaced by barely audible Klezmer melodies, the folk songs of the Eastern European *shtetl*. After the performance, we asked one member of the company why this particular play had been chosen. "Because it says some important things about the relationship of the individual and the army," he replied, with a knowing wink. The implication was clear, and true to the old Russian tradition of Aesopian discourse: the troupe was talking about intimidation and ethnic prejudice in the contemporary Soviet army, a subject that could be approached only obliquely, by staging a play that criticized the same things in the American army of forty-five years ago.

Another play, *The Red Corner*, raised the question of education in an even broader philosophical mode. In Russian peasant homes, the red or, in its traditional meaning, "beautiful" corner is the one where the icons hang and to which each entering guest pays homage. In Soviet parlance, it is the corner or room in each organization or factory where newspapers and other politically edifying literature are available.

The play has only two characters, both women. One, dressed in a businesslike suit, holds the post of "educator" at a factory dormitory. Her charges are *limitchiki*, young women workers whose registered residence is outside Moscow but who are recruited to work in the factory in return for humble accommodations and a chance to live in the "Big Cabbage." We watch her trying to "reeducate" a young woman who does nothing each day after work but return to her bunk and drink herself into a stupor. The dorm supervisor tries all the moral pronouncements and cultural blandishments—

theater tickets, museum excursions—that the Soviet regime has put at her disposal. The drunk, hilariously
canny, manages to demolish them one by one. What
other sensible alternative is there in a life like hers, she
argues, than to get drunk every day? She manages to
convince us and, ultimately, her tormentor as well.

As in the United States, the largest segment of the
Soviet moviegoing audience is student age or younger.
So it is not surprising that many of the newest Soviet
films have heroes in their teens or early twenties. But
unlike the current spate of American "youth movies,"
their Soviet counterparts don't pander to their audience;
rather, they reflect society's preoccupation with the generation that grew up in the era of stagnation. What values have they internalized? What do they live by and
for, and how has their parents' generation failed them in
this regard? The new youth films are merciless in condemning the effects of the high divorce rate and parental
alcoholism, showing the younger generation fresh, talented, but already deformed or discouraged by the
world.

In 1987, *Courier* won the grand prize at the Moscow
film festival and was voted best film of the year by the
readers of *Soviet Screen*. For a Soviet audience, it plays
much the same role *The Graduate* did for an earlier
American generation. The hero, Ivan, lives with his di-
vorced schoolteacher mother; his father has married a
younger woman and gone off to work on a Soviet construction project in Africa. The mother focuses all her
remaining hopes on her son and his educational career.
But Ivan will have no part of the traditional Soviet route
to "making it" and intentionally fails the entrance exam
for the uncompetitive pedagogical institute. Though
he's bright and imaginative—indeed *because* he's
bright and imaginative, the film implies—Ivan sees no
place for himself in the stultifying society that surrounds
him. There's not a single sympathetic adult in the entire
film, no hint of the wise mentor figure.

Why should he get involved in anything anyway, asks Ivan, when in a few months he'll have to go into the army? So he eases into the job his mother has found him as a messenger boy in the office of an academic journal. On his first assignment, he takes three hours off to go skateboarding. The beautiful daughter of a "distinguished professor" is attracted by Ivan's brashness and unconventionality. When her father and his friends ask "What is your goal in life?" Ivan stuns them by parroting their own agenda: "A soft job, a good apartment in the center of town, a car and a dacha." But having used his young hero to "unmask" the spiritual emptiness of his parents' generation, director Karen Shakhnazarov has no more idea than Ivan himself of what to do with him. In a final powerful though enigmatic sequence, Ivan wanders the night streets aimlessly, only to encounter a Soviet soldier, suitcase in hand, obviously returning from Afghanistan. Ivan and the soldier stare into each other's eyes for a long moment of recognition, then the soldier looks down in embarrassment.

While in the past self-congratulatory films or war epics won official recognition, these mercilessly pessimistic films are winning the prizes under *glasnost*. A State Prize was awarded last year to *Games for Children of School Age*, made by a talented Estonian director, Arvo Iho, and a young Russian scenarist, Marina Sheptunova. The film is a semidocumentary, set in an orphanage like the one in which Iho himself grew up, and it uses only one professional actor. The tragedy of Soviet orphanages is that few of the children are in fact orphans—their parents, often alcoholics or prisoners, either cannot or will not care for them. Though the children in the film live in pleasant enough physical circumstances, rather like a boarding-school dormitory in a country setting, there is a severe shortage of both staff and human kindness. Left to their own devices, some of the children engage in psychological terrorism, giving back to the world the cruelty it has shown them. In one particularly

horrifying moment, a group of older girls stuff a younger
girl into a clothes dryer and turn on the power.

If Phoebe had stayed longer than four days in her Soviet school, we might have more to say about elementary
education and the changes afoot there. As it was, those
four days taught us a good deal. The school happened to
be one of the best-known "special" English schools in
Moscow. Generals and Party luminaries, we were told,
pulled strings to get their children and grandchildren
admitted. Jane's visit to the school during her November
1987 visit left no doubt that the director was an authori-
tative lady accustomed to dealing with such pressures.
Our discovery that she knew little or no English made
us wonder what other qualifications had brought her the
job, but though brusque, she was perfectly cordial. She
assured Jane in confidence that "we aren't allowed to
turn down American, English, or Canadian children."
One of Phoebe's fellow students was Katya Lichova, the
much-touted "Soviet Samantha Smith."

A week after we arrived, Jane walked Phoebe to her
first day of school. It was a cold, dark January morning,
and Phoebe, dressed in a Soviet school uniform inherited from the daughter of American journalist friends,
was not enthusiastic. She dawdled and dragged her feet.
We got to school a few minutes late, greeted by the
director's stern admonition that we not be late again,
and by the duty student who sat in the hall, jotting down
the names of latecomers. Not an auspicious beginning.

What we had been told about the use of English as the
language of instruction in other subjects turned out not
to be true, at least in the fourth-grade class, which
Phoebe attended. Her major subjects were math, Russian language, Russian literature, Soviet history, and
English. Minor subjects were nature study, physical education, music, and "labor." The teachers themselves
could not have been nicer or more helpful; the Russian-

language teacher spent individual time with Phoebe every day, despite a class of thirty-nine children. Phoebe's favorite class, for obvious reasons, was English. In math, the material was roughly on her level— so much for the Soviets' vaunted math superiority. With minimal Russian, she had no idea what was going on in her Russian literature and Soviet history classes, and after we took a look at her unrevised textbooks, we were rather glad she didn't. We of course did not know, and Phoebe did not have enough Russian to tell us, whether the teacher was teaching with or against the text.

Phoebe reported that the school had far more rules and regulations than either her school in Amherst or the Anglo-American school in Moscow. But behind this façade of strict order lay elements of permissiveness, especially from teachers who seemed restive themselves in the face of bureaucratic rigidity. The school schedule itself was exhausting, as if designed to wear students out rather than encourage imagination and initiative.

Phoebe's second day began with a double period of physical education; in January, that meant cross-country skiing. We had brought our skis along with us, so off Phoebe went, apprehensive about her ability to keep up. "Don't worry," Jane said in a phrase Phoebe would never let us forget, "just because they're Russian, it doesn't mean that they're all excellent skiers." For two full hours, they ran ski races in the park behind the school. Phoebe's game struggle to keep up may have contributed to the flu that struck her down a few days later. Though our opening-day encounter with the director had left us intimidated, we later discovered that the demands on foreign children are negligible, and they would readily have excused Phoebe from any activity.

Dismissal time was variable, depending on how many forty-five-minute lessons were on the schedule, but it was generally between one and two o'clock. In midmorning the children were given a snack, usually tea with either a roll or a piece of bread with sausage. After classes they went home to dinner, the major meal of the day, or to an after-school program, for which they could sign up on a day-to-day basis at minimal extra cost, featuring dinner followed by crafts and recreational activity. The shorter school day was balanced by the fact that classes met on Saturday as well. Phoebe found this the final indignity. (Some Soviet schools are now experimenting with a five-day week.)

On Phoebe's first Saturday, a double "labor" class was scheduled. Phoebe's new friends Katya and Lena informed us that the girls would be sewing aprons, and she should bring in a meter of cotton cloth. And what would the boys be doing? "Oh, they'll be doing a woodworking project." Phoebe never made it to school that Saturday. The accumulated strains of jet lag, skiing, and hours of class in an unfamiliar language took their toll, and the Moscow flu was coming on. There was the added pressure of being a celebrity, surrounded at each class break by crowds of schoolmates eager to try out their English and befriend an American girl. She was barraged with questions about her knowledge of rock groups. One boy asked ten times, "Do you like ice cream?" Perhaps, we explained to the puzzled Phoebe, it was his only English phrase.

But Katya and Lena remained loyal friends, phoning throughout Phoebe's illness to find out how she was, then coming by the apartment nearly every day to invite her to play with them outside. Phoebe soon had a delightful band of girlfriends in the neighborhood; among other new games, they taught her the Russian version of hopscotch. We, in turn, took Katya and Lena to see *Crocodile Dundee* and introduced them to popcorn. When spring came, Phoebe donned her roller skates and set off on the still-muddy paths around our building. Within days, the other girls—all from privileged academic families—managed to acquire skates too.

During the spring, the press frequently published proposals for educational reform; one full-page piece in *Literaturnaya gazeta* on "the ideal institution of higher education" described a small, intimate community of professors and students much like Amherst College. Still, the idea of a liberal arts education is foreign to Russian soil and slow to take root there. Almost four hundred years ago, the first young Russians were sent abroad to study on state scholarships; on their return, they would repay the state through government service. The notion of education for citizenship takes on different meanings in the two societies; an allegedly forward-looking educator, taking part in a *Literaturnaya gazeta* round table, still described the purpose of Soviet education as "the production of scientific workers in various fields." When we were asked, as American educators, to comment on this round table for a follow-up piece, we stressed the American idea—a myth perhaps, but an important one—that education aims at producing critical, thinking citizens who can take full part in a democratic society. Along the way, we quoted Jefferson to the effect that education is the best defense against tyranny. With no reference books at hand, we crossed our fingers and hoped this remark was indeed Jefferson's. The Soviet professor who had been commissioned to do the article revised it to "Jefferson and V. I. Lenin." We certainly didn't remember such a quote in any Lenin *we'd* ever read, we said, but we were in no position to deny that he'd ever said it, either. When the interview appeared, the quote was still there, but so were both Lenin and Jefferson.

FRESH
ENCOUNTERS,
MORE MYSTERIES

L ike the first, pre-Andreyeva phase of our spring
in Moscow, the third, post-Andreyeva period
posed more questions than it answered. Earlier, we had
attempted to find answers by consulting friends or reading the newly revivified press. Now the press was part
of the puzzle: Just how far could it go? Our friends were
somewhat more optimistic than before, but within the
limits of a basic skepticism. We tried to arrange new and
different encounters in the hope that they would shed
new light. We talked with Foreign Ministry officials, a
Party *apparatchik* and his wife, managers and management specialists, and several members of the working
class. We also met a man reputed to be one of the foremost Russian fascists.

Bill met the Soviet diplomats at Spaso House, where
an American specialist on Soviet military affairs, Professor Condoleeza Rice of Stanford University, was giving

a talk comparing the Soviet General Staff and the American Joint Chiefs of Staff. Professor Rice was elegant, young, black, and female, not exactly the kind of expert from whom Russians were used to taking instruction on military matters; a good turnout was not guaranteed. Five years ago, we were told, the embassy used to invite a hundred Soviets three weeks in advance of events and no one would agree to come, whereupon the then ambassador, Arthur Hartman, would invite dissidents and refuseniks who had little to lose. Nowadays Spaso can be filled with Soviet officials on a few days' notice. And so it was in April, with assorted *institutchiki*—mostly specialists on American foreign policy but a few on Soviet military affairs—and several middle-level officials from the Foreign Ministry.

Rice's lecture was straightforward, informative, and delivered in impeccable Russian. The questions from the floor were respectful. The three Foreign Ministry men at Bill's table were mellow after a long day in the ministry's Stalinist tower. It seemed the perfect opportunity to see how far the diplomatic corps had restructured itself. Bill's mistake may have been to be too aggressive, challenging his tablemates to agree that Stalin was his country's own worst enemy. Either that or they feared to come clean in the presence of each other or of a KGB bug assumed to be within earshot. In any event, one of them counterattacked, charging that the United States had wanted to use Soviet POWs captured by the Germans against the USSR in a new war to follow directly upon World War II. After that, the tension didn't abate until the subject shifted to cooperative restaurants.

We encountered the Party official and his wife in April through a roundabout route and found ourselves in their apartment late one Sunday afternoon. Both were as liberal as they were hospitable. He couldn't emphasize enough the importance of the battle going on in the Party. The country's past was almost unbelievably

bleak, he said. Now a much brighter future was coming.
His wife seemed an equally militant believer. Her firsthand family acquaintance with the failed reforms of the
1950s and 1960s convinced her that this time they would
succeed. We were inspired by their enthusiasm—until
they added vodka to the cigarettes they had been smok-
ing nonstop since we walked in. Both could hold their
liquor, but their optimism began to fade. She turned out
to be a tortured soul. He began reciting all the reasons
the reforms could fail. Suddenly they both looked much
older.

"Have you ever heard of Nina Andreyeva?" he muttered, his speech by now noticeably slurred. "She and
her kind lost this time around, but no thanks to us. We
didn't struggle enough. We weren't scared until *Pravda*
spoke out; we were just fatalistic. We knew she had to
be fought. But we didn't know how to fight." A Party
official who didn't know how to fight? "We're white
crows," said our hostess. "We're not like the others."
Did she have in mind their liberal views, their inapti-
tude for a quarrel, their weakness for drink, or all three?

As our downbeat friend Seryozha had said, the economy holds the key to the future of reform. The question
is not only whether it will deliver the goods, but
whether enterprising managers and skilled workers, the
logical constituencies for change, will fight for reform.
Reformers place great stock in workers' participation in
management, hoping that the chance to shape their own
working lives will provide substitute gratification until
more goods appear in the stores. The danger is that managers will resist the change, and that workers inured to
taking orders will too.

An April visit by a management consultant friend of
ours, formerly with the World Bank in Washington,
more recently a teacher of labor relations, gave us a
glimpse of the Soviet workplace. John Simmons is con-

vinced American capitalism has something to teach Soviet socialism about democracy. Several years ago, the
Russians would have rejected that idea out of hand. But
events in both countries had combined to alter the situation. The Japanese miracle, achieved in large part
through worker empowerment and participative management, has taught Americans the kind of lessons the
Russians might now learn from us. American experience
suggested that the biggest barrier to improving produc-
tivity and performance was not resistant or recalcitrant
workers but the lack of top leadership willing and able
to insist on change. From that point of view, the Soviets
had a big advantage in Gorbachev himself.

Because John knows no Russian and we were curious,
either Bill or Jane accompanied him to see economists
and management specialists at the elite Academy for the
National Economy, the State Committee on Labor and
Social Affairs, and two of Moscow's most successful factories. The people we met ranged from old-style propagandists to hidebound bureaucrats to imaginative
would-be entrepreneurs. In the end, John went home
much more optimistic than his hosts. Our close Soviet
friends couldn't believe that John could believe in Soviet-style democratization. Now at last they had proof of
what they had suspected from observing us—Americans
are crazy enough to think that *demokratizatsiya* just
might work.

Students at the ten-year-old Academy of the National
Economy included plant managers, directors of industrial combines, ministers and deputy ministers, and
other central planners. In any given year, a thousand of
them enroll for anywhere from two weeks to two years
in courses ranging from management to psychology to
agriculture to law. John's host at the academy was the
head of the management department. Seated in a luxurious little conference room, which an attentive female
functionary kept well supplied with tea and pastries, he

minced few words. Democratic management was a great thing, but most Soviet managers didn't think so. "What in hell is going on?" he quoted one manager as saying. "I used to be able to conclude a collective bargaining agreement in one day. Now I've got meetings piled upon meetings, and I've got to explain, explain, and explain." Participatory management was "the most unpopular subject" in the academy's curriculum. Up to 90 percent of the faculty were also skeptical. Both teachers and students would have to learn from the few managers and management specialists who had become true believers.

Heroes like these are regularly publicized in magazines like *Ogonyok,* and an editor there arranged for John and Bill to meet one of them. Since the man was leaving for Eastern Europe the next morning, he kindly agreed to come out to the academy, where he had an adjunct professorship. John and Bill were to call him from there to set a specific time. Arriving late, they asked a friendly woman from the academy's foreign department to make the call. But there was evidently a misunderstanding; when their interview was over at five o'clock, the call still hadn't been made. The woman seemed slightly less friendly when asked again to make the call, but she agreed. "He's not at home, no one answered," she reported a few moments later. By the time John and Bill said their thanks and goodbyes, it was almost six. The foreign department agreed to make one more attempt, but with the same result.

In pre-*perestroika* days, appointments routinely evaporated for political reasons, especially those rare rendezvous that were arranged without going through channels. Either the person you were to see would think better of it, or his institution's foreign department would. But this was April 1988! The interview had not been set up secretly, it was to take place at the Academy of the National Economy, and a magazine with nearly two million readers had helped arrange it. Bill decided to see if the missing specialist had left a message at *Ogonyok*. No help there; as far as the editor knew, the man was at home being interviewed by other journalists.

So Bill himself called. The man *was* home, and had been there all afternoon waiting for John's call. It was now quite late, he lived on the other side of town, but he was still willing to make the trek. He asked Bill to hand the phone to someone from the academy so as to find out where to meet. By now Bill was thoroughly suspicious of the foreign department woman, but she was nearest to the phone. Her face was grim as she picked up the receiver and her voice grimmer still: "Only through the foreign department!" Bill heard her insist. "Only through the foreign department!" she repeated several times.

She had never called the man at all. She had taken it upon herself to sabotage the appointment simply because it was not made through the foreign department. In the old days, she would surely have prevailed. This time, the expert was apparently mad as hell, or so it sounded to Bill, who had gotten closer to the phone. When the conversation finally ended, the woman muttered, "Wait a minute, please," and stalked off. Several minutes later a man appeared, not to apologize but to inform Bill and John, as if nothing untoward had occurred, that the scheduled interview could proceed after all. But by this time John had decided that his innocent interlocutor-to-be had suffered enough. The man was still willing to keep the appointment, but it didn't take much convincing by Bill before he agreed to put it off.

The whole affair was a bucket of cold water in the face for us as well as for John. We knew such things could happen, even in the warmth of Moscow Spring, but were nonetheless shocked when they did. All the management specialist had tried to do was exchange views with an American from whom he might have learned something useful to the Soviet system. Why should anyone object? Probably Bill and John should have made a scene. But neither is the confrontational type. Both prefer getting even to getting mad. During the rest of our time in Moscow, we told the story again and again.

The next day at the State Committee on Labor and Social Affairs, a typical old-style central planning agency with a vested interest in the status quo, John and Bill met two labor-relations specialists, middle-aged, heavyset, jowly, the very image of the bureaucratic enemy of reform. But this first impression proved only partially correct. The senior Soviet described the typical Russian workplace in roseate hues, as if the new legislation had already accomplished miracles. His junior colleague admitted that the reforms had hardly begun to take effect, and that the main obstacle was "us, our own habits, our own way of doing things."

The best case we heard for reform came from a grizzled blue-collar worker we met in Leningrad while waiting for a bus. We asked him for directions and struck up a conversation that moved into a grubby nearby cafeteria. He had retired after working his way up from lathe operator to foreman, but recently found part-time work driving a delivery truck. He remembered all too well the last time reform had been tried. "That fool Khrushchev" had ruined things. But this time was different. "Anyone who is willing to work, instead of collecting his pay for loafing and drinking, will admit that. Some of the guys are impatient. I keep telling them: 'You have to wait five or six years.' They say what's needed is order and discipline. Sure—and they're the guys who bitched most when they cracked down on alcohol and absenteeism. I mean, discipline *is* needed. You can get away with murder these days, especially the youth. But we don't need Stalin's kind of discipline—you know, jail for coming to work five minutes late. People used to respect Stalin a lot more than they do now.

Trouble is, they didn't know enough about him. Nowadays, people can speak out on the job. I did it myself just the other day. Our boss was no good. He didn't know how to relate to people, to treat them with dignity. The new law says we workers don't have to take that. So we had a meeting about it. I was the first to speak up. The guys respect me because I'm older; they know I fought in the war and got my education afterward. They supported my views. Pretty soon, we'll be getting a new boss. Can you believe that?"

We could.

What we couldn't believe was that a man who we were assured by several friends was a foul, right-wing national chauvinist was in fact just that. Unfortunately, we cannot say much about him. To reveal anything about our meeting, he said, would be to place him and us in danger. We were stunned. In the 1970s we met from time to time with liberal dissidents, but though we didn't broadcast these encounters to the KGB (which probably knew about them anyway), we were never sworn to silence. What was so striking about this man was that at the very moment barriers seemed to be crumbling all around us, he was more frightened than anyone we ever met during the bad old days.

He was the scourge of liberals; reportedly, he was linked to the anti-Semitic Pamyat society. We would not have thought to seek him out, nor did we expect him to have any interest in us. When we were offered the opportunity to meet him, we at first declined, surprising ourselves. In general, we have eschewed grand moral gestures in our dealings with Russians. Bill, especially, takes it as his Sovietologist's duty to meet Soviets of all stripes, no matter how unattractive, the better to understand the system about which he is allegedly expert. The man in question was too much for even Bill. But as weeks and months passed, Bill kept returning to the subject. If he was supposed to know the "Communist

enemy," then the least he could do was to meet that
enemy's right-wing enemy as well.

So at last we agreed, and to our surprise and chagrin,
we found ourselves almost liking the man. Like some
but not all Russian nationalists we had heard or read
about, he was as anti-Stalin as our liberal friends. The
difference was he wept for the destruction of a glorious
Russian past that liberals thought had never existed. He
was by no means as hostile to *perestroika* as we had
expected. He applauded the campaign to save the Russian people from drinking themselves into national ob-
livion and the efforts to preserve the natural
environment; he praised *glasnost* and proposed reforms
to limit Party control over all aspects of life. He was still
full of bile about liberal dissidents, but equally bitter
about establishment figures who had denounced liberals in the 1970s and were now trying to pass as liberals
themselves. His fatal flaw, we decided, was that he had
too good a mind, the kind of curious, critical mind that
refused to settle into a prefabricated political niche. If
his bent had been scientific, he would have had more
freedom to cut his own path. But his real forte was politics, and in that field orthodoxy reigned supreme. So he
found an outlet for his acerbic brilliance by excoriating
Western-style reformers.

WELCOME TO
THE PROVINCES

The fresh encounters we sought included new places as well as people. How far had *perestroika* penetrated beyond the capital? Local newspapers were said to be far less venturesome than the central press. Provincial reformers reportedly kept their heads down, waiting to see whether Gorbachev would prevail in Moscow.

We decided to go to Leningrad, Tallinn, and Odessa, all of which either or both of us had visited in the past. Ever since Sergei Kirov was assassinated there in 1934, Leningrad has had the reputation of a city under tight control; we found it looser than that. Tallinn, on the other hand, is supposed to be a hotbed of independent-mindedness, and for the most part it was. Odessa was the most instructive of all. Along with an ecological crisis of disastrous dimensions and a group of academics notably more cautious than their capital counterparts, we encountered a small group of marvelous, creative intellectuals who were asking themselves the same question we were: How many of them were left in the still cosmopolitan but visibly crumbling city by the Black Sea?

It was snowing hard when we arrived in Leningrad in late April. We and our children came with John and Adele Simmons and two of their children. Phoebe would leave with them in a few days to return to Amherst, and we wanted to introduce her and Alex to the city's architectural and cultural treasures. Even touring the town taught political and economic lessons. At a huge indoor market recently given over to the new cooperatives, a young man named Borya introduced himself as the "king of black denim." He claimed to have cornered the market. That allowed him to sell his Soviet-made jeans for 100 rubles a pair (though we didn't see anyone buying). Since we didn't represent the competition, Borya confided a couple of his secrets. Wages of individual coop "members," a necessary ideological euphemism for people who would be considered "exploited" if they bore the label "employees," were taxed at a very stiff rate—as much as 600 rubles on the first 1,500 earned, and at 90 percent above 1,500. The way he got around that was to use the coop's "development fund" to buy desirable items and then rent them to members at a nominal fee. What if he got into trouble? He would consult a new cooperative in Moscow whose business was to help other cooperatives start up and keep going.

We went to Repino, in an area that until 1945 was part of Finland, to find the dacha where Kornei Chukovsky had lived before 1917. It had burned to the ground two years earlier due to the carelessness of its tenants, but we visited the nearby home, now a museum, of the great Russian painter Ilya Repin. A middle-aged guide said what we had so often heard before, but not once in the

spring of 1988: "All was well with us until the war," she
sighed. "The war brought us great losses. We are still
recovering. That's why we have problems today." She
was right about the war, but it neither explains the current mess nor began the bloodletting. Nowadays almost
everyone admitted that, not only in Moscow but in Leningrad.

Ina was intelligent, warm, attractive. She worked as a
typist to support her husband, Grisha, a freelance writer.
Grisha was a decidedly un-Soviet type, a citizen of the
world, wise and learned, whose interests spanned national boundaries and who knew enough languages to
follow his interests wherever they led. Several years ago
he had a run-in with the authorities, and spent some
time in prison. For a long time they thought of trying to
emigrate. Now, when it might be possible for them to
do so, they couldn't bear to leave *perestroika.* "For the
first time in my life," he confided, "it's interesting to be
alive."

Over dinner at their tiny apartment, the talk was lively
and easy. Ina had attended a wild and raucous meeting
at the Perestroika Discussion Club that Leningrad television had taped. Several people called for a second political party, others for some kind of national front or
union of democratic forces. Rumors had swept the hall
that Gorbachev was trying to delay the Party conference,
so he could strengthen his position before it began.
Those at the meeting decided to send a *nakaz* to the
conference, the sort of instruction voters or Party constituencies send to their "elected" representatives. If the
club had its way, its message would be delivered by a
local Leningrad sociologist who had several years ago
been a dissident.

According to Ina, there had been a mini-scandal at the
meeting. In the interest of letting many people be heard,
club organizers had limited the time of each speaker.
Unfortunately, one of the few to be cut off was an ob-

viously working-class speaker who got red in the face
and shouted that "damn intellectuals" were putting him
down. The man reminded Ina of a conversation she'd
had recently on a train in the provinces. Her compart-
ment-mates had no use for reform and assured her that
no one else did either, with the exception of a few egg-
heads in Moscow and Leningrad. She feared they might
be correct. Grisha had heard about a recent poll that
showed only 10 percent of the population favoring Gorbachev's reforms, 25 percent against, and 75 percent on
the fence. If so, the last thing reformers should be doing
was to be alienating a worker emancipated enough to
attend Perestroika Club meetings.

On the way to Tallinn, an overnight train ride along
the Baltic coast, Alex got up at 3:00 A.M. and spent the
rest of the night chatting with several young conductors.
At one station, they fought a snowball battle with the
train engineer. Another first for Moscow Spring! And a
portent of the remarkably relaxed atmosphere that
awaited us in the Estonian capital.

Annexed by the Soviet Union during World War II,
Estonia has never forgiven the Russians for deportations
that claimed thousands of lives, for "crimes against humanity," as an Estonian document prepared for the
Party conference calls them. The Estonians think their
living standard would approach that of Finland, whose
television programs reach them unimpeded across a sev-
enty-mile stretch of sea, if they were left to their own
devices. They blame the Russian-imposed Soviet economic system for holding them down.

Bill had been in Tallinn twice before, in 1973 and
1978. Each time, Estonian nationalism had been palpable; he learned that this was no place to practice speaking Russian. Identifying yourself as an American, on the
other hand, brought smiles and warm hospitality. Even
in English, however, there were limits. Estonian Intour-

ist guides were required to inform you that the "bour-geois" Estonian republic that existed between the wars was politically bankrupt and that Estonia joined the USSR voluntarily. If you tried to engage them, or other Estonians you didn't know very well, in conversation about the truth, the conversation came to an abrupt end.

The spring of 1988 was different. Virtually every Es-tonian we met hoped for a new status for Estonia in the USSR. This took some getting used to, especially since our invitation to Tallinn came from a protégé of Belou-sov, Bill's erstwhile nemesis. But by the time we arrived in Tallinn, Belousov was long gone, and his former col-league could not have been more hospitable. He ar-ranged for Bill to give a seminar at the Estonian Academy of Sciences, interviewed him on Estonian TV, and took us to dinner in the Gothic old town. In Estonia, even Academy foreign-department officials talked frankly about Estonia's predicament and its hope for the future.

Estonians form a shrinking proportion of their own republic's population. Part of the problem, they admit-ted, was their own low birthrate, but we detected a tinge of racist nationalism in their complaints about the grow-ing influx of Russian and Central Asian workers needed to man Estonian industry; before the war, Estonia had been mostly agricultural. Estonians accepted a certain amount of industrialization, but powerful Moscow min-istries which ran Estonia's plants had insisted on more than that. We saw a multipart documentary film about groundwater pollution caused by a huge phosphate strip-mining operation which threatens the ecology of a whole region. We commented that the film seemed rep-etitious and slow-moving. We were told that this was the only way such politically explosive material could make it to the screen; all seven segments were not al-lowed to be shown together.

Some Estonians had proposed that the whole republic

be declared an autonomous economic zone, on the
Chinese model, which would build up its own economy,
trade on its own terms with the West, particularly with
Scandinavia, and contribute to the general Soviet welfare in a more mutually equitable way. Another radical
proposal called for the formation of a mass-based popular front. Under Stalin, so-called popular fronts had been
used in Eastern Europe to disguise Communist rule.
The term still conjured up an empty shell. But that was
before the Tallinn Spring outdid its Moscow counterpart. What "popular front" now suggested was Poland's
Solidarity. As in Poland, Estonian intelligentsia and
workers were more or less united in national pride and
hostility to Russia, or at least to a Russia that insisted on
defending its Stalinist past and depriving Estonians of a
chance to determine their own future.

Shortly before we arrived in Tallinn, the republic's
creative unions—artists, writers, cinematographers, etc.
—had held a joint meeting to which the whole Estonian
Politburo was invited. Only a couple of Party leaders
had attended. The intellectuals' response was loud and
bitter, and it may have contributed to the dismissal, later
in the spring, of Estonian Party leader Karl Vaino. About
the same time, the Estonian Popular Front came into
being, summarizing its aims this way: "We want to be
able to live happily in our own land, deciding for ourselves what constitutes happiness." As the date of the
Party conference approached, the Front organizers
asked conference delegates to come to a meeting to say
whether or not they accepted the Front's program. Only
a handful attended. "Nevertheless," the Front's chairman told a Western newsman, "you will see that in Moscow the others, too, will support our line. Otherwise,
they would not dare return to Tallinn."

The program called for, among other things, "economic self-government and self-management" and the
granting to all Soviet republics of the right "to commu-

nicate freely with foreign countries, to be represented in international organizations, and to maintain, if need be, representation in neighboring countries."

The program was issued after we left, but we could feel it coming. However, the Estonians' very success in raising their national banner—quite literally in May when the blue, black, and white flag of independent Estonia was hoisted aloft in public for the first time in forty-eight years—poses a threat. For the moment, Communist leaders in Moscow seem to accept burgeoning Baltic nationalism. If and when a crackdown comes, it may have more local supporters than one would think. When Bill gave his Academy talk on American views of *perestroika*, he expected a spirited response. But only one or two of the assembled scholars rose to the occasion. The others sat silent and left as soon as they could. "Don't be offended," we were told. "They're just not used to sessions like this." But we weren't entirely reassured. If people were afraid to engage us, what else did they still fear?

Odessa is a once-beautiful city. Founded less than two hundred years ago, it was built on a bluff overlooking the Black Sea and settled by wealthy merchants and grain traders who knew how to enjoy life. They built elegant villas on the hill with a view of the sea. As a busy port at which foreign vessels dock and to which Soviet sailors return with Western goods, the city has a cosmopolitan air. There is street life aplenty, and people look well dressed, especially the young women smartly turned out in Western attire. A spicy ethnic mix—Russians, Jews, Armenians, and others living side by side with native Ukrainians—adds to the brew.

Odessa's tradition of humor was observed this year on April 1 with the second annual humor festival. Odessa-born stand-up comic Mikhail Zhvanetsky has replaced Arkady Raikin as the Soviets' favorite funnyman. While sharing Zhvanetsky tapes with us, our friends confided that it's getting increasingly hard to find targets for humor under *glasnost* because so much can be said directly in the press. The stories they had to tell were hardly funny. One former Party boss, they told us, held a wedding with over three hundred guests on an Odessa-based cruise ship and made the shipping company pick up the tab. The same public servant had a wide suspension footbridge built linking his palatial home overlooking the sea with that of his mother-in-law. It is known locally as the Mother-in-Law Bridge.

Odessa is the saddest city we visited. Except for a few nicely restored palaces, it is remarkably dirty and drab, a striking contrast to the *joie de vivre* of its people. It is also, we learned, a disaster area ecologically. We knew, of course, of Chernobyl. One of the effects of *glasnost* was a stream of pieces in the media on Chernobyl's second anniversary. But Chernobyl is only the most glaring example of problems that have been accumulating in the USSR for many years and significantly worsened during the Brezhnev era. The impact of the ecological crisis on both our daily lives and the consciousness of our Soviet contacts surprised us.

The Soviet regime has always had a love affair with technology, a sense that man can master and transform his environment for the good of all. The contrary notion, that nature has laws of balance that can be broken only at great peril, is just now beginning to be given voice. In Soviet theory, socialism allows central planners to protect the environment. But when real-life planners give priority to industrialization, there are no autonomous environmental groups, of the sort found in Western societies, to resist. Instead, huge, ambitious projects are spawned in Moscow by engineers and bureaucrats with little concern for the local consequences of their decisions. Only recently did public pressure finally succeed in forcing the cancellation of one of the most ambitious of these ill-conceived projects—a plan to reverse the flow of Siberian rivers to irrigate Central Asia.

Moscow's environment was bad enough. A few days before our January arrival, there was a chemical spill of some sort into the Moscow River, upstream from the reservoir that provides the city with water. Official government sources were silent as usual, but residents noticed a distinct kerosene-like smell to the tap water. The U.S. Embassy recommended that Americans temporarily not drink the water. After a while, we did, but never without boiling it first.

The air in Moscow is worse than in many American cities because Soviet industry gravitates toward big cities, where housing and services are more plentiful. From our fourteenth-story window, we watched three giant smokestacks of an electric generating plant spew smoke in our direction. Soviet cars, trucks, and buses evidently have no pollution-control devices. The clouds of acrid black smoke emitted by aged vehicles made walking along major roadways unpleasant at best.

But Muscovites complained less about environmental damage than did our friends in other cities, each of which had its own pet disaster. In Estonia it was the phosphate mine; in Leningrad, an immense flood-control dam built several kilometers out into the Baltic Sea, designed to protect the city from disastrous floods of the sort immortalized in Pushkin's narrative poem *The Bronze Horseman*. The pet project of former Leningrad Party chief Grigory Romanov, built over the initial objections of local experts, the dam is already partially operational, and its disastrous effects are beginning to be felt. What it does is trap the sewage released from the city in the outer harbor, from which it is backing up into the river and threatening the city's water supply. What's worse, even dynamiting the dam would not solve the problem, for the rubble would remain on the ocean bottom and continue to impede water circulation. In response to this mess, plus the Leningrad city fathers' arbitrary decision to tear down a historic hotel in which the poet Sergey Esenin committed suicide, independent environmental and preservation groups sprang up in Leningrad in the first months of *glasnost*. Others were forming around the country.

When Jane was in Odessa in November 1987, her group had been housed in a grand pre-revolutionary hotel in the lovely downtown area. This time, our local host, to save us the exorbitant cost of the local Intourist hotel, housed us in a guest suite at the Odessa State University dormitory for graduate and married students. Although built relatively recently, the dormitory façade was chipped and the front steps were crumbling. The lobby was pervaded by the distinct odor of sewage and garbage. We were given what seemed a perfectly adequate two-room suite, with kitchen and bath. When we arrived, a janitor was hanging curtains, frantically trying to put the rooms "into shape" for us. But much was beyond her powers. There was a large TV set, which didn't work, and a telephone, which didn't work either. The kitchen stove leaked gas. The bathroom taps provided only cold water, and that of a suspicious odor and color. The hall toilet consisted of two holes in the floor.

In the warmth of mid-May, we also noticed something that had escaped Jane's attention in November—the pervasive odor of sewage throughout the town. The trouble, we were told, was Odessa's leaky sewage system; built over a hundred years ago, it has had little maintenance since. There is only one sewage treatment plant, and when it breaks down, untreated waste spews into the sea a mere two kilometers from the shore. Even when the plant is working, up to 30 percent of the city's sewage leaks into the ground and eventually finds its way to the sea. Water pipes are said to leak too, and the combination probably accounts for the mysterious intestinal ailments of which several residents complained.

The cost of repairing the pipelines will be 300 million rubles at the very least. As usual, the Moscow authorities have been slow to respond. But a campaign by local scientists and journalists, including an angry appearance on television, seemed to have gotten Moscow's attention. In the meantime, however, the Black Sea around Odessa is dying. As of May 1988, only the top twenty meters can support life. If current trends aren't reversed, we were told, the whole sea will be dead sometime in the twenty-first century.

Standing atop the bluff, strolling past pleasant health sanatoria in what were once private villas, looking down at a string of beaches hugging the shore, we found the bad news hard to believe. But our guide was a specialist in the field, and when we took an excursion boat ride along the shore, we could see the damage for ourselves.

Making matters worse were giant breakwaters constructed by project-happy engineers. Designed to protect the beaches from wave damage, they actually serve, like the Leningrad dam, to increase pollution by cutting off water circulation. In the distance, on a nearby peninsula, our guide pointed out a giant phosphate plant built in the Brezhnev years by American entrepreneur Armand Hammer. Russia's great American benefactor could not have built such a plant in the United States because of environmental controls, our guide explained.

Ecological issues are becoming mixed with national issues, particularly by Soviet minorities who feel their national health is being sacrificed for the benefit of the Great Russians. The Armenians, for instance, first welcomed large chemical combines in the belief that they would benefit the local economy and provide good jobs. The result has been Yerevan air pollution ten times over the permissible standard, and a rising rate of birth defects. After many years of protest, the giant Yerevan chemical plant believed to be among the worst offenders was finally closed down in 1988. In Uzbekistan, concern is rising about rates of miscarriage and birth defects in the children of local women who work in the cotton fields, where agricultural chemicals are used with a heavy hand. Odessa is too cosmopolitan to allow this sort of national-ecological blending. As we learned about the political life, or lack thereof, in the city, it seemed even more surprising that local activists succeeded in mounting the campaign they did.

People we encountered officially and semiofficially were warm and informal, but their openness seemed to come to an end where *glasnost* Moscow-style began. Our academic host in Odessa was a witty, sophisticated scholar of international affairs with a bright and charming wife. Yet dinner at their home reminded us of occasions in the 1970s when one felt that at least some of the plentiful warmth and hospitality was designed to keep risky political talk at bay.

Our host introduced Bill to the university rector, Igor Petrovich Zelinsky, whom Jane had met the previous autumn. A geological engineer by training, he helped design several mammoth Soviet hydroelectric stations as well as others in Iraq. Entering graduate school at the age of thirty-seven, he completed the course in a year and a half and worked his way up from instructor to vice-rector only to resign, during the depths of the Brezhnev stagnation, on grounds of "ill health." "Whose health?" they had asked at the Ministry of Higher Education in Moscow. "Yours," Igor Petrovich had replied. He had recently been elected rector by the university faculty and staff in accordance with *demokratizatsiya.*

Unlike Moscow bigwigs, who can be impossible to get to see, Zelinsky took two hours from the first day of his vacation to chat. Talk ranged from his horrendous childhood (as a nine-year-old he had watched from the bushes as Nazi killers mowed down villagers and stacked and burned the corpses) to the geology of beach erosion (he diagrammed for Bill the reasons why the

Black Sea coast can't accommodate hordes of shivering
northerners seeking the southern sun) to inside details
of university administration. Economic reforms now require Odessa State University to cover more of its own
costs, which he calculated at 10,000 rubles per student
per year. Part of that sum is still covered by Moscow.
Part comes in payment for research and other services
provided by faculty to local plants and agencies. The
rest he had resolved to get from enterprises spread out
across the country from Lvov to Vladivostok, to which
OSU students were "distributed" upon graduation.

Another example of the university's newfound independence involved Americans: The Ministry of Higher
Education in Moscow had informed Odessa State that it
would have a sister-college relationship with Vassar, in
Poughkeepsie, New York. The rector had written to Vassar but received no answer. When Johns Hopkins University and Goucher College in Maryland proposed a
similar arrangement, he had agreed and so informed
Moscow, without, he added proudly, asking the ministry's permission.

Clearly the rector was in tune with the times. Smart,
energetic, informal—he was on a first-name basis with
Bill in five minutes—he seemed just the sort of man to
push *perestroika* over the top. To test this impression,
Bill asked what he hoped for from the Party conference.
His answer was a string of clichés about "generalizing
from previous experience and moving forward from
there." Did he favor greater democracy within the
party? "No parties are entirely democratic," he said.
"Even the Republican Party in the United States is organized on 'democratic centralist' principles." So much
for the rector's knowledge of American politics. Or had
he come up against the limits of *glasnost* in Odessa and
was playing it safe?

Equally ambiguous were the reactions to two talks
Bill gave in Odessa, one in the university history de-

partment, the other to an interdisciplinary group of in-
ternational-relations specialists who gathered once a
month in the House of Scholars. Bill needled his university hosts about the lack of *glasnost* in Soviet foreign
policy. The younger scholars present shot agitated
glances at each other and at their department chairman.
Apparently it was their first encounter of this kind, and
they weren't sure how to respond. The senior man
vaguely agreed that foreign policy *glasnost* could go further, but gave no particulars.

The downtown seminar was a more formal occasion,
with fifteen or so participants sitting around a long ma-
hogany table. This time Bill talked about the upcoming
Reagan-Gorbachev summit. Gorbachev was the first Soviet leader since the war, he said, to be willing to meet
the Americans halfway. Bill was critical of Stalin,
Khrushchev, and Brezhnev, but mostly to contrast them
with Gorbachev. He was surprised when his hosts felt
obliged to defend Gorbachev's predecessors. The senior
Soviet at the table seized on a Washington news item
reported that day in the Soviet press. The U.S. Senate
had put off further work on ratifying the Intermediate
Nuclear Forces Treaty pending certain clarifications in
Moscow. "This step cannot but put us on guard," he
said. "It looks to us like blackmail designed to get us to
make more concessions." He was right about how the
American move might look in the USSR, but he should
have known there was a more benign explanation—the
treaty had gotten temporarily caught up in the conflict
between the executive and legislative branches and the
two parties in the Senate. "Your job is not to rush to
worst-case conclusions," said Bill. "Your job is to try to
explain to the Soviet people how the American system
works."

A young historian demanded to know why the United
States had worked so hard and long to deny the USSR
"political parity." Political parity means equal political

influence. Certainly the United States has long tried to deny that to the USSR, while trying to extend its own influence worldwide. But why should a young Russian demand it in retrospect for the likes of Stalin and Brezhnev? The whole point of Moscow Spring was that Soviet citizens themselves were reassessing their own leaders' credentials to speak for the national interest.

On the whole, however, reformers in Odessa seemed less prone to discouragement and cynicism than those in Moscow, even though there were fewer of them. They seemed closer to each other as well as to other Odessites who shared their views but weren't ready to act as forcefully as they were.

Lena is a young journalist who had interviewed Jane in November 1987. Jane wasn't sure the piece would be printed, let alone that it would offer a faithful account of what she had said. But when it finally reached us in Amherst, we found it was a full and faithful transcript, using Jane's criticisms of Soviet higher education to advance the cause of educational reform. Equally rare for a Soviet newspaper article, it conveyed both Jane's feeling for Odessa and Lena's warm response to Jane. When we arrived in Moscow the following January, Lena called to invite us all to visit her in Odessa.

Lena is tall and attractive as well as bright and brave. She has an equally winning husband and small daughter. The little girl spends more time in the state kindergarten than her parents would like, so that they can devote endless hours to *perestroika*. All three of them crowded around a tiny dinner table with us in their living room. Lena told us how she and her colleagues tried to help people who had no one but the press to appeal to, and she showed us an article she had written on the May Day parade. It was the first piece to say what people had been thinking for years—that the compulsory celebrating was an empty, costly ritual. How had she managed to get the piece in the paper? Her editor, she said, was a man known for miles around as a fighter for reform.

Much of the evening we spent discussing the fast-approaching Party conference. Bill had been trying to figure out from contradictory press accounts how the delegates were to be chosen. Lena explained excitedly that the procedures allowed for more democracy than ever before. The rest of the conversation could be reconstructed from our notes, but it was much more dramatically reported in an extraordinary front-page article of Lena's published in the May 18 edition of the *Evening Odessa*. The article appears under the standard rubric, "Toward the XIX Party Conference." In other years, what usually followed was an account of how workers and collective farmers were preparing to greet the occasion by overfulfilling their production plans. Lena's article, subtitled an "Open Letter to Amherst College Professor William Taubman," reported with some chagrin that her assurances to Bill had proved premature.

Lena prefaced her open letter with an account of our dinner conversation. Bill's question about delegate selection, she wrote, had been on her mind as well. Instead of electing delegates according to the old quota system (so many workers, so many intellectuals, so many milkmaids), Gorbachev had urged they be chosen, regardless of occupation, from among champions of *perestroika*. But where was the "guarantee," Bill had asked, that this procedure would in fact be followed? Lena had answered that all candidates would be nominated "from below," at meetings in factories, universities, and other local institutions. City and provincial Party committees would eventually pick the delegates, but only from among those so nominated. Gorbachev had also suggested that candidates' views be publicized in the press and discussed by the public before the actual elections. But, Lena wrote, Bill saw a flaw in that too: there wouldn't be time to publicize candidates and their views before the elections were held, nor any way to ensure that the Party committees paid heed. Lena recalled showing us an *Evening Odessa* article that named May 21 as election day. "You see," Bill had said, "there will be no time after all." Lena had promised to write Bill telling him how the nominations and elections actually went. Why not make that letter part of the article as well?

"Dear Bill," the open letter began. "Yesterday, a Party cell meeting held elections at Odessa State University where you visited two weeks ago." The meeting had gone wrong from the very start, when it was announced that the district Party committee had granted the university the right, as the biggest institution in the district, to nominate a candidate for conference delegate. Did that mean smaller institutions had no such right? Any collective could nominate, said a Party *apparatchik*, but most didn't bother because they knew the district committee wanted someone from the university or a huge nearby construction trust.

What happened next was disturbing and embarrassing. The university's Party cell nominated Rector Zelinsky and recommended that those present vote to approve him. "That's all," wrote Lena. "The matter was to be decided without other nominations. Of course, people came forward and said nice words about the rector. But although these words were absolutely justified, Bill, I felt sorry for Igor Petrovich, who was sitting up there at the presidium and looking physically uncomfortable." Fortunately, the vice-rector, who was chairing the meeting, had the presence of mind to invite other nominations after all. "And although the majority was clearly heart and soul with the rector (whom you know, so you'll understand that they weren't paying their respects to his high office but to the man himself, who has few if any equals in that position), they gladly supported those who came forward with more suggestions—at least that made the meeting more interesting."

In the end, of course, the meeting nominated the rec-

tor, an outcome that Lena was sure would please Bill.
But what would happen at the next stage? "Of course, it
is already clear," Lena wrote, "that despite all the promising headlines, such as 'Everything Depends on the
Collective's Will,' the real choice, if we are honest
enough to admit it, depends on the will of the district
committee bureau (which is to say on eleven individuals)."

Zelinsky was eventually chosen as delegate. Lena's
reformist editor, whose name *Evening Odessa* Party
members put forward, was not. City Party authorities
tried to defame the editor and his staff by implying that
they had falsified nomination papers. The same authorities apparently chastised Lena for her "Dear Bill" letter.

How many Lenas are there in Odessa? Not only we
but she and her friends—artists, musicians, and journalists—asked that question. One of them, an art historian,
took us to a high-tech cooperative called the Video Café.
Customers sit in leather easy chairs recycled from
Odessa-based cruise ships and watch music videos
brought back from abroad by Odessa sailors. Friendly,
efficient waiters—the kind rarely found in the state sector—serve delicious mushroom soup and Ukrainian
dumplings. As our coffee arrived, the art historian posed
the sort of question we had associated until then with
books on possible civilizations in other galaxies: "Are
we alone? How many of us are there?" There seemed to
be hardly anyone. Even concerts, which used to be well
attended, now played to nearly empty halls. Few
showed up for lectures at the House of Scholars. But
really good books, the kind one would die to get hold of,
sold out half an hour after they went on sale. "Who is
buying them?" she continued. "We often ask ourselves
that question. We don't know for sure. But someone
must be out there!"

TOWARD THE

CONFERENCE AND

THE SUMMIT

By the time we returned from Odessa in mid-May, Moscow Spring was spinning even faster than when we left. Events were rushing toward a seeming climax, two of them in fact. The one that got the most attention outside the USSR was the Reagan-Gorbachev summit scheduled for May 29 through June 2. But in Moscow, the summit seemed a sideshow to the main event, the Nineteenth Party Conference set for late June. Yet a third extravaganza would be the millennium of the Christianization of Kievan Russia.

Party conferences, like Party congresses from which they need to be distinguished, are large gatherings that bring five thousand or so delegates from all over the USSR to the marble-and-glass Kremlin Palace of Congresses. Party congresses, held every five years, are theoretically the most important Communist conclaves. In fact, congresses have had little or no power ever since the 1920s, especially during the late Stalinist period, when the dictator bothered to convoke only one of them between 1939 and 1953. More power resides in the smaller (about three hundred members) Central Committee, which meets several times a year, but most is arrogated to itself by the ruling Politburo (with thirteen voting and six nonvoting members in the spring of 1988), which gathers every Thursday afternoon for meetings that reportedly last late into the evening. Conferences used to be called fairly frequently when important matters needed to be addressed in the interim between congresses. But the Eighteenth Party Conference was so long ago (1941) that no one was quite sure what a conference's powers actually were. The issue would have been entirely academic, except that this conference seemed likely to make a difference.

Gorbachev had used the Twenty-seventh Congress, held in February 1986, to enunciate a reformist program and consolidate his political position. But both the reforms and his own power required further reinforcement—the kind best accomplished at a big conclave which could alter the composition of the Central Committee in his favor—and the next congress was still several years away.

During our first two months in Moscow, hardly anyone we knew was thinking about the conference. Even Gorbachev's most fervent supporters assumed they would have no role to play. The Party apparatus would select the delegates. The reason that prospect didn't create alarm was ironic. Most people considered the Party undemocratic enough to make the conference safe for democracy: they assumed Gorbachev would be able to push through his program against the wishes of many delegates.

By May, all these expectations had changed. The Andreyeva chill demonstrated that reform had powerful enemies. In its aftermath, Gorbachev sounded more militant, and pro-reform people who had been sitting on the fence resolved to come to his aid. But by mid-May he had moved back toward a more centrist position. Rumors had it that there would be no big personnel changes at the Party conference—a sign, it seemed, of Gorbachev's weakness. But we also heard that he had gotten the Politburo to reprimand Ligachev for endorsing the Andreyeva letter and had deprived him of his role as the leadership's specialist on ideology. Whatever was going on in the Kremlin was no cause for complacency. Gorbachevites were now convinced that the conference mattered and that, with the top leadership divided, delegate selection mattered too. So they threw themselves into the process of electing representatives who would fight for radical rather than cosmetic reform.

A surprising amount of all this political action was reported in the press. Our friends wanted to talk about it; sometimes they even asked our advice as people more experienced than they at democratic politics. Bill's social scientist friends were deeply involved; Jane's literary friends were caught up in the drama as well. Almost everyone seemed to have put aside his professional pursuits to concentrate on the conference.

On April 9 the television news program *Vremya* showed Gorbachev speaking at length to a gathering of Party *apparatchiki* in Uzbekistan. He was in a feisty mood. Several times he referred to the "battle" going on in the country, the fact that *perestroika*'s opponents weren't yielding without a "struggle." But as the camera panned over the audience, it became clear many of his opponents sat right there. The more impassioned Gorbachev became, as if trying to inspire them with the sheer force of his personality, the more stony-faced they sat. After a while, a coldness came into his voice to match their faces. If we had only read his text in the next day's paper, we would not have felt the impact. A couple of days later, the Western press reported the Politburo

clash that allegedly ended with a reprimand for Ligachev.

Did it in fact end that way? The theory that Gorbachev
thus settled accounts with high-level opponents comes
up against what he said at a mid-May meeting with editors and writers. Instead of lambasting conservatives, he
was now sympathetic and understanding: "I would not
regard those who have panicked as irresponsible or opposed to *perestroika*. No, comrades, we should approach
these issues seriously, without going to the other extreme, without labeling anyone who has voiced doubts
an opponent of *perestroika*. And I am especially against
those who have put the expression 'enemy of *perestroika*' into press circulation."

What were reformers to do when he told them to love
thine enemy of *perestroika*? Fortunately, that was not
all he told them to do. At the same mid-May meeting he
endorsed the conference election procedures that Lena
later outlined to Bill. He urged that "true champions of
perestroika" be chosen in a way that allowed rank-and-
file Party members to participate. That sounded like a
reference to the same danger Popov, Gelman, and others
had discerned back in April, namely, that if reformers
didn't stand and fight, the conference might end up setting back the cause of change instead of advancing it.
But if that was Gorbachev's message, the further question was just *how* to fight, and on that issue Gorbachevites split into at least two camps.

Both groups shared the same end—a radically re-
formed Soviet system with a largely market economy
and much freer political choice. For the time being, that
choice was to be achieved through a single, democra-
tized Communist Party, but the idea of a multiparty system was not nearly as far beyond the pale as it seemed.
Where the reformers diverged, we were told, was in
their tactics. One group, represented by Popov, Shmelyov, Selyunin, and others, wanted to keep pounding
away at conservatives despite Gorbachev's remon-

strances. Arbatov, Yevgeny Primakov, the director of the Institute on the World Economy and International Relations, and others feared that too much militancy would give Gorbachev's opponents an excuse to move against him. But the militants too thought they were doing the Soviet leader's bidding. Only if they exerted pressure from the left could he portray himself as a centrist; the center itself would drift to the right if there were no action on the left.

Our source told us about an informal discussion-group meeting at which upwards of 350 social scientists had debated these issues. To our amazement, he reported that almost all found a multiparty system theoretically preferable to a one-party state. "Even if they are called Communist Party A and Communist Party B," said our source, "that would still be an improvement." A could unite the two reformist wings; B could bring together conservatives ranging from Ligachev to the non-crazy wing of Pamyat. Gorbachev and Ligachev could then openly contest a new Soviet presidency. Except, our source feared, Ligachev might win. That was one reason why people who preferred two parties in the abstract would just as soon stick with one as long as Gorbachev was its leader.

Didn't the assembled 350 realize that the political legitimacy of the Soviet system had been based for seventy-one years on one-party rule? Of course they did, but they also knew that evils allowed or encouraged by that arrangement had deprived it of moral legitimacy. Some people present argued for letting Misha do it, that is, letting Gorbachev push through democratization in his own way and at his own pace. Others had rightly asked what kind of democracy it is that doesn't well up from the bottom. Yet even they had to admit that if the bottom really did well up, in a country where so much popular sentiment seemed to be authoritarian, there might be a terrible mess.

At times all this talk of democracy struck us as utopian.

Other times it simply seemed inconsistent. But whatever else it was, it was brave. A friend summarized the
reformer's dilemma this way: "We can't not act, even
though it's terribly risky." But when we asked whether
the people at this discussion-group session had been
afraid, he said, "No. There were so many of us there it
was hard to feel threatened. A few people made jokes
about ending up in Siberia, but we felt reassured because we think we're doing what the General Secretary
wants."

A couple of representatives had been present from the
Democratic Union, a small group that has proclaimed
itself a second party, with a platform that includes,
among other things, releasing Eastern European "satel-
lites" from the Soviet orbit. Not long after the meeting,
the KGB swooped down on the Democratic Union and
arrested its leaders. Yet our friend refused to be shaken.
"The Party and the police may not know what the other
is doing," he said. "The KGB may have orders not to
touch informal groups but is probably free to go after
those who call themselves a political party." The implication that Gorbachev did not know what his goon
squads were up to seemed naïve. One didn't have to
assume he enjoyed the idea of bashing heads, one had
only to remember his political situation. The last thing
he needed, during the pre-conference political campaign, was to seem soft on the issue of a second party.

There had been another discussion meeting earlier in
May—Igor Klyamkin and Yury Levada had been among
the main speakers—at which participants talked openly
about the danger of a KGB crackdown on *glasnost* and
what if anything could be done to defend against such a
threat. All over the place, it seemed, reformers were
gathering together and gaining strength and determination from doing so. The press reflected the trend when
it published a flood of proposed changes for the Party
conference to consider and then more correspondence

protesting the way conference delegates were chosen. A cynic would say that this letter blitz was orchestrated to put pressure on the Party apparatus. But if the decision to publish the letters was made higher up, the decision to write them occurred lower down.

Moscow News proposed an age limit of sixty-five years and a maximum of two five-year terms in office for top Party leaders. Both suggestions sound tame to Western ears. But as Arbatov later pointed out at the Party conference, if Stalin had served only two five-year terms, he would have been out of office before the Great Purge began—but not, one must add, until after collectivization and man-made famine had taken millions of lives—and Brezhnev would have retired by 1974.

Sovetskaya kultura's conception of *glasnost* demanded that it publish conservatives too. "Not all the enemies of the Party and the people were destroyed," wrote a man with a higher degree in "philosophical science." "Their offspring are now out to get Stalin. Yes, he was guilty: he did not destroy all our enemies." Even more shocking was a pro-Pamyat worker's combination of anti-Brezhnev sentiment with an injunction to learn from the Nazis: it was "well known that the Nazis took very strong action against thieves, drug addicts, prostitutes and such. What factors allowed Germany to mobilize the vast majority of its people, to focus their wills and actions, and to build such a propaganda and organizational weapon in such a short time? Was it evil aims only? What role was played by the legal restrictions on Jewish participation in sociopolitical life?"

Such sentiments were not just expressed by the lunatic fringe. The new openness allowed freer expression of age-old Russian anti-Semitism. As the millennium celebrations approached, rumors circulated that Russian nationalists would use the occasion as an excuse for pogroms. A friend with an obviously Jewish name told us of a visit by a member of the militia who advised her to

reinforce her apartment door. He didn't say why, but she
promptly had it done without inquiring. Several different sources told us about handwritten notices that had
gone up in stations of a suburban rail line along which
many Jewish families had traditionally rented dachas.
"Jews! Don't rent dachas here this summer!" they
warned, and many had taken heed. As we sat drinking
tea with one young Jewish couple, the phone rang. An
acquaintance was calling to pass along rumors. "Don't
let your children out to play in the yard on June 1st, 5th,
or 7th," the agitated caller advised. (The millennium
celebrations centered on the June 5 weekend.) Our
friends dismissed the warning with a shrug, but their
mood subtly changed.

Glasnost was one thing, actually restructuring the
Party was another. We and our friends waited for the
official Central Committee "theses," which would constitute the agenda for the conference itself. The fact that
they didn't appear until May 27 probably meant the top
leadership was divided. There would hardly be time to
discuss the theses before the conference—so much for
informed choice as a component of democratization.
When the delegate selection process finally began, the
central papers reported widespread irregularities: old-
style quotas—selection of delegates on grounds of social
origin rather than devotion to reform—in Kiev; officials
in Minsk instructing Party cells whom to nominate at
hastily summoned sessions. In Magnitogorsk, they
didn't even bother with meetings but settled on "nomi-
nees" by phone with enterprise directors and lower-
level Party officials. The same sort of electoral violations
that occurred at Odessa State University repeated themselves at Moscow University and elsewhere.

Of the reformers mentioned in these pages, Gavriil
Popov, Tatyana Zaslavskaya, Andrey Nuikin, Nikolay
Shmelyov, Mikhail Shatrov, and Aleksander Gelman
were put forward as delegates only to be denied. Other
well-known progressives made it by a roundabout route,

such as *Ogonyok* editor Vitaly Korotich, who was designated a delegate from Kherson Province in the Crimea. Yury Afanasyev became the subject of another ruckus in which reformers didn't take no for an answer. The Historical Archives Institute's party cell nominated him, only to be told by Sverdlovsk district officials that it had no right to do so. They had given that right to the bigger Party cell at the Mendeleyev Chemical Institute, which proceeded to nominate a fourth-year woman student. With the example of Nina Andreyeva so fresh in their memories, Afanasyev backers could be forgiven their otherwise sexist response. They took their grievance to the papers, specifically to *Evening Moscow,* which reported their protest and added its own.

District officials backed off, agreeing to consider Afanasyev at the district Party plenum, which was then cancelled. Party leaders grilled him and other reform candidates in private for several hours. According to *Moscow News*, the questions were hostile: What had he been doing during the stagnation period? Wasn't he devoting too much time to journalism? The result was predictable: Afanasyev was voted down, only to rise again as the result of an outpouring of protest, including, it was rumored, from Gorbachev himself. When the secret ballots at the Moscow Party plenum were counted, Afanasyev was elected after all. The lesson: if liberals could get that far by dint of new-style lobbying and protest, then old-style Party discipline would put them over the top.

The Moscow protests weren't the only ones. Eight thousand people rallied in an Omsk soccer stadium to protest electoral manipulation by the provincial Party apparatus. On the Pacific coast, another thousand gathered at a Sakhalin theater for a similar purpose. Demonstrations here, petition drives there—we might have thought we were back in the States, except for the way some reformers reacted to their own successes.

Arkady is a senior researcher at a Moscow social sci-

ence institute, a man whose powerful pro-reform writing
has inspired many. Toward the end of May, we were
sitting in his kitchen with him, his wife, and son. Arkady
sighed, recounting the events of the day before at work.
He and like-minded colleagues had made a revolution.
They had gotten their Party cell to endorse a radical,
hard-hitting petition to the upcoming conference. It
hadn't been easy. They first had to convince fellow
Communists to allow non-Party members to take part.
Afterward, Arkady said, he felt absolutely euphoric—for
exactly three hours, before reaction set in. "I started asking myself, 'What have we done?' I knew the answer:
we had dismantled a small piece of the old system. I had
been wanting to do that for years. But now that we'd
done it, I suddenly had doubts. Is it prudent to begin
tearing down before you have something to put up in its
place? Whatever else you say about this regime, it has
kept the lid on. The question is, What will happen if we
succeed in taking it off?"

The same sort of distrust for democracy, the very democracy they were struggling to bring into being, was
visible in late May at a lecture by Tatyana Tolstaya on
"The Russian Literary Emigration." The subject itself
was political. But before long, Tolstaya and the audience turned to politics per se. Afanasyev had just lost
out in his district, she announced. The audience buzzed
with indignation. Mikhail Alexeyev, editor of *Moskva,*
one of eleven conservatives who had hounded *Novy mir*
editor Aleksander Tvardovsky from his post, would be a
delegate. A voice from the hall immediately proposed a
petition protesting Alexeyev's selection. When we
passed it on without signing—we didn't think the signatures of two Americans would help the cause—our
neighbors glared in disapproval.

Then a note from the audience asked Tolstaya what
she thought of the Democratic Union, which had declared itself to be a new political party. Suddenly, she

was scathing. The declaration was "an ego trip and a provocation." It would give ammunition to Gorbachev's opponents at just the wrong time. "Let's try genuine one-party democracy for a while before we start demanding more parties," she said. Tolstaya's tirade was a classic combination of healthy realism and self-defeating Soviet political culture. She was probably right that founding a new political party at this time was not constructive. But to refer to the right of free speech as a "privilege granted by the Party" gave away the game before it began.

Liberals and conservatives hated each other. Each camp distrusted the *narod* (people) while hoping to use popular resentment for its own purposes. The *narod* returned the ill will. Was there any way out of these intersecting vicious cycles? Was self-destruction built into the Russian political psyche? Gloomy thoughts like these kept blending with excitement as our Moscow Spring neared its end and our Soviet friends moved on toward the Party conference. In the midst of it all, Ronald Reagan came to town to cheer everyone up.

If Gorbachev was embattled, he needed successes, and the summit was the biggest success he was likely to get before the conference. But there was danger in the close proximity of the two events. If the summit blew up or broke down, Gorbachev would be particularly vulnerable when he most needed to be strong.

Ideally, he wanted not only to seal ratification of the intermediate-range forces treaty, but to sign a strategic nuclear arms treaty as well. As the summit approached, it became clear there would be no START treaty. The Soviet press never said it in so many words, but U.S. Embassy officials confirmed as much to us. Reagan's penchant for giving belligerent anti-Soviet speeches on the eve of summit meetings irked Gorbachev, too.

Despite the strain, summit arrangements proceeded on schedule. If our friends were less worried than we that the meeting might fail, it was partly because they weren't paying as much attention. So inured are they to their impotence in this field, they don't even complain that national security has been much slower than domestic affairs to come under the glare of *glasnost,* let alone see the dawn of democratization. Several times we tried to start conversations with friends about whether the United States could aid the cause of Soviet reform, and if so, how, only to be told that we probably knew better than they did.

How *can* the United States help Gorbachev? That is not a popular way of putting the question in American policy-making circles. The United States doesn't know enough about Kremlin politics, it is said in Washington, to be sure who the good guys are. Even if we did, we can't know whether our "aid" would actually help or hurt them. We can only protect our own interests and let the Soviet chips fall where they may. Some American conservatives insist Gorbachev is a more dangerous enemy than Brezhnev precisely *because* he is a reformer who is trying to make the Soviet system work. They contend *perestroika* is no different from previous Soviet efforts, under Lenin and Stalin and their successors, to obtain a temporary breathing space from the West before returning to the attack at a later date. This last view has supporters in the USSR too, but we encountered it remarkably rarely. Virtually everyone we met, including former dissidents, agreed that Gorbachev was sincerely trying to change the Soviet system.

At least one good Soviet friend warned against trying to help the Soviet leader. He admitted that Gorbachev means well. He agreed that U.S. behavior could raise or lower Gorbachev's domestic standing. The problem, he said, was that the cause of reform was doomed whatever we did. Therefore, any U.S. concessions that might help Gorbachev in the short run could hurt America after the Neanderthals retook control. "Not if American concessions are minor," piped up a young Russian at the table. "But if they're minor," replied our host, "they won't help Gorbachev anyway."

Another friend wasn't so sure. Aleksey is a fifty-year-old sociologist we met late in the spring after reading several of his pieces in the press. Like so many of his colleagues, he had put aside his academic work to write on Soviet reform. "Have you heard about the latest Novosibirsk research?" he asked, as we entered his apartment. The Novosibirsk study divided *perestroika* into economic and political reform and assessed how various groups felt about each. The only groups who favored both were the top Party leadership and the intelligentsia, discounting, of course, divisions within each category. The huge Party apparatus itself was against radical reform in both areas, as were unskilled workers. Factory managers were said to favor economic reform while opposing political change. The sentiment of skilled workers was unclear.

Aleksey wasn't exactly optimistic, but he was determined to fight on. In the 1970s he and his friends had been more cautious, expressing their dissent in esoteric references that only close readers could catch. Even so, they had troubles—articles censored, political reprimands, the threat of losing good jobs. But compared to someone like Andrey Sakharov, who refused any compromise, they had had it easy. It was partly out of guilt over past compromises that Aleksey would be steadfast this time. "I'm aware of the risks," he said. "I've discussed them with my family. They know it's the last chance I'll have, my last roll of the dice."

For Aleksey, the prospect of American help offered hope. Back in the seventies, he had secretly shared American hard-liners' view that "force is the only thing the Soviets understand." But the most useful thing the United States could do now was to help Gorbachev put something in the stores for Soviet people to buy. Leasing land to peasant families, a change just announced in Moscow, would help eventually, but it had come too late to affect the fall harvest. "Couldn't the U.S. extend us credit for buying consumer goods?" Aleksey asked.

The question struck us as naïve. Moscow had plenty of access to Western credit. Western firms were eager to sell consumer goods. The Soviet government had so far preferred to keep its debt to a minimum and use the credit to purchase high technology. Nonetheless, Aleksey had a point. The fate of his country hung in the balance. The only alternative to reform that he could see would threaten the world as well as the Soviet people.

Bill observed the summit close up as the Cable News Network's expert analyst. He hoped the network would use the event as a window on a society struggling with change. He suggested that CNN interview more than a few of the Soviets mentioned in these pages. Bill thought of the all-news network as having twenty-four hours a day to play with. It thought of itself as having twenty-four one-hour slots, or rather forty-eight half-hour segments, each of which had to cover the world and pay for that coverage with regularly scheduled features. The numerous interviews Bill had dreamed of were cut down to a handful lasting for two minutes each. Sitting next to the anchorman on the outdoor set overlooking Red Square, Bill learned to dread the words, "OK, Bernie, wrap it and head for a commercial," hissed over his earpiece from Atlanta—especially when he suspected they were a response to his having crowded too many subordinate clauses into an otherwise promising "sound bite." But being able to watch every moment of Soviet and American television "feeds" was invaluable.

The story of the summit, as Bill watched it from the studio and Jane tried to follow Soviet reactions around town, was more significant than we had expected. It accomplished things worth accomplishing, and it strengthened Gorbachev's hand at home. The crowd that lined

the President's route from the airport gathered sponta-
neously and reacted with real warmth. Although Soviet
media failed to cover Reagan's every movement, they
didn't miss many. The prime-time evening news usually
lasts about forty-five minutes. One evening it devoted
fifty-five to the summit alone. *Pravda* and *Izvestiya* plas-
tered the President's smiling face, along with those of
his wife and the Gorbachevs, all over their front pages.
Even our most sophisticated Soviet friends were smitten
with the President and First Lady for what seemed to us
the wrong reasons: "He held himself with such dignity!" "Did you see the way they held hands in public?"
"He's so sincere!" "She looks so natural!" But they were
also won over for the right reasons. They were relieved,
actually quite moved, to see the INF treaty go into effect
at last. The personal warmth between the two leaders
came across on Soviet TV. If the two leaders enjoyed
each other's company so much, we heard Russians say,
that must mean peace was at hand, and peace, in a country that has known such devastation from war, is one
cause that really does unite the Soviet people.

Gorbachev himself had other reasons to be pleased.
Like Mao during President Nixon's first visit to China,
Reagan went out of his way to legitimize the new dé-
tente and thus make it easier for his successor to continue it. So useful were this and other gestures that the
Soviet leader even sat still for Reagan's lectures on
human rights. We thought the President came across as
insensitive and condescending in his Spaso House address. But not so the next day at the Writers' Club and at
Moscow University. In both talks, he paid eloquent tribute to Russian culture, dropping great names in literature and the arts and quoting a series of magnificent
poetic lines. Our friends didn't care that his pronuncia-
tion butchered names which someone else had obviously provided him. In his Moscow University
speech, he respectfully brought American experience to

bear on issues the Soviets themselves were debating: the need for intellectual freedom if science and technology are to flourish, the evils of a bloated bureaucracy, the political as well as economic benefits of markets, the virtues of a rule of law based on a separation of powers, the need to institutionalize reforms lest they be eroded or swept aside, the uneasy blend of hope and fear provoked by rapid social change, even, in response to a clever Soviet student's question, the delicate matter of how to get a powerful leader quietly to relinquish the reins of power.

YOU CAN

GO HOME AGAIN

On June 1 we welcomed to Moscow two Russian emigré friends who were returning for the first time. The return of Soviet emigrés, now American citizens, for brief tourist visits is a larger, quieter, but equally important parallel to the legitimation of emigré writers and cultural figures.

Travel abroad for average Soviet citizens, even to Eastern-bloc countries, has been fraught with restrictions, complications, and unpleasantness. On this and previous trips we had frequent conversations on the subject with taxi drivers who wanted confirmation that Americans did not need an exit visa to leave the United States, they could just buy a ticket and go. We were always careful to add that the price of a ticket made such freedom illusory for some, but that was a very different issue.

Our first hint of change came soon after our arrival in

1988. Our friend Anna had not seen her mother or brother, who had emigrated to the United States, for eight years. She had waited anxiously to reach the minimum pension age (only fifty-five for women), which is supposed to make it easier to get a visa, then applied several times, but the visa office always refused to accept her application on some technicality. Now she greeted us with the happy news that she was leaving for a three-month stay in America.

The same story was repeated several times. A literary scholar Jane had met on her last trip was going to Scandinavia for two months to visit a Danish colleague who was not even a relative. A prominent scientist, a member of the Academy of Sciences, who had never before been allowed to travel beyond the Eastern bloc, was off with his wife to Western Europe to visit friends. Another new acquaintance left to spend April in Paris.

Now, for the first time, we felt we might have the opportunity to return the hospitality of some of the people who had done so much to open Moscow Spring to us. Indeed, since our return, the visits have begun. We have to shake off our disbelief; it seems bizarre to be continuing our intense Moscow conversations while showing friends the bucolic beauty of the Connecticut River Valley or the colonial architecture of old Deerfield. It was the same reaction we had to so many events of Moscow Spring—that what was being said or done was, and should be, really quite ordinary. But decades of prohibitions and restrictions had made the newly possible ordinary seem extraordinary.

The most symbolic moment occurred just days before our departure. Sixteen years ago, on one of our first joint trips to the Soviet Union, we met a couple who became our closest Soviet friends. They provided our introduction to many households both in Moscow and abroad. Vika, a literary scholar, had been fired from a low-level job at the Writers' Union in 1966 for circulating a petition in defense of Andrey Sinyavsky. Misha, her husband, was a self-taught dissident, raised in an orphanage. He assumed his parents had starved or been shot during collectivization. He had served a total of fifteen years in Soviet labor camps, in the last of which he met the imprisoned Sinyavsky. When Misha was released, Sinyavsky sent him with messages to his wife, who introduced him to her friend Vika.

When we first met them in 1973, they were already on the margins of society and therefore without fear. We knew they were hoping to emigrate eventually—Misha especially was so alienated from the Soviet regime that he idealized everything American. Vika loyally supported his views. And so, in early July 1978, we found ourselves at the Hartford airport, embracing Vika, Misha, and nine-year-old Marina as they began a new life in America.

They became our "Moscow in Amherst," their apartment a welcoming haven where we could go for endless cups of tea and conversation about developments in Soviet literature and politics. Misha, like most emigrés, was far to our right politically. He himself might have coined Reagan's "evil empire" phrase, and he was constantly accusing us and our fellow Americans of naïveté about the Soviets and their intentions. All they ever understood was force; they were always up to something; they could never be trusted; they would never change. Misha saw little to be excited about in the rise of Gorbachev: "Don't fool yourselves; they're all the same underneath. Anyone who scrambles to the top through the jungle of the Party bureaucracy becomes like all the rest of them, or he wouldn't have survived."

As *perestroika* unfolded and it became clear that real changes were afoot, we realized how difficult it would be for dissidents like Misha to acknowledge the fact. Their whole lives and their decision to emigrate had been based on the conviction that the regime would

never change for the better. When Marina thought about
traveling to Moscow a few years ago with a school group,
Misha vetoed the plan: "I don't trust them to let her out
again." But Vika had left a brother and many close
friends in Moscow, and as the atmosphere improved,
she hesitantly began planning a trip for herself and Marina. Misha with his political convictions and his prison
record would never return, but he would wait for them
in Vienna.

Misha's death in the fall of 1987 deprived him of the
trip to Vienna. But throughout Moscow Spring, we
awaited Vika's arrival with Marina, scheduled for June
1. Would they get their visa? Politics were no longer the
problem, but the date they had chosen months earlier
turned out to be in the middle of Reagan's summit visit.
Thousands of visiting journalists packed all the Intourist
hotels. Groups of tourists had already been turned
down, not only because there were no available rooms,
but because the understaffed Soviet Embassy in Washington could not keep up with the flood of visa applications. The suspense lasted till the last moment. Vika had
promised to call if the visa didn't arrive in time, but no
call came. And so, slightly less than a month short of ten
years after we had met them in Hartford, Jane found
herself at Sheremetyevo Airport, inside the customs barrier we ourselves had crossed so many times since then,
waiting to welcome Vika and Marina.

The plane arrived; tourists trickled through passport
control and began to collect their baggage. Vika's
brother, sister-in-law, and friends craned to get a first
glimpse through the single exit. And suddenly there
they were, looking visibly apprehensive. Vika collected
her luggage and placed it before the customs inspector.
Her face from long habit assumed the stolid, almost sullen expression with which Soviets confront bureaucratic
superiors. Surely as soon as they noticed "Place of birth,
Moscow" in her American passport, they would rip her

luggage apart, humiliate her, confiscate the gifts she had lovingly chosen for friends. The young customs officer ran the suitcases through the same West German fluoroscope machine that examines the baggage of all incoming travelers. He glanced at her passport, stamped her customs declaration, and waved her through. She was being treated like any other American tourist.

They walked into the tearful embraces of friends and relatives. But there was still one more gauntlet—how would Intourist treat her? She went to the Intourist desk, inquired in her native Muscovite Russian, and was politely told that a car was waiting to take her and Marina to the National Hotel, one of Moscow's oldest and most central, just across from the Kremlin at the beginning of Gorky Street. Her fears vanished and a wild giddiness took over. Our caravan of greeters headed for the National, to discover yet another change. Doormen at Intourist hotels have always admitted only foreign tourists, ostensibly protecting their esteemed visitors from the predations of black marketeers or ladies of the night. Soviets trying to visit foreign friends in their hotel rooms were asked to leave their identification papers with the concierge, a procedure designed to intimidate. We had read in the press that this policy was about to be changed, but could we believe it? No one at the National blinked an eye as our procession marched through the halls to Vika and Marina's room.

"We know of people who were allowed out with an exit visa that had expired. But we've never heard of anyone getting out without a visa at all."

It was about noon on Sunday, June 5. Our plane was scheduled to depart at 1:30 P.M. Alex had left several days earlier. Jane was already at the airport with half of our baggage. Bill was in the U.S. Embassy, miles away in the center of Moscow, getting the bad news from a young woman in the consular section. She had just is-

sued him a shiny, navy-blue American passport to replace the one he had lost the day before. But even in the
afterglow of the summit, the U.S. Embassy had not assumed the Soviet government's function of replacing
lost Soviet visas.

"If anyone has a chance to get out without a visa, it's
you," she said, "what with your contacts, your summit
press pass, and your television appearances. But I'd say
the odds are several thousand to one against you. Let's
just call it a test of *perestroika*."

At seven thirty that morning, Bill had reached into his
pocket for his passport and exit visa only to discover that
both were gone. Saturday had been hot and steamy, and
he slung his blue blazer over his shoulder as he walked
around town on a number of last-minute missions. He
had been aware throughout the day of the documents in
his breast pocket and had taken care to hold the jacket
so they would not slide out. They must have slipped out
anyway and fallen to the sidewalk. It was also possible
they had been stolen.

Part of Bill didn't want to leave anyway. Although his
Khrushchev research had gone well, several important
interviews had eluded him. Just two days before, a particularly important source had broken an appointment at
the last minute. There was a possibility of seeing him
later that afternoon at a friend's place outside Moscow.
The dacha wasn't far from the airport. The mirage of
access to Foreign Ministry archives also beckoned. If,
through no fault of his own, he was still around on Monday, perhaps that might yet be arranged. Then there was
the Party conference, by now only weeks away. Could
he conceivably wangle an extension until then?

The trouble was, Bill had obligations at home. His
bags were already packed and loaded in an Academy of
Sciences car, and Valentina Vasilyevna had repossessed
the keys to our apartment. He had gotten used to the
idea of leaving and was too worn out to change his mind.

As usual, the week before departure had been frantic. Besides collecting microfilm at the Lenin Library, mailing home packages of books and notes, and saying goodbye to friends, Bill had spent long hours in CNN's Rossiya Hotel studio. A reporter from *Sovetskaya kultura* wanted an interview; Bill talked to her on the phone. Central Television's *120 Minutes*, an early morning news and entertainment program, broadcast one of Bill's CNN commentaries. That produced what friends said we should regard as the most coveted invitation of all, from *Vzgliad* ("Viewpoint"), the bold, late-night TV talk show.

Vzgliad had asked Bill to appear once before, on a program marking Lenin's birthday. The very idea was startling, especially since they must have gotten wind of Bill's jaundiced view of Lenin's historical role. In fact, a knowledgeable friend later told us, that's exactly why they wanted him, to push the boundary of *glasnost* a little bit farther. We were leaving for Leningrad, so the *Vzgliad* interview couldn't be done live. They offered to tape it the evening before, but at the last moment Bill came down with a twenty-four-hour virus. When *Vzgliad* called back on June 1 and offered to bring its cameras to our apartment on the evening of June 2, he agreed with alacrity.

When Bill got back from covering Reagan's departure on June 2, he had ten minutes to shave, shower, and change his shirt before the Soviet camera crew arrived. In the kitchen, Jane was feeding an American tourist who had come by with greetings from mutual Soviet friends in the provinces; another Moscow friend had stopped in to say goodbye. Perfectly comfortable visiting our apartment in the past, he became suddenly uneasy at the prospect of sharing it with a Soviet TV crew, and was determined to stay out of their line of vision. Two rooms and a kitchen didn't leave much space for that, and Jane began to feel she was directing one of those French bedroom farces with lovers in every closet and under the bed.

While the TV crew set up their lights and microphones, which looked at least a generation behind CNN's equipment, a bright young woman who was to interview Bill chatted with him about the subjects she would raise. The summit was one, of course. Viewers would also want to hear Bill's views on Khrushchev. What else would Bill like to talk about? Lenin, he said, recalling his missed opportunity back in April, particularly the question of his responsibility for the rise of Stalin. No problem, according to the interviewer. And with that the interview began.

Bill answered questions for nearly thirty minutes as the cameras rolled. It was by far his most fluent performance of the spring. But somehow he never got around to Lenin. It wasn't the interviewer's fault; he just forgot. It was the interviewer who reminded him and offered to shoot another short segment. This time, Bill zeroed in. Some people, he said, believed that if Lenin had lived several more years, there would have been no such thing as Stalinism. But there was something gravely wrong with a system in which the only barrier to massive crimes was the continued existence of one ailing *starik* (old man).

Even as Bill said the word, out of the corner of his eye he could see the soundman wince. Afterward, the crew exchanged whispers. "That word will kill it," one of them said to Bill. "They'll allow you to criticize Lenin on the air, but not to call him a *starik*." True enough, Lenin was only fifty-three when he died. But he was the senior Soviet leader, and his colleagues themselves referred to him as *starik*. Should they redo the take? The crew didn't offer. Bill didn't ask. The piece was scheduled to be shown on June 3 or June 10. We sat up with friends on June 3 till the program ended at 1:30 A.M.— but no Bill. Would they ever show it? A Soviet friend

who visited the States later in the month said she had
seen it. Had they left in Bill's comments about Lenin?
She didn't remember. Would they have stuck in her
memory if she had heard them? "Not necessarily," she
said, laughing. "Knocking Lenin is becoming routine."

The woman at the Embassy came in specially on a
Sunday morning to issue Bill his new passport. All the
required paperwork, including applications, photos,
etc., was accomplished in less than an hour. But by now
it was 12:15, and the clock was running. The Academy
driver, a bulky middle-aged woman, didn't look remotely capable of the feats she performed on the way to
the airport. Careening along at high speed, weaving between lanes, swerving onto the shoulder to pass slower
traffic, she got there by 12:45. Racing into the terminal,
Bill waved to Jane. She had already cleared customs and
checked in for the joint Pan Am/Aeroflot nonstop to New
York; she'd even managed to get Bill a boarding pass
and a seat assignment. With scheduled departure only a
half-hour away, the rest of the passengers had already
passed through passport control. The only hopeful development was an announcement on the departure
board that the flight would be delayed.

To whom should we appeal? Our Academy escort,
Borya, was eager to help. But the same qualities that set
him apart from pre-Moscow Spring escorts—his long
hair, graying beard, and elegantly disheveled denim
jumpsuit—reduced the chances he could talk the KGB
border guards into waving Bill through. Nevertheless he
gave it a try. He hurdled a barrier, ran over to the chief
border guard, a young blond officer with a broad Slavic
face, explained the situation, and asked whether there
was any way Bill could leave without a visa. "Absolutely
not, it's out of the question!" The words could not have
been uttered with stonier finality.

Bill almost gave up, but we remembered the advice of

an American journalist friend: "In this country, you can talk your way out of almost anything." At this point, Jane came to the rescue. She recounted the situation to the chief customs agent, using her best Russian and her most feminine manner. She and her husband had come together on the academic exchange, she explained, stressing that they had arrived together, shared an apartment, and were to depart together. All the data on her visa was identical with his. Their children—she paused significantly—had already gone home to America and were eagerly awaiting their reunion. Somehow she managed to hint at her reluctance to undertake the rigors of transatlantic travel alone. As soon as contact had been made on a human level, the situation changed entirely. "Married couple? Children waiting at home? I see. Let me talk with him." Taking Jane's passport and visa, off he went to the KGB major. Five minutes later the two of them were back; the major's expression had already begun to soften, and suddenly his previous "No way" wasn't so categorical at all. "Here's what you do. Call your embassy and have them call the duty officer at the Ministry of Foreign Affairs to explain the situation and vouch for your story. The ministry knows what to do. If they approve, they'll call permission down the line to me."

Bill called the embassy, and we began to wait. By now it was past one thirty, but the plane was still delayed. "Don't worry," said a friendly Soviet woman who worked for Pan Am. "It hasn't even arrived yet. And when it does, it'll take a lot of time to turn it around." Half an hour later, Bill called the embassy again. According to the Foreign Ministry, as quoted by the embassy duty officer, the chain of command down which word had to pass was more complicated than we had thought. The ministry would have to clear it with KGB's Chief Administration of the Border Guards, which would then call the airport. All of which assumed, of course, that someone somewhere would take responsibility rather than covering his or her ass in traditional bureaucratic fashion.

There were no chairs in sight. With no passengers around, the customs man had no objections to our sitting down on the baggage counter. He even chatted pleasantly with us about the summit. After Bill slipped away to buy soft drinks, he switched the subject to whether Soviet Pepsi was the same as the American original. On all our previous trips we had lived in fear of unsmiling Soviet customs agents. We had nothing to hide, except an occasional volume of Russian poetry, but we had seen enough people get the third degree, including body searches, that we held our breath each time we had to run the gauntlet. On our two trips in 1987, we noticed a new breed of younger and more pleasant agents with better command of English. But never did we imagine that one day we would sit around chatting with some of them, or that they would adopt our cause as their own, encouraging us with a cheery word, perking up every time the KGB major strolled across the hall in our direction.

By three o'clock there was still no word. By now the plane was boarding, with departure announced for 3:45. Bill called the embassy one last time. No further news from there. Finally, at 3:20 the major emerged from his office and walked our way. A radiant smile transformed his once impassive face. "You can go!" he exclaimed, holding his arms aloft in a sign of victory.

EPILOGUE

The Nineteenth Party Conference held in Moscow from June 28 to July 1, 1988, is the logical conclusion to our story. Not only did it bring to a climax the events and developments we describe in this book, it also marked the end of the first three years of Mikhail Gorbachev's leadership. It signaled, we think, the beginning of a new phase of Moscow Spring. It also made clear that the time ahead would be even more tumultuous than our months in Moscow.

When the conference was held, we were in Amherst, but we could imagine our friends' reaction to the first spontaneous, unrehearsed Party conclave in six decades. During the conference one of our Moscow friends passed through Amherst on a cross-country American visit. Watching scenes of the conference on U.S. television, catching a glimpse of a mutual friend demonstrating on a Moscow street, she gave us a sample of the excited reaction we were missing.

The conference approved substantive reforms, aimed at reducing the Party's role in the economy. The delegates voted to limit the tenure of Party officials to two terms, and approved a monument to Stalin's victims. Much more important was the example the conference set of a new kind of Soviet politics, a politics of pluralism and protest, of thrust and counterthrust, of dramatic clashes in the hall, charges and countercharges on prime-time television, delegates voting "No!" for the first time in sixty years.

All these innovations built on trends we had witnessed. They also sharpened the dilemma we had observed. Reformers could not fail to be encouraged. But their leader failed utterly to get the personnel changes he must have wanted. The conference spotlighted the strength of Gorbachev's conservative opponents and their appeal to the Soviet people at large. Each side emerged from the affair more determined than ever.

The important September 30, 1988 Central Committee plenum also sent mixed signals. This time, Gorbachev was able to remove conservatives Andrey Gromyko and Mikhail Solomentsev from the Politburo, to shift Yegor Ligachev and KGB chief Viktor Chebrikov to less critical assignments, and to get himself appointed to the soon-to-be-strengthened post of Soviet President. But in comparison to the tumultuous June conference, the September plenum was tame. There was no debate and no dissent. The whole proceeding, which endorsed changes in Party and government structure as well as in personnel, took but an hour to complete.

The fall plenum underlines the paradox of Moscow Spring: Can democracy really be promoted by such undemocratic means? In today's Soviet Union, can it be fostered in any other way?

Amherst, Massachusetts
December 1988

INDEX